The UNIX System Administrator's Guide to X

Eric F. Johnson
and Kevin Reichard

M&T BOOKS

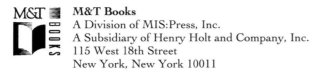

M&T Books
A Division of MIS:Press, Inc.
A Subsidiary of Henry Holt and Company, Inc.
115 West 18th Street
New York, New York 10011

Limits of Liability and Disclaimer of Warranty
The Author and Publisher of this book have used their best efforts in preparing the book and the programs contained in it. These efforts include the development, research, and testing of the theories and programs to determine their effectiveness.

The Author and Publisher make no warranty of any kind, expressed or implied, with regard to these programs or the documentation contained in this book. The Author and Publisher shall not be liable in any event for incidental or consequential damages in connection with, or arising out of, the furnishing, performance, or use of these programs.

All products, names and services are trademarks or registered trademarks of their respective companies.

Library of Congress Cataloging-in-Publication Data

Reichard, Kevin.
    UNIX system administrator's guide to X / Kevin Reichard, Eric Johnson.
        p. cm.
    Includes index.
    ISBN 1-55828-347-1 : $49.95
        1. UNIX (Computer File)   2. X Window System (Computer system)
I. Johnson, Eric (L. Eric)   II. Title.
QA76.76.O63R445   1994
005.4'3--dc20   94-13565
                                                                        CIP

97 96 95 94   4 3 2 1

Publisher: Steve Berkowitz
Associate Publisher: Brenda McLaughlin
Development Editor: Laura Lewin
Copy Editor: Suzanne Ingrao
Production Editor: Patricia Wallenburg
Associate Production Editor: Cari Littman

Dedication

From Eric

To Halloween and to the Platypus Society—devoted to praise, preserve, protect, and promote those fuzzy little platypi.

From Kevin

As always, for Penny, Sean, and Geisha.

UNIX System Administration and X

Welcome to the *UNIX System Administrator's Guide to X*! We hope this book aids you through some difficult times, as you navigate the challenges posed by the integration of UNIX and X.

First of all, let us extend our sympathies. We know how difficult it is to perform basic UNIX system-administration duties. We also know that the inclusion of the X Window System into a UNIX network makes your job so much more difficult.

That's why this book exists—to make your job go a little smoother. We cover the difficult situations you're likely to encounter when you perform your daily duties and offer practical advice. We focus on the challenges posed by the X Window System when it comes to a UNIX network, such as security. And we emphasize troubleshooting techniques we've picked up along the way, during our many adventures in X.

This book is unique in its devotion to the use of X in a UNIX environment, with the specific emphasis on system-administration tasks. There are several other books on the market that cover X "administration" (including our own *Using X*, also from MIS:Press), but none explicitly written for the UNIX system administrator.

What is X?

The X Window System is a graphical windowing environment originally developed at the Massachusetts Institute of Technology and currently under control of the not-for-profit X Consortium Inc. The X Window System is also known as X11 or X (*never* refer to it as X Windows). X is distributed free of charge in source-code form—anyone on the Internet can download it from *ftp.x.org*—and serves as a building block to other products, such as Motif.

X is built on the model of distributed computing: An application (called a *client* in X parlance) communicates with a *server*, which can reside anywhere on the network. The server then sends output to a *display*, which also can reside anywhere on the network.

Notice that the client, server, and display aren't automatically the same machine. This is one of the major appeals of X on a UNIX network: It allows applications to be run anywhere on the network and displayed anywhere else on the network. For instance, your users could run a graphics-intensive client on your machine and display the results on their own.

This flexible arrangement dates back from the days of big iron, when the large machine sat in the middle of the network, with relatively limited power on the desktop. The idea was to distribute computing power more efficiently across the network and allow any user access to adequate computing power. Today, as the prices of UNIX workstations, personal computers, and X terminals plummet, the notion that computing power be centered at a network location is superseded.

However, there are other computing trends that make X an appealing tool on UNIX networks. For starters, there's the growing importance of *client/server* computing schemes, particularly in the database-management field. Here, the notion is simple: Some of the computing chore can be done on the desktop, while the heavy-duty work is done on the server.

The power comes at a cost, of course. X adds another layer of complexity to a UNIX network, both literally and figuratively. Structurally, X communications between clients, servers, and displays are managed by the X

Protocol, which runs on top of TCP/IP, UNIX domain sockets, or DECnet. The X Protocol entails a performance hit on the network, as the graphical routines managed by the X Protocol tend to be rather hefty.

X is still predominately a programmer's environment, unfortunately. As a user environment, X leaves a lot to be desired, which is why you'll need to tackle a lot of tough issues, such as resource files, and provide more assistance to users than you're probably used to. You'll need to put out many more fires among users, however, especially if your users love to tinker and cause a little trouble for themselves.

In the commercial world, X comes in many flavors. Sun Microsystems includes X as part of its OpenWindows environment. Hewlett-Packard includes X as part of its VUE user environment. Motif, from the Open Software Foundation, is based on X Window.

X and Hardware

Depending on your hardware configuration, the level of difficulty you'll encounter with X will vary. Relatively speaking, X on the workstation isn't automatically a problem child; as mentioned, many UNIX workstation vendors have integrated X within their user environments. Throughout the text, we've noted several areas where user environments from Sun and Hewlett-Packard vary from the default configurations.

However, there are other hardware configurations that can cause more headaches for you, as X terminals and personal computers gain in popularity as desktop systems on UNIX systems. X terminals are either smart terminals or dumb PCs; either way you look at it, an X terminal is set up solely to run an X server and perhaps a few local applications, such as a local window manager. X terminals emphasize graphics performance and network connectivity at the expense of local computing power (many X terminals lack a local hard drive, for instance). Typically, X terminals will cause you the most headaches during the configuration process; when X terminals are up and running, there are some issues, such as performance, that you simply won't be able to solve. However, X terminal vendors have been working on configuration and performance issues (such as placing a hard drive on the X terminal to handle local clients, which cuts down on the number of network requests), which should eventually make your life a little easier.

Unfortunately, the same can't be said for PCs running X servers. If you've administered PCs on your UNIX network, you already know what sort of problems PCs pose for the system administrator: weird third-party graphics boards, inconsistent TCP/IP configurations, multiple software layers (DOS, *Windows*, TCP/IP, X), and the inevitable tug of war between the computing power needed for UNIX and X and the lack of relative horsepower of a PC. However, PCs are an attractive proposition for many corporations, especially for the accounting and purchasing departments of many corporations. Therefore, chances are good that at some point you'll need to deal with PCs and X. In this book, we've covered both PC X servers and XFree86, a free implementation of X for Intel-based PCs running UNIX.

How This Book is Organized

Section 1 introduces X Window and the challenges presented by X to your work as system administrator. We begin this book by spending a little more time explaining the X Window System in Chapter 1, while detailing all the fun you can look forward to as a UNIX system administrator working with X in Chapter 2. If you're starting an X environment from scratch, the first challenge you'll face is actually installing X onto your UNIX network, which we cover in Chapter 3.

Since a good many problems caused by the X Window System have to do with environment issues, we spend the majority of Section 2 covering such basic tasks as starting and stopping X (Chapter 4) and setting up user accounts (Chapter 5).

Once X is up and running, your next major task will be to properly configure X, as discussed in Section 3. Part of that configuration process, interestingly enough, involves determining exactly what sort of X environment you currently possess, so we cover this exploration process in Chapter 6. This chapter is a very important one, as we also explain our nominations for a UNIX administrator's toolbox, including utilities like *xdpyinfo*, *xlswins*, *xwininfo*, *xlsclients*, *xprop*, and *xload*. With these tools in hand, you'll be able to tackle such configuration issues like fonts and the font server (Chapter 7); resources, resource files, and command-line parameters (Chapter 8); the keyboard, keys, and key bindings (Chapter 9); colors and color names (Chapter 10); and bitmaps and icons (Chapter 11). Finally, we end the section with an important issue of security (such as it is) and the X Window System in Chapter 12.

Section 4 covers topics relating to X terminals, a popular piece of computer equipment that you'll probably encounter in the course of your work. We spend Chapter 13 explaining X terminals and the problems they might cause on a UNIX network, while Chapter 14 details X terminal utilities and the process of configuring X terminals.

A close cousin to X terminals—a PC running X on top of UNIX, DOS, or *Windows*—is covered in Section 5. Software that adds X Window capabilities to DOS- or *Windows*-based PCs is covered in Chapter 15 (focusing on *DESQview/X* and *HCL-eXceed/W*), while XFree86, a popular method of adding X to UNIX-based PCs, is detailed in Chapter 16.

Since there's a ton of free software out there—the best of which we collected for the accompanying CD-ROM—you would be foolish not to take advantage of it as the need arises; hence the coverage of this software in Section 6. Chapter 17 covers the methods for obtaining free X sources, if you ever need something not contained on the accompanying CD-ROM. Chapter 18 details the process for building the free sources, using the *make* and *imake* tools. Chapter 19 details system-administration utilities like *netload*, *xsystats*, *xmeter*, *spacetool*, and *xfedor*. Chapter 20 covers some nifty scripting tools like Tcl/Tk, *xgen*, and Wcl, which allow you to create graphical front ends for text-based applications. Chapter 21 briefly covers screen-locking programs, which prevent others from using your system. Chapter 22 discusses *xmon* and *xscope*, two debugging tools that you'll find essential when problems occur. Chapter 23 covers miscellaneous utilities like *xman* (for reading online manual pages), *xfed* (for editing fonts), free clocks (X Window users are obsessed with clocks, for some reason or another), and an X utility, *workman*, which allows you to play audio CDs from your CD-ROM drive. Finally, the book ends with Chapter 24's discussion of X Window tools (*xmosaic*, *xarchie*, and *xgopher*) used when connecting to the Internet with X.

Conventions Used in This Book

Book titles, machine names, font names, and software titles, such as *DESQview/X*, are printed in *italic* type. Filenames, script names, and general UNIX commands are printed in **bold** type. Commands that are meant to be typed directly into the system's command prompt are printed in a monospaced font.

How to Reach the Authors

We'd love to hear your feedback about this book. You can send electronic mail to *kreichard@mcimail.com*.

Introducing X

This beginning section introduces the X Window System from the UNIX system administrator's point of view.

Chapter 1 provides a basic introduction to X, for those system administrators who are unfamiliar with X and want a basic overview.

Chapter 2 encompasses an overview of the UNIX system administrator's tasks when it comes to the X Window System and also goes into file locations and other meaty X issues.

The section closes with Chapter 3, which covers an X installation from beginning to end.

What is X?

Topics covered in this chapter include:

* A gentle introduction to the X Window System
* The X client–server model
* Networking with X
* X displays
* The X environment
* Motif and Open Look interfaces
* Window managers
* Determining which window manager is running
* Making windows active
* Icons

The X Window System

This chapter provides a gentle introduction to the X Window System, explaining the main concepts and providing an overview of the X environment. If you're already familiar with X, then you can jump ahead to Chapter 2, which begins the specific discussion of X and the UNIX system administrator.

The X Window System is a operating-system-independent set of graphical routines. The X Window System began life at MIT's Project Athena as a tool for linking different types of computers from different manufacturers. Development and distribution of X is now overseen by X Consortium, Inc. (see Appendix A for details), which makes it available free of charge to anyone. As such, X ships in source code and is compiled for specific operating systems.

The X Window System is also known as X and X Window, but *never* as X Windows—anyone caught using the term *X Windows* will immediately be recognized as someone rather unfamiliar with X.

N O T E

X was built with a philosophy of mechanics, not policy. This means that X doesn't dictate the exact look and feel of a graphical display, but rather provides the building blocks for those who want to provide a look and feel of their own. While this has lead to a distressing fragmentation in the X marketplace—Motif, Open Look, and straight X all have had their adherents over the last few years—it has led to a situation where the marketplace has decided which look and feel to embrace: Motif, an offering from the Open Software Foundation. (We'll discuss Motif later in this chapter.)

Virtually every major operating system supports X, ranging from MS-DOS and the Macintosh operating system to Cray supercomputers and everything in between, though increasingly this support occurs in the form of Motif. The bulk of this support, however, occurs in the UNIX world, where X has been adopted as the de facto graphical-interface tool of choice.

Which is why you, the UNIX system administrator, need to become acquainted with the X Window System and variants. If you're not yet working with X Window or Motif, you probably will in the near future, as most new systems and software packages are increasingly centered around X and Motif.

However, be warned that X will intensify the complexity in your life. (As if it weren't complex enough!) One of the key features of X is the high degree of flexibility and configurability. This gives you, the administrator, a lot of freedom and power, but you pay a price in increased complexity.

Client–Server Graphics

The complexity begins with X terminology and structures.

The X Window System was a pioneer in the practice of *distributed processing*, where the resources on a network are viewed as potentially accessible to anyone on the network. Instead of clustering processing resources in the mainframe, there might be several servers interconnected in the network.

X was designed from the beginning to provide graphics over the network, and it does so by dividing up the graphics chores along client and server lines. However, be warned that X treats the terms client and server in slightly different ways.

In the rest of the computer world, a *server* is usually a hardware device (VAX, AS/400, Novell file server) in the middle of the network, distributing files and processing power to networked users. These users have main access to the server, with incidental and indirect access (such as mail and network messages) to other users.

With X, however, the server (sometimes called a *display server*) is a continually running program on a local machine. The server communicates with other machines on the network via the X Protocol, and it's responsible for sending output to the display (explained in the following section). *Clients*, or applications (the two are used synonymously in X), communicate with the server. This means that you can run applications on one system and display them on another system. For users, this means running a complex application on a powerful server while displaying the results on the workstation at your desk. (Or, better yet, it means running CPU-intensive games on your boss's machine and displaying the results on your own machine.) For UNIX administrators, this means that you can work on any UNIX system on your network while sitting at your desk.

In practice, this allows you to access any machine on a network — which can actually ease your system-administration tasks. You can perform many (but alas, not all) administration tasks remotely from a workstation at your desk instead of trudging around your entire site.

The fact that the X server is all you need locally allows for single-tasking DOS boxes to run the X server and yet be a workable solution on your network. This also allows for the creation of special devices called *X terminals*, which provide the X server locally in a smart graphics terminal. See Chapter 13 for more on X terminals.

The Display

When experts talk about X, they'll often use the terms *display* and *screen* in unfamiliar ways. A screen is a physical monitor. A display is a much broader term, which includes:

✱ A keyboard

✱ A pointing device, usually a mouse

✱ One or more screens (almost always just one)

Basically, each X user sits at an X display, so the display includes all the necessary hardware for one user to run X.

You'll rarely see displays with more than one screen, except in high-end CAD systems. These multiheaded systems usually include one keyboard and mouse, but two or more physical monitors.

Don't confuse multiple screens with multiple displays. In the simple case, each UNIX workstation has a single monitor (the console), keyboard, and mouse. This is the X display.

N O T E

Usually the pointing device is a mouse, and that's our assumption throughout this book, even though your pointing device might be a trackball, stylus, or graphics pad.

The X Environment

Users run multiple applications on their workstations and display them on their X display. A typical user session involves a number of very large X application processes, which drain system resources. (X programs rarely clock in at smaller than a megabyte, although shared libraries help immensely.)

Accessories like *xclock* (which places a clock on the screen) are always popular, frills like *xeyes* (which opens a window containing a pair of eyes that follow the cursor movement across the screen), thanks to their novelty value, are frequently embraced by novices, and applications themselves frequently open up multiple windows on their own.

Most users run the X server (usually a UNIX process named *X*), a window manager (which we cover in the next section), and a number of X terminals. You'll also commonly see clock programs, calendars, and file managers, as shown in Figure 1.1.

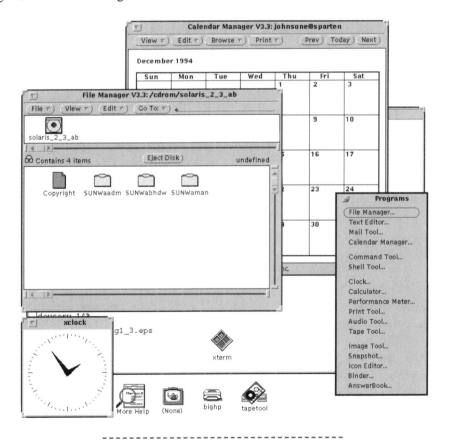

Figure 1.1   A common X environment.

The Root Window

The background of Figure 1.1 is the *root window*. You can configure a system to display a graphic of some sort in the root window. Many session managers (software that provide a greater amount of control over the look and feel) cover the screen background with a session background, however. Programs that change the root window, like *xsetroot*, still work, but their results are obscured by the session manager's background. If your users complain that *xsetroot* doesn't work, this is probably why. In such a case, you need to use the session manager to change the screen backgrounds.

User Interfaces on X: Motif and Open Look

Computer users love a good battle. Witness the war between Macintosh and Windows users over the last few years.

Similarly, there has been a battle between proponents of Motif and Open Look. Motif, created by the Open Software Foundation and marketed by members of the foundation (most notably Hewlett-Packard, IBM, and DEC), had the advantage of a greater market share. Open Look, a crucial element in the larger offering from Sun Microsystems called OpenWindows, had the advantage of support from the largest UNIX workstation vendor, Sun.

Both are based on the X Window System—a crucial fact that most participants in the wars usually ignored. We always felt that the war was based on some faulty assumptions: The two were never mutually exclusive, and with a little clever coding a programmer could build applications that would run under both.

The two offer a slightly different look and feel, as shown in Figures 1.2 and 1.3. As the screen dumps indicate, there are some basic similarities between Motif and Open Look. Both have titlebars at the top of the window, indicating the name of the application or the file. And both feature scrollbars on the right side and on the bottom of the window, allowing you to move through the entire window.

Past these, however, there are some cosmetic differences between Motif and Open Look, as well as some basic operational differences. Motif adheres to the IBM Common User Access (CUA) guidelines, as do Microsoft

Windows and IBM OS/2. A Window menu in the upper-left-hand corner controls the window sizing and positioning, while **Minimize** and **Maximize** buttons control window sizing. Open Look, on the other hand, places a different Window menu on the upper-left-hand corner, while resize handles are placed on every corner of the window. And the actions associated with mouse buttons are totally different—for instance, the left mouse button under Open Look runs the default choice in the nearest menu, while the left mouse button under Motif selects whatever the mouse is positioned over.

Figure 1.2   A Motif application window.

As we write this (the beginning of 1994), the war between Motif and Open Look has been minimized due to the emergence of Common Open Software Environment, or COSE. As part of COSE, Sun Microsystems has agreed to embrace Motif as the preferred look and feel, while elements of OpenWindows are being incorporated under the hood. While Sun has warned that support for Open Look will end shortly, there are still a lot of Sun sites still dependent on Open Look applications. Since change occurs slowly in the computer world, it's still important to know about Open Look, so discussions of Open Look are included throughout this book.

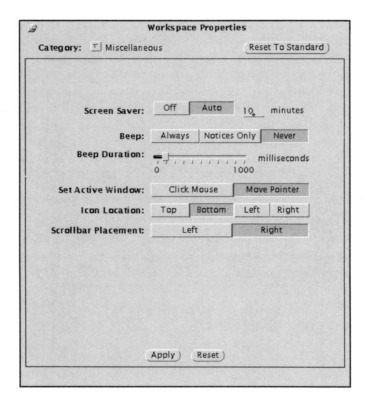

Figure 1.3   An Open Look application window.

Window Managers

The window manager is a key concept that every administrator must understand. A *window manager* is a program that users run to control the layout and
placement of windows on their screen. The key concept is that this window manager is a separate UNIX process and not part of the basic X server. You can only
run one window manager per screen and usually only one per X display.

  The window manager has the final say over how much of the screen any
program can occupy, although most window managers don't interfere too
much with application programs. The window manager also places the title-

bars across the top of application windows and allows you to iconify, move, and resize windows on the screen. It is the window manager that determines the style, size, fonts, and colors users see on the titlebars.

Unlike almost all other windowing systems, X doesn't build in any form of window manager. Instead, the user is free to run any of a number of common window managers. Since the window manager provides a good deal of what the user perceives as the look and feel of the workstation, you'll be surprised at how much variation there is—even on the same system, as different users run their preferred window managers. Even so, the vast majority of users simply run the default window manager for their system.

The most common window manager your users will run is a variation of the Motif window manager, *mwm*.

The Motif Window Manager

Mwm looks and acts much like Microsoft Windows and OS/2 Presentation Manager—no surprise, since all three follow IBM's CUA guidelines. While they all look similar, there's a lot more you can configure with *mwm* than with Windows or Presentation Manager.

Mwm comes from the Open Software Foundation and is standard equipment on most commercial UNIX systems. In addition, the Common Open Software Environment uses a *mwm* variant as part of its Common Desktop Environment (or CDE). *Mwm* provides a common Motif look and feel for the titlebar and decorations it places on your application windows. And, to the user, *mwm* distinguishes itself by the look of these decorations, which are illustrated in Figure 1.4.

Though they can be rather subtle, there are many distinctive characteristics to a window managed by *mwm*. The top of the window is called the titlebar, and it (not surprisingly) identifies the window by a text string called a title.

To the left of the titlebar is the Window menu button. You can use this control to pull down a Window menu, which allows you to **Move**, **Resize**, **Lower**, **Iconify**, and **Close** (quit) the window.

To the right of the titlebar are two buttons. The small button, called the **Minimize** button, iconifies a window; that is, replaces the current window with a small picture (or icon at the bottom of the screen). The large button, called the **Maximize** button, resizes the window to the largest size possible.

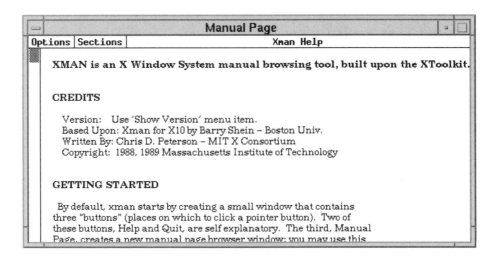

Figure 1.4   The Motif window manager titlebar.

Projecting Three Dimensions in Two

Another noteworthy aspect of *mwm* is its three-dimensional look and feel. Windows are shaded as to appear to pop off the screen to trick users into think that they are pressing real buttons instead of using a mouse to click on an area of the screen. Most other X window managers provide some form of three-dimensional look, including the Open Look window manager.

The Open Look Window Manager

Another common window manager is the Open Look window manager, or *olwm*. Use of *olwm* should drop dramatically as COSE systems become the norm for Sun Microsystems, the main Open Look proponent. For now, though, you'll still find *olwm* on many Sun systems, particularly since Sun users seem slow to convert from SunOS to Sun's newer Solaris 2.*x* operating system.

Olwm has a distinctive, rounder look, as shown in Figure 1.5.

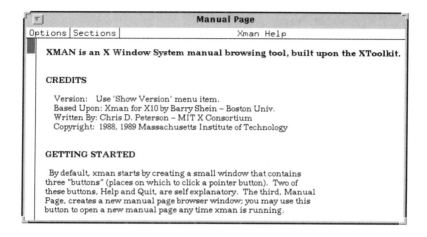

Figure 1.5   The Open Look window manager titlebar.

The Tab Window Manager

Many users, particularly at academic sites, use the free window managers that come with the X Window System's source code from the X Consortium. The most commonly used window manager that comes with the X sources is *twm*, the Tab window manager. *Twm* provides a simpler look and feel, as shown in Figure 1.6.

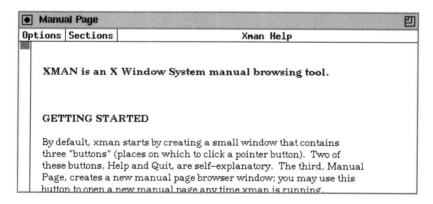

Figure 1.6   The Tab window manager titlebar.

Other Window Managers

There are many other window managers, but most, such as Silicon Graphics' *4Dwm* and Hewlett-Packard's *vuewm*, provide some variant on the Motif look and feel. We list some of the main window managers in Table 1.1.

Table 1.1   Common X window managers.

Program	Window Manager	Used Mainly With
dtwm	DeskTop window manager	COSE CDE systems
dxwm	DECwindows window manager	DEC workstations
4Dwm	4D window manager	SGI workstations
mwm	Motif window manager	Motif-supported workstations
NCDwm	NCD Window manager	NCD X terminals
olvwm	Virtual Open Look window manager	X11R5
olwm	Open Look window manager	Sun workstations, pre-COSE
twm	Tab window manager	X11R5, R4
tvtwm	Virtual tab window manager	X11R5
vtwm	Virtual tab window manager	X11R5
vuewm	HP VUE window manager	HP workstations
XDSwm	Visual window manager	Visual X terminals

Determining Which Window Manager is Running

Every window manager has *wm* in the name of the executable program. This means you can determine what window manager is running by generating a process listing and searching for the string *wm*. For example, on System V UNIX systems, you can use the following command:

```
% ps -ef | grep wm
```

You'll see a response something like:

```
erc   185   180   0 11:36:48 ?          0:01 mwm
```

This tells you that *mwm* is the window manager. Users can run only one window manager at a time on a given display.

Active Windows

When you have multiple windows, you still need a logical method for organizing the windows. Even though you may have multiple windows on your display, only one is *active* or has the *keyboard focus*; that is, only one accepts your direct keyboard input. This active window (also referred to as the *window with focus*) usually will be colored differently than other windows on the display (the exact color changes depend on your system configuration), and the cursor will usually change shape when placed over the active window. For instance, if you've opened an *xterm* window (a popular X Window command-line terminal-emulation client) to perform some command-line processing on your own machine or another networked machine, the cursor will change to an I-beam cursor, indicating that text entry and editing occurs in that window.

The window manager controls which application receives the keyboard focus, and the window manager controls how this active window is highlighted. The window with focus automatically receives all of your keystrokes, no matter where the pointer is positioned. However, not every window accepts keystrokes. In the case of an application like *xeyes* or *xclock* made active for some reason or another (you might have moved or resized the window, for instance), your keystrokes will simply be ignored.

Many window managers follow this *click-to-type* model of window management: An active window stays active until the user explicitly clicks on another window, which then becomes the active window. (The converse of this model is *focus follows pointer*, where the active window is automatically the window underneath the mouse pointer. The window manager controls which mode is used.)

Icons: On-screen Symbols

Icons play a very important role in X, if only to allow you to organize the inevitable screen clutter when working in a multitasking graphical environment. If you're like us, you're going to be doing more than one task with your computer—which means opening multiple windows on your display. By iconifying a window, you replace it with a small symbol on the bottom of the screen. The application is still in your computer's memory, and, depending on the application, it may or may not be actively working (for instance, some applications block input when the window is iconified). When you click on the icon, the window reverts to its full size. If you look closely at the icons in Figure 1.7, you'll see a text string on the bottom of each icon; this *label* (usually the name of the application) identifies the icon through an application name.

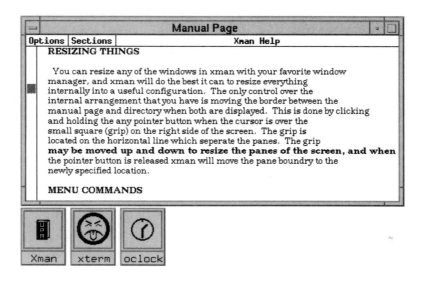

Figure 1.7   An X display with a full window and iconified windows.

Summary

This chapter introduced the X Window System and explained its importance to the UNIX system administrator. Particular attention was paid to window managers, a crucial area for system administrators to master.

The next chapter provides an overview of the X tasks that UNIX administrators need to perform.

The X Administrator's Job

Topics covered in this chapter include:

* ❋ An overview of the X administrator's tasks
* ❋ Getting a handle on X
* ❋ X from the system administrator's point of view
* ❋ X from the software developer's point of view
* ❋ Platform layout differences
* ❋ Sun Microsystems file configurations
* ❋ Hewlett-Packard file configurations
* ❋ IBM file configurations
* ❋ SGI file configurations
* ❋ COSE extensions to the X environment

Take This Job and...

The very nature of the X Window System makes it hard to administer. X applications can reside on one machine and display their output on another. This seemingly simple concept opens a series of Pandora's boxes in the areas of network configuration, security, and, of course, system-administration tasks.

This chapter provides a brief overview of the tasks a UNIX system administrator must perform to set up and configure X systems properly. We also describe X from the point of view of the UNIX system administrator.

X Tasks For the Administrator

The basic X-related tasks required of an UNIX system administrator include:

- ❖ Installing X
- ❖ Setting up your own X-based configuration
- ❖ Setting up X on UNIX workstations
- ❖ Configuring user accounts to start with X on login
- ❖ Installing fonts and perhaps a font server
- ❖ Messing with the dreaded X resource files
- ❖ Trouble-shooting keyboard quirks with X software
- ❖ Securing your X environment
- ❖ Installing and manage X terminals, including PCs configured as X terminals
- ❖ Installing X application software from third parties

We'll briefly discuss each of these tasks in this section. In addition, these topics will be covered in depth throughout this book.

Installing X

Over the years, X has become much easier to install. It still takes about 100 megabytes—that's right, *100 megabytes*—of disk space, though. Most commercial UNIX vendors now incorporate X installation as part of a larger UNIX installation or upgrade, so you may not need to install X on your systems.

Setting Up Your Own X-Based Configuration

There's a host of things you need to configure on a given X environment. Luckily, users can perform many of these tasks. However, chances are they'll be asking *you* how to do them.

 You'll need to set up the proper permissions and paths so that users can run the neat (and not so neat) programs that come with X.

N O T E

Setting Up X on UNIX Workstations

Whether or not you need to install X, there's still a number of tasks necessary to get X properly set up in a networked environment. You'll need to verify that X actually starts and runs and, more importantly, that your users can start X.

Setting Up User Accounts to Start-Up with X on Login

Once X is set up properly, you need to set up user accounts to work with X. Of paramount importance is ensuring that X, along with the user's X environment, starts when a user logs in. When the user quits this environment, X should stop and the user should be logged out.

On modern workstations, X has become the user environment. X, along with vendor-supplied software like Sun's OpenWindows desk set or the COSE Common Desktop Environment, is now the primary way users interact with their UNIX workstations.

Installing Fonts and the Font Server

The default X Window System comes with a dizzying array of fonts, more than you'll probably ever need. Even so, some applications require additional fonts or they simply won't run. In addition, X won't accept new fonts unless they're installed properly.

Along with fonts, you may need to set up the font server. New with X11 Release 5, the font server provides font information on demand for the X server. Normally, font servers support Adobe Type 1 and Bitstream Speedo fonts.

Messing with the Dreaded X Resource Files

X resource files are a great strength and a terrible problem. Users and administrators can customize huge portions of most X applications (that is, today's UNIX applications, which tend to be X-based) by editing an external ASCII resource file. For example, you can change font sizes, colors, and even some of the text messages used by your applications. Administrators can set up sitewide defaults that cater to your particular needs. That's the good part.

The bad part is that the syntax for setting X resources can be confusing at best. Once you master the syntax, you also have to deal with the plethora of locations where X resource files can reside.

Trouble-Shooting Keyboard Quirks with X Software

Using the keyboard should be a no-brainer, right? Not with X. Many times you'll need to diagnose, change, or pound into shape the keyboard on your X-based workstation. Often, users need to enter foreign characters, and you must convince the keyboard to allow this. Other times, especially for users of the *emacs* text editor, you'll need to configure the keyboard and perhaps remap some of the keys.

Left-handed users can remap the mouse buttons, reversing them if necessary. Users can set up programs to use older, more familiar key combinations.

Securing Your X Environment

X, developed in an academic community, has been faulted—and rightly so—for being lax when it comes to security. Just think about it: every single keystroke entered at an X workstation—including the superuser password—is being sent out over a network transport. If this transport layer is not secure, your system is compromised.

In addition, even if malicious users cannot gain access to the network packets, they often can gain access to your X display. This allows users to see everything you do and may even allow them to damage your system.

> 🚫 In recent years, security in X has advanced a great deal, but you still
> need to be aware of the problems and risks.
>
> WARNING

Installing and Managing X Terminals

X terminals can be administered from a central site, but they increase the
complexity of your system. Users at X terminals must log on to other systems
on the network and compute there. In fact, users at X terminals (or any X
workstation) can log on to a number of machines on the network and display
all the results on the X terminal on their desk.

The system that allows for X terminal users to choose which system to
log on to and to present the login banner is called the *X Display Manager*, or
XDM for short. You'll need to set up XDM and secure it in order for users
to log in.

Installing X Application Software

Most commercial UNIX applications these days are also X-based. These
applications should come with complete installation instructions. Even so,
you may still have problems—particularly where the application intersects
with X, such as when using a shared X library.

Most free software packages don't come with complete instructions, so
you're left more on your own with this class of software. No matter what the
instructions, administrators are expected to install any package necessary.

With all that said, this book will help you perform these and many more
X administration tasks.

Getting a Handle on X

What is this X thing that you need to install and configure? From a system
administrator's point of view, you may consider X your worst nightmare.
There isn't a single application that can be termed X, although the X server
executable is typically named with a single *X*. There isn't a single directory
where you can find all X-related files. Different vendors ship radically different configurations. You'll find the same X programs located in wildly differ-

ent directories on systems from different vendors. You'll find that some vendors fiendishly remove some simple X programs from their systems, just when you least expect it. For example, many vendors don't ship *imake*, a Makefile generator commonly used to compile free X programs. Because of all this, you'll have to be ready for differences in your system's presentation of X.

From a system administrator's point of view, then, X is:

❋ The X server program named *X* (or *Xsun*, or *Xsgi*, etc.).

❋ A number of user applications, usually including a window manager, like *mwm*, *dtwm*, or *olwm*.

❋ An often-conflicting set of system preferences for attributes like colors and fonts.

❋ An often-conflicting set of user preferences, usually stored off the user's home directory, for attributes like colors and fonts.

❋ A huge set of configuration files, including more fonts than you ever thought existed.

Where Does X Reside on Disk?

In a default configuration, various aspects of X reside all over your disks. In the next few pages, we'll cover aspects of X from both a user's and a software developer's perspective. Since many UNIX workstations are used primarily for software development, X provides a number of tools, include files, and libraries for developing X programs. We won't cover them all, but we'll show you where to find them.

Once we've presented the default configuration that ships with the generic X Window System, we'll show you how four major UNIX vendors — Sun Microsystems, Hewlett-Packard, IBM, and Silicon Graphics, Inc. (SGI) — have modified the generic configuration for their systems. We then cover the COSE changes to the default X layout.

NOTE

Always remember that previous administrators (or even yourself) may have customized the X configuration and locations for X files at your site.

X from the System Administrator's Point of View

From the system administrator's perspective—and also for users—the two most important directories for X files are **/usr/bin/X11** and **/usr/lib/X11**. Most X programs are stored in **/usr/bin/X11**, and most X configuration files are stored in **/usr/lib/X11**.

Common X Programs

You'll be surprised at the primitive state of most of the programs that come with X. Some X applications are surprisingly sophisticated, but most are simple to the extreme. Table 2.1 lists the more useful X programs you should find on your system. These programs are covered under the appropriate headings in later chapters.

Table 2.1   Common executable programs found in /usr/bin/X11.

Program	Use
X	X server; often named something like *Xsgi* or *X386*
bdftopcf	Converts bitmap font file to binary X server font file
bitmap	Bitmap editor
fs	Font server; can scale fonts for X server
fsinfo	Prints information on font server
fslsfonts	Lists font-server fonts
fstobdf	Converts a font-server-scaled font to a bitmap font file
mkfontdir	Sets up a font directory
mwm	Motif window manager
oclock	Rounded-corner clock program (displays current time)
resize	Reconfigures an *xterm* window for a new size
startx	Shell script to start X (used on some systems)

continued

Program	Use
twm	Tab window manager
xauth	X security program
xbiff	Mail notification program
xcalc	Calculator
xclock	Program displays current time
xconsole	Displays console messages
xdm	X Display Manager
xdpr	Captures screen dump and prints picture
xdpyinfo	Outputs information on your X environment
xedit	Primitive text editor
xev	Prints output on keys you press; used to diagnose keyboard problems.
xeyes	Eats up CPU cycles
xfd	Displays characters in a font
xfontsel	Allows you to choose a font graphically
xhost	X security program
xinit	Starts X server on some systems
xkill	Kills an X program
xload	Displays system load graphically
xlsclients	Lists running X programs
xlsfonts	Lists available font names
xlswins	Lists windows on display; used to find hidden windows
xmag	Magnifies the bits on part of the display
xman	Displays UNIX man pages
xmodmap	Modifies keyboard and mouse button mappings
xpr	Prints out a captured screen image
xprop	Lists X properties on a window
xrdb	Loads a resource file into X server

continued

Program	Use
xset	Sets various X server parameters like screen saver
xsetroot	Changes screen background color or image
xstdcmap	Creates standard colormaps; useful with PEX applications
xterm	UNIX terminal emulator; provides a UNIX command-line under X
xwd	Dumps (captures) a screen image to disk
xwud	Undumps, or displays a captured screen image

As always with X, your system probably doesn't offer all these programs.

X Configuration Files

Most X configuration files are stored in subdirectories of **/usr/lib/X11**. The most common subdirectories are listed in Table 2.2.

Table 2.2   Configuration subdirectories under /usr/lib/X11.

Subdirectory	Contains
app-defaults	System default X resource files
fonts	X font files
nls	International text messages
xdm	XDM configuration

X Font Files

The **fonts** directory usually has a number of subdirectories, each containing a different font format or font sizing. The X font formats have one step in the past and one in the future: The older font formats sized fonts at 75 dots per inch (dpi) or 100 dpi. Newer font formats are tied to the vendor—PostScript fonts from Adobe and Speedo fonts from Bitstream—on purpose, such as the fonts used by PEX. Typically, the **/usr/lib/X11/fonts** directory will occupy a lot of space on disk. Table 2.3 lists the most common font directories.

Table 2.3   Font directories under /usr/lib/X11/fonts.

Subdirectory	Contains
75dpi	X font files tuned for a 75 dots-per-inch display
100dpi	X font files tuned for a 100 dots-per-inch display
misc	Miscellaneous X font files
PEX	Fonts for the PEX 3D extension to X
Speedo	Bitstream scaled fonts for font server
Type1	PostScript scaled fonts for font server

The **75dpi**, **100dpi**, and **misc** directories contain bitmap fonts, where each font file contains a given face with a given style at a given size. Contrary to what you'd expect, there are no restrictions on using fonts from the **75dpi** directory on a 100-dpi monitor (or vice versa). These fonts are just tuned to look better on displays of the given type. X places no restriction on their use, though.

The **PEX**, **Speedo**, and **Type1** directories contain scaleable fonts. The **/usr/lib/X11** directory also contains a number of key configuration files that you'll refer to again and again, as listed in Table 2.4.

Table 2.4   Configuration files stored in /usr/lib/X11.

File	Use
XErrorDB	Database of X error messages
XKeysymDB	Extra logical keys defined for the keyboard
Xconfig	Graphics hardware information for Intel-based systems
rgb.txt	Text version of color database
rgb.dir	Binary color database information
rgb.pag	Binary color database information

The **XKeysymDB** file is crucial for Motif programs to operate correctly. You'll often find this to be a problem on Sun systems that have yet to be upgraded to Solaris 2.3 or higher.

On Intel-based 386, 486, and Pentium systems, the **Xconfig** file is often used to specify what kind of graphics, keyboard, and mouse hardware are available.

X from the Software Developer's Point of View

From a software developer's point of view, the key X files are the necessary include files needed for compiling and the libraries needed for linking X applications. There's also a number of X applications that can aid software developers. Since it's likely that a good portion of your users will also be programmers, you'll need to know the location of these files and their availability. Table 2.5 lists a number of these programs.

Table 2.5   Common programs found in /usr/bin/X11 that are useful for software development.

File	Use
imake	Program to generate Makefiles from Imakefiles
lndir	Creates linked directories; used when installing X
makedepend	Generates dependencies for Makefiles
xmkmf	Shell script that invokes imake

For include files, X provides two main directories in which you should look. The two main X include directories are listed in Table 2.6.

Table 2.6   X include file directories.

Directory	Contains
/usr/include/X11	X and Xt include files, for compiling X programs
/usr/include/Xm	Motif include files

Under the **/usr/include/X11** directory, you'll also find a number of subdirectories, where various X library include files are stored. Table 2.7 lists these directories.

Table 2.7   X include file directories under /usr/include/X11.

Directory	Contains
extensions	Include files for X extension libraries
PEX5	Include files for PEXlib 5.*x*
phigs	PHIGS include files for PEX
Xaw	Xaw (Athena) widget set include files, for compiling X programs
Xmu	X miscellaneous utilities library include files

Not all directories will be available on all systems.

X libraries, used for linking X applications, are usually stored in **/usr/lib**, like most normal UNIX libraries. Some systems, such as those from Sun and Hewlett-Packard, store these libraries in nonstandard locations (see below).

In addition, the **/usr/lib/X11/config** directory should contain the necessary files for configuring *imake*. You'll find that *imake* is often necessary for compiling X programs, especially free X software.

Platform File Layout Differences

The disk layout previously described is the default setup for the generic X Window System. Unfortunately, the main UNIX players highly customized this layout. In the following sections, we'll just go over differences from the norm.

Sun Microsystems

Sun Microsystems, the leading supplier of UNIX workstations, chose to place all X files under one top-level directory, by default **/usr/openwin** (you can alter this when installing Sun's OpenWindows, which is Sun's name for its X package). Table 2.8 lists the main subdirectories under **/usr/openwin**.

Table 2.8   X include file directories under /usr/include/X11.

Directory	Contains
bin	X programs
etc	Miscellaneous configuration files
include	Include files for developing X applications
lib	Shared libraries used by executables; also used for linking
man	Online manual pages
share	Actual location for **etc**, **include**, and **man** directories

X applications are stored in **/usr/openwin/bin**. Some interesting programs in **/usr/openwin/bin** are listed in Table 2.9.

Table 2.9   Interesting Sun X applications.

Program	Use
answerbook	Displays Sun on-line help
calctool	On-line calculator
cm	A calendar manager
kbd_mode	Fixes a locked keyboard after running X
mailtool	Graphical front-end to mailx
pexdpyinfo	Presents information on PEX 3D extension to X
olwm	Open Look window manager
Xsun	X server

The **/usr/openwin/lib** directory contains the usual libraries for linking X applications. Since Sun makes extensive use of shared libraries, you'll need these files to run X applications, since virtually all Sun X programs are dynamically linked and expect these shared libraries. In addition to the libraries, the **/usr/openwin/lib** directory also contains a number of default start-up files used by OpenWindows, including **openwin-init**, the default start-up script, and **openwin-menu**, which holds the default menu definitions for the Open Look window manager, *olwm*.

The **/usr/openwin/lib/X11** directory corresponds to **/usr/lib/X11** on more generic systems. This directory contains the usual X configuration files and the fonts subdirectory. Sun systems provide an extra font directory, **F3**, for F3-format fonts.

Hewlett-Packard

Unlike Sun, which places all X files under one top-level directory, Hewlett-Packard (H-P) chose to distribute X files throughout the UNIX file system. In addition, H-P extended the basic X interface with the Visual User Environment, or VUE. VUE provides a nice front-end to the traditionally cryptic UNIX operating system, but VUE has its own quirks.

Like most X systems, you'll find the main X applications stored in **/usr/bin/X11**. Some notable applications include *datebook*, an online calendar, and *xhpcalc*, a calculator program that looks and feels like the popular H-P handheld calculators.

Most configuration files are stored in **/usr/lib/X11**. Many, though, are instead part of the VUE configuration.

The VUE Configuration

Most VUE files are stored under the **/usr/vue** directory, in a number of sub-directories (there's also a **$HOME/.vue** subdirectory for each user). The subdirectories under **/usr/vue** are listed in Table 2.10.

Table 2.10   H-P VUE directories.

Directory	Contains
app-defaults	X resource files for VUE programs
bin	VUE programs

continued

Directory	Contains
config	XDM configuration
dialogs	VUE dialog definitions
examples	Example user configuration files for VUE
help	VUE help files
icons	VUE icons
newconfig	VUE installation information
nls	International VUE text messages
palettes	VUE color palettes
types	Information on file types and actions

The **/usr/vue/config** directory contains much of what you find in **/usr/lib/X11/xdm** on other systems.

Software-Developer Files on Hewlett-Packard Systems

Software developers will be constantly trying to track down the necessary files on H-P systems. The key software-developer directories (starting with HP-UX 9.01) are listed in Table 2.11.

Table 2.11   H-P software-developer directories.

Directory	Contains
/usr/include/X11R5	X include files, also needed for Motif
/usr/include/Motif1.2	Motif include files
/usr/lib/X11R5	X libraries, also needed for Motif
/usr/lib/Motif1.2	Motif libraries

IBM

IBM systems store most X files under the **/usr/lpp/X11** directory, but maintain symbolic links back to the more traditional directories. For example, **/usr/bin/X11** points at the **/usr/lpp/X11/bin** directory, where the X programs are really stored. This directory structure allows IBM to store all X files under one directory hierarchy and yet still to present a system that looks like other X systems.

The program *xdt3*, stored in **/usr/lpp/X11/bin**, starts the AIX Windows desktop. Most other IBM programs are the traditional X programs you'd expect.

In addition to **/usr/lpp/X11/bin**, IBM systems also have a **/usr/lpp/X11/Xamples** directory, where many of the simpler X programs are stored in source and binary format. You'll also find the *imake* configuration files under this directory.

X include files are stored in **/usr/lpp/X11/include/X11** and **/usr/lpp/X11/include/Xm**.

SGI

SGI provides the most true-to-form layout for its X files. X programs are stored in **/usr/bin/X11**, and X configuration files are stored in **/usr/lib/X11**. SGI also provides a number of neat graphical programs with its system, some of which are listed in Table 2.12.

Table 2.12   Interesting SGI applications.

Program	Use
4Dwm	Silicon Graphics window manager
Xsgi	X server
endsession	Writes to an X property in a way that causes X to quit
toolchest	Provides menu access to many X and system functions
xwnmo	Input manager for Asian languages

COSE Systems

In addition to their own individual quirks, the main UNIX vendors (including Sun, H-P, IBM, Novell, and SCO) are migrating to the Common

Desktop Environment, or CDE. Part of COSE, this environment is based mainly on H-P's VUE interface, along with many of the Sun *deskset* applications, like the calendar manager and the electronic mail front-end *mailtool*. All of these applications, though, are written with the Motif toolkit under the CDE.

When fully installed, the CDE promises to eliminate many of the annoying differences between UNIX systems. Unfortunately, it will be years before all sites get upgraded. In addition, the COSE system-administration tools are on a much slower release cycle than the user environment. This means that COSE will make your users' lives easier far sooner than it will make your life as an administrator easier.

The nice thing about the COSE CDE, though, is that the environment looks remarkably similar on all the supported platforms. This is especially important for Sun and Novell UNIX users, as the Open Look interface is now dying a slow death, to be replaced eventually by a Motif interface. Any such form of standardization can only make your job easier—when implemented and distributed to all your systems.

The Common Desktop Environment

The CDE is built on top of the X Window System and the Motif toolkit. The CDE window manager, *dtwm*, acts very much like the Motif window manager and even more like the Hewlett-Packard window manager, *vuewm*.

By default, all COSE CDE files are stored under **/etc/opt/dt** and **/opt/dt**. The session configuration files go into **/etc/opt/dt**, which holds much of the same information as **/usr/lib/X11/xdm** in generic X. All other COSE files go into **/opt/dt**, which contains a number of subdirectories, as shown in Table 2.13.

Table 2.13   Main COSE CDE directories under /opt/dt.

Directory	Use
app-defaults	X resource files for CDE applications
appmanager	Application files used to launch programs by clicking

continued

Directory	Use
backdrops	Files for screen backdrops
bin	CDE executable programs

You can install the CDE anywhere on your disk. The default locations are **/etc/opt/dt** and **/opt/dt**.

In addition, in many of the CDE directories, you'll see subdirectories named **C**. These directories hold files for the "C" locale (really US English). If you have other locales installed, such as German or Japanese, you'll see other directories in parallel with the C directories.

Software Development with COSE

The include files for CDE development are located in **/opt/dt/include**, which contains a number of subdirectories, as shown in Table 2.14.

Table 2.14   CDE include directories under /opt/dt/include.

Directory	Use
Bento	Apple Bento files (used to store collections of objects)
Dt	CDE desktop function include files
Mrm	Motif resource manager include files
Tt	ToolTalk include files
X11	X include files
Xm	Motif include files

CDE libraries, including shared libraries, are stored in **/opt/dt/lib**.

Summary

This chapter introduces the main aspects of X Window configuration for UNIX system administrators. These tasks include:

❋   Installing X

❋   Setting up your own X-based configuration

❋   Setting up X on UNIX workstations

❋   Configuring user accounts to start with X on login

❋   Installing fonts and perhaps a font server

❋   Touching the dreaded X resource files

❋   Trouble-shooting keyboard quirks with X software

❋   Securing your X environment

❋   Installing and managing X terminals, including PCs configured as X terminals

❋   Installing X application software from third parties

Also covered in this chapter were the default file locations for a generic X installation, a Sun Microsystems installation, a Hewlett-Packard installation, an IBM installation, and an SGI installation.

This chapter ends with a short discussion of file locations for the COSE Common Desktop Environment, or CDE. The next chapter covers the first main task for X administrators: installing X.

Installing X

Topics covered in this chapter include:

* What you need to install X
* Steps to installing X
* Configuring the installation
* Configuration options explained
* Building the X Window System
* Build options explained
* Installation options explained
* Installing the newly built version of X
* Configuring *xterm*

Installing the X Window System

This chapter covers the time-consuming task of installing the X Window System from the source code that's freely available from the X Consortium. We cover the initial preparation needed before installation, as well as the building and installing processes.

Before installing X, though, be sure to ask the basic question: Do you really need to install X? Just about every commercial version of UNIX now comes with X. UNIX vendors modify the basic X sources to perform better on their displays and to enhance the X baseline.

Sun Microsystems, for example, adds Adobe's Display PostScript extension to X into the Sun version of X. Other vendors add video extensions. You won't get these extra features if you install the generic X Window System from the X Consortium.

For the majority of readers, the vendor-supported version of X will suffice. If it does, there's probably no sense installing X on your system, unless you're a glutton for punishment. A vendor-supported version of X may perform better and install much easier. In addition, you'll be running what the vendor has tested.

However, vendors are notoriously slow to upgrade their versions of X. You may be running X releases that are many years old and have no upgrade in sight. Some users, though, need to run the latest version of X and perhaps take advantage of special optimizations or bug fixes that your vendor doesn't support. These are good arguments for installing the generic X Window System on your corporate computer.

 Bottom line: X is the most highly portable windowing system we've seen, but it still can be a daunting task to get X built on your workstation.

N O T E

Check Your Disk First

While you may want to install X, it may not be possible due to lack of disk space. The X Consortium divides the X release into *core* (essential) and *contrib* (software donated by others outside of the X Consortium) sets. The core set requires about 100 megabytes of disk space. You may need even more while compiling the X sources. The contrib set requires about 140 megabytes of disk space, but few people bother to compile all of the contributed software. With a few exceptions (see Chapters 17 through 24 for more on this), you'll never need, nor use, nor want to use the vast majority of the free X programs.

X Versions

This chapter covers installing X11 Release 5 (known as X11R5 or just R5), the latest version of X. By May 1994, you should be able to get the source code for Release 6 (or R6) of X, a significant upgrade. You might think that you need the latest and greatest version of X, but we suggest you wait until after the initial release. Each release of X is followed by a flurry of patches and fixes to solve problems that early adopters discover.

Unless you want to be one of these early pioneers and deal with all the problems entailed in a major new software release, we suggest you wait a month or two until the release stabilizes. Once the release stabilizes, though, you'll probably want to upgrade. X improves with each release, which improves performance and adds neat new features. Vendor-supported versions of Release 6 should trail the X Consortium release of R6 by up to a year.

Even though the next release of X will add many new features, the installation process should be very similar to what we outline in this chapter. In fact, we noticed that the Release 4 and Release 5 installation processes are very similar, so we expect Release 6 to follow the same concepts.

What You Need to Install X

To install X, you'll need the following:

- ❋   The X Window System source code
- ❋   A supported operating system
- ❋   Enough disk space, about 100 megabytes for the core release
- ❋   A C compiler
- ❋   The *make* program

Since Release 5 came out in August 1991, you'll find that many modern operating systems simply aren't supported by the base release. On Sun systems, for example, R5 is only supported on SunOS 4.1.1, not the newer Solaris. Still, you'll find a host of patches available that support newer releases of operating systems, such as Solaris 2.*x*.

The full list of supported operating systems is shown in Table 3.1.

Table 3.1   R5-supported operating systems.

Vendor	Operating Systems
Apple	A/UX 2.0.1
AT&T	UNIX System V Release 4 V2
Cray Research	UNICOS 5.1
DEC	Ultrix-32 4.2, VAX 4.3bsd
HP	HP-UX 7.0 on 9000/s300, Apollo SR10.3
IBM	AIX 2.1.5
OMRON	Mach 2.5 Version 1.13
SGI	IRIX 4.0
Sony	NEWS-OS 4.1, NEWS-OS 5.0U
Sun	SunOS 4.1.1
Tektronix	UTek 4.0

Much of the hardware that runs these operating systems isn't even built anymore, such as Hewlett-Packard's Series 300 workstations and the Sun-3 family. This is a tribute to the fast-paced computer industry. If you'd like more information concerning support for the above systems, you should read the X11R5 release notes, which come with the R5 source code.

Don't be discouraged by Table 3.1, as most modern operating systems are supported by X. Just about every form of Intel-based system running just about every form of UNIX is supported by a project called XFree86. If your operating system isn't on the previous list, you'll need to check some of the locations for the freely available X sources for the proper patches for your system.

The reason we repeatedly mention the 100MB or more disk space requirement for X is because few people have over 100 extra megabytes of disk space on most systems.

The X source code is written in the C language, the most common programming language on UNIX systems. We mention a C compiler and *make* just because many commercial versions of UNIX skimp on software development tools. Sun's Solaris, for example, unbundles the C compiler. If this is the case for your site, you'll need to get a C compiler. (Solaris users can use the free *gcc* compiler.)

Installing X: A Checklist

To install X, you need to:

- ✳   Obtain the X source code
- ✳   Unpack the sources, if necessary
- ✳   Read the release notes
- ✳   Determine if you have a supported operating system
- ✳   Determine where on disk you're going to install X
- ✳   Prepare the X directories
- ✳   Determine which parts of X you'll build
- ✳   Set up the X configuration files
- ✳   Build the world of X
- ✳   Wait for a long time
- ✳   Verify that your build completed successfully
- ✳   Install the newly built version of the X Window System

Obtaining the X Window Source Code

You can get the sources for the X Window System from different locations, at a variety of price points, including the following:

- ✳   Use anonymous FTP to transfer the files to your system from an Internet site. This, of course, requires an Internet connection.

❋ Purchase a set of tapes or a CD-ROM with the X sources. We've seen prices as low as $29.95 for a CD-ROM. Tapes are usually much more expensive, due to the higher media cost.

❋ Purchase X in binary form from a third-party vendor. Many vendors sell X for Intel-based UNIX workstations. This is very useful in that some of the Intel-based UNIX vendors are notoriously slow to upgrade their versions of X.

Look in Chapter 17 for more information on obtaining X. First, check if X is already installed on your system. Virtually all UNIX systems come with some form of X, even if they give it a different name—Sun makes it part of the OpenWindows environment, while Interactive UNIX calls it EasyWindows. If you find the vendor-supplied version of X acceptable, you can save yourself a lot of work—and disk space—by just using what's already installed on your system.

Unpacking The X Sources

If you order the X sources on tape or ftp the sources from an Internet site, you've probably picked up a set of compressed and split files. The files are split into smaller chunks that work better for sending over a network. If so, you'll need to unpack the sources. If you have the X sources on a CD-ROM, this step should already be done for you.

There are four basic directories, or parts, to the X Consortium core release, stored in subdirectories **mit-1**, **mit-2**, **mit-3**, and **mit-4**. (Prior to its spin-off as a separate corporation, the X Consortium started out at the Massachusetts Institute of Technology, hence the frequent use of *MIT* in file and directory names.) The contents of these directories are listed in Table 3.2.

Table 3.2   Contents of the R5 packed core release.

Directory	Contains
mit-1	Everything else not in the other parts, **mit-2**, **mit-3**, and **mit-4**

continued

Directory	Contains
mit-2	**clients**, **demos**, **rgb**, and **server** subdirectories
mit-3	Fonts from **fonts/bdf**
mit-4	Documentation in **doc** and **hardcopy**

To unpack the first part, use the following commands:

```
cd mit-1
cat mit-1.?? | uncompress | (cd top_src_dir ; tar xfp -)
```

where *top_src_dir* is the top-level source directory you want X to be in, such as **/usr/local/src/X11R5**. You then repeat this process with the **mit-2**, **mit-3**, and **mit-4** directories. Use a similar command for the contributed directories.

After doing this, read all the X release notes. You'll be very sorry if you don't. The instructions in this chapter come from our experiences building X, particularly on Sun workstations. The X source code you get may differ from the version we used, and—we hope—the problems we faced may have been solved, especially if you purchase a tape or CD-ROM of the X sources from a commercial vendor.

Also, a number of fixes have been released by the X Consortium, solving many problems faced by users. You'll want to get the latest set of fixes from the X Consortium as well. (Most X source code vendors include the latest fixes on their tapes or CD-ROMs, although the older the tape or CD, the less up to date you'll be.)

The fixes are usually applied to the source using a program called *patch*. Before compiling the X release, you should ensure that you have applied the proper patches, both general fixes to X and patches specific to your operating system, such as Solaris 2.*x*.

Your release notes may conflict with the instructions presented in the rest of this chapter. When in doubt, use the instructions that came with your X sources. You may very well have a more recent release than we had (we hope so) and the instructions may have changed. As always, common sense helps.

Read the Release Notes

Yes, we really want you to read them. Don't even think of installing a system as complicated as X without performing a little bit of preparation. The release notes describe the X installation process in great detail; read it and follow it.

In fact, you have your choice of format for the release notes, which appear duplicated in three separate files, listed in Table 3.3.

Table 3.3   X release notes formats.

File	Format
RELNOTES.PS	PostScript
RELNOTES.TXT	ASCII text
RELNOTES.ms	Troff (using -ms macros)

Preparing to Build the X Window System

The first step in preparing to build X is to determine whether your operating system is supported. If you run a system that isn't listed in Table 3.1 — and chances are this is the case, as the list is very old — you'll need to do some extra digging. Many of the X fixes added support for newer operating systems.

Other operating systems have special patches, such as the XFree86 and Solaris patches. When in doubt, check. Where should you check? If you have FTP access to the Internet, you can check **ftp.x.org**.

The next step is to decide where on disk you intend to build and install X. You need a disk location with enough space.

If your system is anything like ours, disk space is at a premium. If you have a multisystem site (and who doesn't), we recommend you share the source directories over a network, using NFS or other network file systems, as the X source code is so large. You'll also probably want to build the X sources in a separate set of directories, instead of the default source directories. The **lndir.sh** shell script helps with this. This shell script creates a local shadow set of directories that mimic the X hierarchy. Then the script creates links between the source code (stored on the remotely mounted disk) and the local directory (used to keep the object modules while compiling).

To use the **lndir.sh** shell script, first, create your top-level build directory, then change to this directory and execute the following command:

```
top_src_dir/mit/util/scripts/lndir.sh mit_src_dir
```

where *top_src_dir* is the top-level source directory you placed the X sources in, such as **/usr/local/src/X11R5**.

Determining Which Parts of X to Build

You have many choices when building X. You can decide to build the X server, the client libraries and programs, or both. You can build the PEX 3D extension to X or skip it. Table 3.4. summarizes the most important options.

Table 3.4 Parts of X you can build.

Part	Impact
Server	Necessary to run the X server locally
PEX	Used for 3D applications; usually safe to exclude
Font server	Can't use scaleable fonts
Libraries	May not be able to compile applications
Debug libraries	Cannot get at debugging information
Lint libraries	*Lint* won't understand X libraries and will complain

You can build or not build each X library, such as the Xt Intrinsics or Athena widget libraries. The problem is determining which libraries to exclude. X programs often require nearly all the libraries provided. Your best bet for reducing space is to eliminate the debugging libraries (extra copies of the X libraries built with C debugging information) as well as the lint libraries (extra copies of the X libraries built with lint information). You normally don't really need these nearly so much as you need the basic libraries themselves. It's also usually safe to exclude PEX, a very large extension to X, if you're short on disk space.

Configuring the Build

Once you've determined the basic areas to build, you need to set up the configuration files for building X. These build configuration files are stored in *top_src_dir*/**mit**/**config** in the source directories, where *top_src_dir* is your top-level X source directory (and, by default, **/usr/lib/X11/config** *after* installing X).

These are two main configuration files you need to edit: the **site.def** file and a platform-specific file, such as **sun.cf**. The **site.def** configures the X build for your entire site; that is, for every target system. The **site.def** file transcends platform-specific issues. In addition to the **site.def** file, there are a number of platform-specific files that configure the X build for a given platform and operating system. Usually these platform-specific files have names that immediately tell you which platform they're intended for, such as **sun.cf**, **hp.cf**, and **ibm.cf**.

When you edit the configuration files, put all platform-independent definitions for your whole site into the **site.def** file and all platform-specific definitions into the proper platform file.

Identifying the Configuration Options

There is a number of configuration, build, and installation options that you can place into either the **site.def** file or the platform-specific file, based on whether you want the option to apply to your entire site or just to a single platform. Table 3.5 reviews the most important options. A full set of more options than you'll ever need to deal with is listed in the **README** file in the *top_src_dir*/**mit**/**config** directory.

Configuration Options

The main configuration options usually apply more to a particular platform than to your entire site. These main options are listed in Table 3.5.

Table 3.5   Main configuration options.

Option	Use
BootstrapCFlags	C preprocessor symbols you need to define to get going
CcCmd	Command to invoke the C compiler
HasGcc	Set to **YES** if you use *gcc*, **NO** otherwise
HasLargeTmp	Set to **YES** if you have a large **/tmp** space; **NO** otherwise
HasSharedLibraries	Set to **YES** if your system has shared libraries; **NO** otherwise
HasShm	Set to **YES** for System V shared memory; **NO** otherwise
HasSockets	Set to **YES** if your system has BSD sockets; **NO** otherwise
OSMajorVersion	Set to major version number of operating system
OSMinorVersion	Set to minor version number of operating system
OSName	Operating system name, such as "HP-UX 9.01"
SystemV	Set to **YES** for systems that are at least SVR2; **NO** otherwise
SystemV4	Set to **YES** for SVR4 systems; **NO** otherwise
HasXdmAuth	Set to **YES** for using XDM-AUTHORIZA-TION-1; **NO** otherwise.

Set the **BootstrapCFlags** option to any missing symbols that your C pre-processor needs. Usually the existing platform-specific configuration files, such as **ibm.cf**, contain examples of this option. If you have immediate problems in the build, you probably need to set a new value for this option.

The **CcCmd** directive holds the command necessary to invoke the C compiler. Usually, this is simply set to **cc**. On some systems, you may use a different command to invoke the C compiler.

The **HasGcc** directive tells the X build process whether or not you are using the GNU C compiler (*gcc*). If you use the GNU C compiler, then uncomment this definition:

```
#define HasGcc    YES
```

This flag is intended mainly for an older version of *gcc*, where you had to run the **fixincludes** script to fix the include files for *gcc*, or you'd get serious errors with X networking. Newer versions of *gcc* don't share this problem. (Check your *gcc* installation notes to see if you need to run the **fixincludes** script.)

If you set **HasLargeTmp** to **YES**, then the X build will put together some very large C libraries, using the UNIX **ar** library archiver, in **/tmp**. If your **/tmp** is not large enough, or if you fill up **/tmp** during the build, set **HasLargeTmp** to **NO**. This tells the X build to use the current directory for placing object modules into libraries with **ar**.

Set **HasSharedLibraries** to **YES** if your system supports shared libraries. Shared libraries dramatically cut down the size of the installed X executable programs. Without shared libraries, these programs would each normally take up at least a megabyte of disk space each. With shared libraries, you can cut this significantly.

Many imaging programs try to use shared memory to avoid large—and slow—data transfers between the client application program and the X server. If the memory can be shared between the client and server, then performance improves. Set **HasShm** to **YES** if your system supports System V UNIX shared memory.

Set **HasSockets** to **YES** if your system supports Berkeley UNIX-style sockets. Virtually all commercial versions of UNIX do, except for low-end Intel-based UNIX systems, where networking is often an extra-cost option.

Set the **OSMajorVersion** to the major version number of your operating system, such as **2** for Solaris *2.3*. Similarly, set the **OSMinorVersion** to the minor version number, such as **3** for Solaris *2.3*. Set the **OSName** to the text name for the operating system. For example, with Solaris 2.3, you'd set the following values:

```
OSName Sun Solaris 2.3
OSMajorVersion    2
OSMinorVersion    3
```

With the major efforts for unifying the disparate versions of UNIX, the next two options are becoming less and less important. Set **SystemV** to **YES** if your system is at least at UNIX System V Release 2 or higher. Virtually all commercial versions of UNIX are at this level today. If you have System V Release 4 UNIX, set **SystemV4** to **YES**.

The **HasXdmAuth** option controls whether or not to build using the XDM authorization scheme known as XDM-AUTHORIZATION-1. This DES-based authorization scheme is not available on all systems, particularly if you live outside the United States, due to export restrictions. To use XDM-AUTHORIZATION-1, set **HasXdmAuth** to **YES**. If you do this, make sure that you have the key source-code file, *top_src_dir*/**mit/lib/Xdmcp/Wraphelp.c**. If you don't have this file, don't set **HasXdmAuth** to **YES**.

Build Options

In addition to the configuration options, there are a number of build parameters you can use to customize those parts of X that are built and install them accordingly. The most important build options are listed in Table 3.6.

Table 3.6   Main build options.

Option	Use
BuildFonts	Set to **NO** to disable building PCF fonts
BuildFontServer	Set to **NO** to disable building font server
BuildPex	Set to **NO** to disable building all PEX-related code
BuildPexClients	Set to **NO** to disable building PEX clients/demos
BuildPexExt	Set to **NO** to disable building PEX extension
BuildServer	Set to **NO** to disable building X server
BuildXInputExt	Set to **YES** for building X Input extension; **NO** otherwise
BuildXInputLib	Set to **YES** for building X Input library; **NO** otherwise

continued

Option	Use
BuildXsi	Set to **YES** for building Xsi input method; **NO** otherwise
BuildXimp	Set to **YES** for building Ximp input method; **NO** otherwise
MotifBC	Set to **YES** to enable bug-compatibility mode for Motif

The **BuildFonts** directive determines whether to build up the fonts. The PCF format, new in X11 Release 5, allows for sharing fonts between machine architectures, something that wasn't possible with older versions of X. If you have already built a set of PCF fonts, you can turn off building the fonts again by setting the **BuildFonts** directive to **NO**. These fonts occupy a lot of disk space, so you may want to share them between systems. Note that you may incur a performance penalty when doing this, though.

The **BuildFontServer** option determines whether or not to build the font server, which is new in X Release 5. The font server is a separate program that serves fonts to the X server. The main point of all this is that the X server only understands bitmap fonts. It is the font server that scales fonts and then provides the bitmap equivalent of the newly sized font to the X server. If you want scaleable fonts, you need to build the font server.

We've had numerous problems building the PHIGS 3D Extension to X, or PEX. The PEX code is known to blow away many C compiler limits for static table sizes, at least on some systems. If you have problems and cannot solve them, you can build without PEX by setting the **BuildPex** directive to **NO**, which prevents you from displaying PEX applications on your X server.

You can also control building PEX to a greater degree by building only the PEX client programs or the PEX extension to the X server using the **BuildPexClients** and **BuildPexExt** directives, respectively. The **BuildServer** directive determines whether the X server should be built (this can be overridden, as most parameters can, in the vendor file). It defaults to **YES**, so you only need to change if you don't want to build the X server.

You can control building the X input extension with the **BuildXInputExt** and **BuildXInputLib** options. The X input extension is used to provide a standard means for connecting alternative input devices, such as digitizing tablets, dials, and boxes of buttons. Most of these devices are used in the CAD industry. **BuildXInputExt** controls whether to build the input extension in the X server. **BuildXInputLib** controls whether to build a library so that you can create programs that use this extension.

If you run Motif programs, it's a good idea to allow for backward compatibility with older Motif 1.1 applications. To do so, set the **MotifBC** directive to **YES**. Most Motif programs should be at version 1.2 or higher, but there are still a large number of old applications to support.

X11 Release 5 adds support for international text input, especially for Asian languages. While nowhere near perfect, you can run X in Japan with full Japanese text input and output. The key to this is software called an *input method*, which translates the user's keystrokes into the necessary characters in the target language. For example, Japanese users type in a syllable using Roman letters, such as *ka*. The input method then converts this syllable into Japanese Kana. When the user enters enough Kana, the input method presents a list of available Kanji characters that match the Kana. Text input in Asian languages is not easy, but it's better than having a keyboard with tens of thousands of characters.

X11 Release 5 provides two main input methods, both incompatible (Release 6 should fix this problem): *Xsi* and *Ximp*. By default, all but Sony systems use *Xsi*. You can set one of the input method directives, **BuildXsi** or **BuildXimp**, to **YES**.

In addition to these options, you can control whether to build each C library in the X release. You can build the normal library, or you can build libraries with debugging, profiling, and lint information, all of which take up more disk space.

Installation Options

Once you've configured the build options, the next step is to configure the options that control the final installation of X on your system. Table 3.7 lists the main installation options.

Table 3.7   Main installation options.

Option	Use
ExpandManNames	Set to **YES** to expand man pages names to long form; **NO** otherwise

continued

Option	Use
InstallAppDefFiles	Set to **YES** for installing new app defaults files; **NO** otherwise
InstallFSConfig	Set to **YES** for installing **fs** config file; **NO** otherwise
InstallLibManPages	Set to **YES** for installing library man pages; **NO** otherwise
InstallXdmConfig	Set to **YES** for installing *xdm* config files; **NO** otherwise
InstallXinitConfig	Set to **YES** for installing *xinit* config files; **NO** otherwise
ManSuffix	Filename extension for manual pages
ProjectRoot	Specifies where to install runtime files
StripInstalledPrograms	Set to **YES** for stripping executables; **NO** otherwise

The **ExpandManNames** directive tells whether or not you want the online manual page files expanded for the long names. Most X functions, in particular, have very long names. The length of these names may exceed what your system allows (some UNIX systems allow for only 14-character filenames). **Set ExpandManNames** to **YES** to expand out the names; **NO** otherwise.

If you've changed the application defaults (that is, X resource files) for the main X applications, you may not want to overwrite these files with the new versions that don't contain your changes. If so, you can set **InstallAppDefFiles** to NO.

The X resources in these files changed dramatically between Release 4 and 5 of X. We expect even more changes for Release 6. It's probably better to simply save your existing files and install the new ones. You'll have to modify these new files later, but this avoids problems, such as the common problem where *xterm* menus appear in minuscule windows.

NOTE

Set the **InstallFSConfig** directive to **YES** to install the font-server configuration files. By default, the font-server configuration files are not installed, which seems odd to us.

The X programming library online manual pages take up a lot of space on disk. If users at your site won't be developing X applications, you can skip installing these manual pages by setting the **InstallLibManPages** directive to **NO**.

The two main ways to start up the X server are through *xinit*, which starts X locally on a per-user basis, and *xdm*, which controls both local and network logins. *Xdm* is necessary for X terminals. Since you'll most likely spend a lot of time configuring these programs, the X install process doesn't want to overwrite your changes. By default, neither the *xinit* nor the *xdm* configuration files will be installed. You can change this by setting **InstallXdmConfig** or **InstallXinitConfig** (or both) to **YES**. Again, we suggest you back up your existing configuration files and then install the new X files. You'll need to merge your changes back into the new configuration files, but you won't be missing out on new features.

The X online manual pages, by default, have a filename extension of *.n*, which places the manual files into the **mann** subdirectory. You can change this with the **ManSuffix** directive. To place the manual files into the **man1** subdirectory, for example, and use *.1* as a filename extension, set **ManSuffix** to **1**.

The **ProjectRoot** directive specifies where the X runtime files should be installed. If you want to use the defaults, **/usr/bin/X11**, **/usr/lib**, **/usr/lib/X11**, **/usr/include/X11**, and **/usr/man**, leave **ProjectRoot** commented out between the /* and */ comment delimiters. If you want to place all X files in a special disk partition or directory, uncomment **ProjectRoot** to read:

```
#define ProjectRoot your_base_directory
```

where *your_base_directory* is the base directory for all the X files to be installed. The X files will be installed in *your_base_directory*/**bin**, *your_base_directory*/**lib**, *your_base_directory*/**include/X11**, and *your_base_directory*/**man**.

For example, if you choose a **ProjectRoot** of **/usr/local/src/X11R5**, then X will be installed in the following directories:

✳ **/usr/local/src/X11R5/bin**

✳ **/usr/local/src/X11R5/include/X11**

✳ **/usr/local/src/X11R5/lib**

✳ **/usr/local/src/X11R5/man**

By default, the X executable programs include the symbol table information, which makes the program files much bigger. You can strip out this extra information by setting the **StripInstalledPrograms** directive to **YES**. Debugging information will not be available—but you'll rarely need to debug the standard X programs.

If you install different releases of X on the same system, you probably want to use different top-level ProjectRoot directories to separate the versions and to avoid overwriting any key files from previous versions.

Setting Up the Site Configuration File

Oddly enough, the two main directives you need to set in the site configuration file include **HasGcc** and **ProjectRoot** (both covered previously). We expect that both of these values will change depending on the different platforms you support. The expected location for this information is in the **site.def** file. Inside this file, you'll see two sections. The first section is checked *before* reading in the platform-specific configuration file. The second section is checked *after* reading in the platform-specific configuration file. This allows you to override values set in either file, if you're careful. In the latter part of the **site.def** file, you'll place most of the build directives, such as **BuildServer**, **BuildFonts**, and **BuildPex**.

Before changing any of these configuration files, make a copy. It's far too easy to mix up the entire build process, so make a back-up and save yourself a lot of grief.

Setting Up the Platform Configuration File

The appropriate vendor-specific platform configuration file to use should be self-explanatory—use **sun.cf** on Sun Microsystems workstations, **sgi.cf** on Silicon Graphics workstations, and so on.

In this vendor file, such as **sun.cf**, first set up the operating-system version numbers to be the version you're using by setting the **OSName**, **OSMajorVersion**, and **OSMinorVersion** values we just described.

Then set any other platform-specific directives. If your operating system is supported by the X release (see the list presented in "What You Need To Install X"), then the platform-specific configuration file probably is already configured for most of the necessary options for your system.

After configuring the **site.def** and platform-specific configuration files, other files you should look over include **Imake.rules**, **Imake.tmpl**, **Library.tmpl**, **Project.tmpl**, and **Server.tmpl**. Edit them if necessary *before* you try to build X.

Building X with Imake

Once you've configured the proper files, the next step is to build the X sources.

Most UNIX C software uses a program called *make* to compile and link programs. *Make*, in turn, uses a Makefile to tell it which files to compile and how to compile them, as well as adding any necessary customizations.

X, instead, uses a program called *imake* to generate Makefiles. *Imake* generates the Makefiles from Imakefiles, files that tell *imake* what to do. These Makefiles generated by *imake* are customized to your system configuration. Then, and only then, *make* uses the newly built Makefiles to build the software. To configure the X build for your systems, you need to provide enough information for *imake* to create an Imakefile in each subdirectory of the X sources. If you've set up the **site.def** and platform-specific configuration files, as we described previously, then you're probably done with setting up *imake*.

The whole purpose of *imake* is to have a way to deal with both platform-specific differences as well as any peculiarities at your local site. *Imake* looks in the ***top_src_dir*/mit/config** directory (where ***top_src_dir*** is your top-level X source directory) to find the necessary information that tells it about differences for your system. *Imake* also uses the Imakefile to tell it what it's trying to build. The output is then a Makefile, which is then used by the tried and true *make* program to build X. See Chapter 18 for more than you want to know about *imake*.

Building the World of X

When you build X, you run *make* in the top-level X source directory. The first step performed by *make* is to call *imake* to build all the necessary Makefiles in all the numerous subdirectories. Then *make* builds the source code in each directory, creating libraries and executable programs along the way. There are many of X sources to build.

Building X takes a long time, to say the least. First, change to the top-level source directory where you placed the X sources. You'll need to be logged in as **root**. Use a command like the following to build the whole thing, the world of X:

```
make World >& world.log &
```

If you have problems, you may have to use:

```
make World BOOTSTRAPCFLAGS=-DNOSTDHDRS >& world.log &
```

Set the **BOOTSTRAPCFLAGS** to whatever is necessary to get the code to compile. In our case, we needed the -**DNOSTDHDRS** option for *cc*.

Both *make* commands above send their output to a file named **world.log**, which contains important information about what is being built and what works are in the build. This file will grow immensely as the build process proceeds. To monitor this file, you can use the following command:

```
tail -f world.log
```

There is a lot of output in this file, so it's hard to track down if there are any problems. Generally, you can scan for words like *error* and *warning*. If the X build fails, it will come to a halt—but it may take a very long time before halting. Sometimes the build is so slow you can't tell if it's halted or not. Just be patient and wait until the process stops and you get back some sort of status message.

You'll have to wait for a long time; a *very* long time on some systems. The length of time that X requires to build varies greatly depending on the speed of your machine and the system load.

TROUBLE-SHOOTING

If something goes wrong in the build process, the best bet is to try to fix the problem and then try make World again, sending the output to a new log file. This may seem inefficient, but it ensures that all the necessary steps are performed using the current configuration.

If something really goes wrong and corrupts the top-level Makefile, don't panic. There's a copy in **Makefile.ini**, so you can copy this back to a Makefile, using a command like:

```
cp Makefile.ini Makefile
```

Don't try to build directly from the backup **Makefile.ini** or you may corrupt that file, too.

Verify the Build

Once built, verify that your build was completed successfully. Check the log file you used while building (**world.log**, usually) for any errors. If you find none, and it looks like the build succeeded, then you're ready to install X.

Installing X

You install X from the same top-level directory where you built X. You'll also need to be logged in as **root**. Before installing, you probably want to check one last time for available disk space. Most X files go into, by default, the following directories, listed in Table 3.8.

Table 3.8   Default X installation directories.

Directory	Use
/usr/bin/X11	for X programs
/usr/lib	for X C libraries
/usr/lib/X11	for X configuration, resource, and font files
/usr/include/X11	for X C language include files

All of this occupies a lot of space on your **/usr** partition. You can change the installation using the **ProjectRoot** directive just described.

To install X then, run **make install**. Again, we suggest you capture the output into a log file. You can use a command like the following:

```
make install >& install.log
```

If you change any configuration files, especially if you change the ProjectRoot directive for placing the installed files, run the following command first:

```
make Everything >& everything.log
```

This will rebuild the Makefiles (as well as act much like make World). Then run make install as previously described.

To install the online manual pages, run:

```
make install.man >& installman.log
```

Before moving on, check all the log files for errors. You may have a problem and not know about it, especially if you let X build overnight.

Setting Up Xterm

Once installed, you may need to perform a little more work to get the *xterm* program set up properly. *Xterm* is one of the most frequently used X programs because it provides access to the UNIX command-line shell. We normally run three or more copies of *xterm* in our daily computing.

Xterm uses its own (ASCII) terminal definition, so you need to ensure that your **/etc/termcap** and **/usr/lib/terminfo** databases are properly configured for *xterm*. If these databases are missing entries for *xterm* (this is very rare on modern UNIX systems, however), you can find sample entries in the ***top_src_dir*/mit/clients/xterm** directory (where *top_src_dir* is your top-level X source directory).

If you run System V UNIX, you may need to compile the entries with the tic **utility. Consult your system documentation for further information.**

N O T E

In addition to the terminal-type database entries, you may also need to ensure that there are enough pseudoterminals for *xterm*. Since each *xterm* run requires its own UNIX pseudoterminal, you may need to increase your system's allotment (you'll want at least 32). Each version of UNIX configures pseudoterminals differently, so consult your system documentation for more on this.

Summary

This chapter covers the time-consuming task of installing the X Window System from the source code that's freely available from the X Consortium. We cover the initial preparation needed before installation, as well as the building and installing processes.

To install X, you'll need the following:

✳ The X Window System source code
✳ A supported operating system
✳ Enough disk space, about 100 megabytes for the core release
✳ A C compiler
✳ The *make* program

To install X, you need to:

✳ Obtain the X source code
✳ Unpack the sources, if necessary
✳ Read the release notes
✳ Determine if you have a supported operating system
✳ Determine where you're going to install X on disk
✳ Prepare the X directories
✳ Determine which parts of X you'll build

❄ Set up the X configuration files

❄ Build the "world" of X

❄ Wait for a long time

❄ Verify that your build was completed successfully

❄ Install the newly built version of the X Window System

Each of these steps was covered in detail in this chapter, along with a discussion of *xterm* configuration.

In the next chapter, you will learn what to do once you've successfully installed X on your systems.

Workstations and X

This section covers what to do with your X workstations once you've installed X.

Chapter 4 delves into issues of starting, stopping, and remotely accessing X.

Chapter 5 describes how to set up a user account to run X and how to get the user's X environment configured properly.

Starting and
Stopping X Sessions

Topics covered in this chapter include:

* ❋   Strategies for starting X
* ❋   Starting X with *xinit*
* ❋   Display names
* ❋   Starting X with *startx*
* ❋   Starting X on OpenWindows under Solaris
* ❋   Starting X with *xdm*, the X Display Manager
* ❋   How to stop the X server
* ❋   Connecting to other X servers
* ❋   Using the *-display* command-line parameter
* ❋   Setting the DISPLAY environment variable

Configuring X to Launch Automatically

Whether or not you install X, there are still a number of tasks necessary to integrate X properly into a networked environment: verifying that X actually starts, making sure X runs, and, most importantly, that your users can start X. This chapter covers strategies for starting X through various programs and startup scripts, as well as stopping X.

Before your users can run X applications, they need to start the X server. The X server takes over control of the display: keyboard, mouse (or another pointing device, such as a graphics pad or a trackball), and at least one monitor—sometimes more in multiheaded systems. It also must communicate with a variety of proprietary graphics controllers and other assorted hardware.

However, launching the X server is merely a starting point—a crosshatch pattern and an X cursor aren't very valuable on their own. You'll want to enable your users to launch a number of X applications, including a window manager, when they start the X server. This means that you must master the mechanisms for launching X applications and window managers at startup, both to initially configure systems for your users and to fulfill the inevitable customization requests from your users. If you're introducing X or Motif to your computing environment, these are the issues that you'll face immediately.

Strategies for Starting the X Server

The two main tools for launching the X server are *xinit*, which starts X locally on a per-user basis, and *xdm*, which controls both local and network logins. (*Xdm* is necessary if X terminals are used.)

Of the two, *xinit* is easier to understand, and it also provides an introduction to the concept of starting X. *Xdm* is considered to be the preferred method for starting X, but we're going to cover it after covering *xinit*: While *xdm* embraces similar concepts, it involves more complicated networking issues.

Starting the X Server with *Xinit*

As we stated in Chapter 2, the X server is usually a program called *X*, normally located in **/usr/bin/X11**. On many systems, the real X server program is named something else, like *Xsun* or *Xagi*, with a symbolic link to *X*.

The program named *X* must exist, obviously. Most likely, this means you must link one of the available X server programs to *X*.

N O T E

The first thing *xinit* does is start the X server process. Users run *xinit* from their start-up scripts, such as **$HOME/.login** (C shell) or **$HOME/.profile** (Bourne or Korn shells).

Basically, *xinit* is not very complex. All it really does is:

* ❊   Start the X server, *X*, which takes control of graphics hardware
* ❊   Run the **$HOME/.xinitrc** script, or just *xterm* if no script is available
* ❊   Terminate when **.xinitrc** script exits, which also kills the X server

Xinit Options

While most users will run *xinit* without any options, there still are a few available. *Xinit* accepts three forms of command-line options: *xinit* options, X server options, and options that control the starting X client program (in lieu of running the **.xinitrc** script).

The main *xinit* option involves a display name, with the *-display display_name* option. X display names follow a simple syntax:

```
hostname:server_number.screen_number
```

In real life, the command line would look something like this:

```
xinit -display eric:0
```

where the workstation has the hostname *eric*.

The single colon (:) denotes Ethernet-style networking with TCP (or UNIX domain) streams. Two colons (::) denote DECnet protocols. The 0 stands for the first X server on machine *eric*.

The optional .0 means to use the first screen on the given display or X server. Screens can be confusing, but a screen is really just a physical monitor. Most workstations have only one monitor, so always use the screen number .0. Don't forget that a single X server can control a number of monitors at once; these systems are often referred to as multiheaded systems, found mainly in the CAD field.

Display Name for a Local Workstation

X uses a special syntax for a local workstation's display name. The purpose of this special syntax is to allow the X library to choose the best transport mechanism and to allow for a simple name for the local machine.

If you're running X11 Release 5 or higher, this default display name is :0 — skip the hostname. If you're still running X11 Release 4, the default name is unix:0.

This is one place where you need to know which version of X you're running. The best way to determine this is to check your vendor documentation or the online manual pages. Checking the manual page for X (*man X*) should help you determine your system's default server name.

Both default names allow the application to use the best local transport mechanism. For some systems, this means using a shared memory link, which is typically a lot faster than using a TCP/IP network link.

Normally the *-display* command-line parameter isn't needed to connect to a local display. Just use *-display* to connect to another X server. For the local machine, use the DISPLAY environment variable.

You and your users will almost never use the *-display* option. Why? Because the X server is usually launched locally, not on another machine.

Many new X users assume that when you login a remote machine, you also have to start X. This is an incorrect assumption: X is started at your local machine. X programs run remotely and are displayed on your local machine.

> **This tends to get confusing. As an administrator, you need to ensure that when users login their X environment gets started.**

X server options begin after a double dash (--). Any options that follow, to the end of the command line, are passed to the X server started by *xinit*. The first option passed usually is which X server to run, such as:

```
xinit -- /usr/openwin/bin/Xsun -l
```

N O T E

The X server name, such as *Xsun*, must start with a period (.) or slash (/). Anything else is assumed to be a command-line parameter to pass to the default X server. You'll want to add the complete path to the X server—hence our use of /usr/openwin/bin/Xsun in the previous example.

The previous command starts an X server named *Xsun* and passes the *-l* command-line parameter to *Xsun*. In general, any options following the X server name, such as *-l* in this case, are passed to the X server process.

If the X server name with the double-dash (--) options is not passed to *xinit*, then *xinit* will look for a file named **.xserverrc** in the user's home directory. This **.xserverrc** file must be a shell script that starts the proper X server. Commands can be placed inside this shell script.

If there is no **$HOME/.xserverrc** file (which is highly likely, unless you take the time to set them up, and few users set up such a file), then *xinit* starts the X server named *X*, passing *:0* as the display name.

To specify an X application to run in the place of **.xinitrc**, list it after a display name but before the double dash:

```
xinit /usr/bin/X11/xterm -geom \
      80x24 -- /usr/bin/X11/Xsgi
```

This command line starts the *Xsgi* X server and then runs *xterm* in place of the commands in the **$HOME/.xinitrc** file. *Xterm* is an arbitrary choice on our part; you and your users can run any X program in place of *xterm*. However, most systems that use *xinit* set up an **.xinitrc** file.

NOTE   The program name must start with a period (.) or slash (/). Anything else is assumed to be a command-line parameter to pass to the default program (which also happens to be *xterm*). Add the complete path to the program—in this case, **/usr/bin/X11/xterm**.

To run *xterm* instead of executing the **$HOME/.xinitrc** file, use the following simpler version of the command:

```
xinit /usr/bin/X11/xterm -geom 80x24
```

This command starts X using the default X server and then runs *xterm* instead of executing the **.xinitrc** script.

The XINITRC environment variable overrides the **$HOME/.xinitrc** file. This environment variable should name the file to run in place of **$HOME/.xinitrc**. This new file must be a Bourne shell script.

NOTE   Another environment variable to note: The XSERVERRC environment variable specifies a different file for the **$HOME/.xserverrc file.**

Start-Up Scripts with Xinit

Unless it's overridden, *xinit* executes the programs listed in the file **$HOME/.xinitrc**. If you use *xinit* to start the X server, the **.xinitrc** script is the accepted means to start an X session. The **.xinitrc** file lists the programs to start when the X server starts. In addition, each user will probably want to edit this file to add individual preferences (and, of course, they'll ask you to edit the file for them).

With very few exceptions, every user will run a window manager; your local needs and system configuration will determine the window manager you run. Because of the state of UNIX graphical interfaces, every user probably needs at least one terminal emulator, such as *xterm* (we normally start three or four *xterm* windows). Most vendor-supported UNIX systems come with some form of file-manager interface to UNIX, and many users will want these programs started as well. Quite a few like to use one of the graphical clock programs, such as *xclock* or *oclock*, to display the current time on the screen. And, of course, you'll want to launch your mainstay applications— database managers, graphical editors, and so on.

Since **.xinitrc** is a shell script, all the programs it launches—except the last—should be run in the background, with an ampersand (&) trailing the command. Why exclude the last program? If every program in **.xinitrc** is run in the background, then **.xinitrc** will quickly terminate, and so will your X server. (This, in essence, is how you stop X. In this situation, however, you don't want to stop X.) Commands that execute quickly and then exit, like *xsetroot*, need not be run in the background.

The program chosen to run in the foreground should be a program that the user will likely keep around for the entire X session. Usually this is a session or window manager (often the two functions exist in one program, such as in *vuewm*, the combination session manager and window manager on Hewlett-Packard systems).

There are two main reasons for ending the **.xinitrc** file with a window manager, like *mwm*. First, users want a window manager running during their entire X session. Second, most window managers provide a menu choice that allows users to control when they exit. Most window managers, like *mwm*, also provide a dialog to allow users a chance to double-check that they really want to quit their X session. If a window manager runs as the foreground program in the **.xinitrc** file, exiting the window manager is the means the user has to exit X.

If a number of long-running programs run in the foreground in a **.xinitrc** file, then users will probably be confused. Consider the following example **.xinitrc** file, which we include as an example of how *not* to set up an **.xinitrc** file:

```
/usr/bin/X11/xterm -geom 80x40 &
/usr/bin/X11/xterm -geom 80x40+300+300 &
/usr/bin/X11/oclock -geom 120x120+900+10 &
/usr/bin/X11/xsetroot -solid bisque2
/usr/bin/X11/mwm
/usr/bin/X11/xterm -geom 80x50+30+100
```

The previous example file starts two copies of *xterm* and one *oclock* in the background and then runs *xsetroot* in the foreground. Because *xsetroot* runs in the foreground, the execution of **.xinitrc** waits for *xsetroot* to complete. Since *xsetroot* completes very quickly, the **.xinitrc** shell script will soon proceed to the next command. This should cause no problem, unless the script file is ended with the *xsetroot* command, in which case the user's X session would end prematurely.

The next command starts the window manager, *mwm*, in the foreground. When the user later chooses the *mwm* **Quit** option, *mwm* will exit, and the **.xinitrc** script will proceed to the next command, which is to launch an *xterm* window. By that time, the user will expect to exit X. Instead, the user will see a new *xterm* window running without a window manager. The user will then have to quit this *xterm* window to quit X. Furthermore, there's nothing special about this *xterm* window that distinguishes it from the other two copies of *xterm* started earlier. Thus the user will have no clue as to which program to quit to end the X session. This is probably not a good idea, unless you want to be deluged with questions about the mystery *xterm* window.

The lesson: Be careful about the commands placed in the foreground in the **.xinitrc** file.

Editing .xinitrc

WARNING

A word of caution to you and your users: If *xinit* is used to launch a current X session, be careful when editing the **.xinitrc** file. Since *xinit* executed that file to start X, you're asking for trouble if you edit that file while it's still in use.

The simple way to avoid trouble is copying **.xinitrc** to another file, such as **.xinitrc.new**, and then editing this new file. Once the editing is finished, quit X and *then* copy your new file, **.xinitrc.new**, to **.xinitrc**.

An Example .xinitrc File

Use the following file as an example when creating **.xinitrc** files:

```
# Sample .xinitrc
#
#
# Load in X resources to
# set up X environment.
#
/usr/bin/X11/xrdb -load $HOME/.Xresources
#
# Start three xterms. Start the
# third as an icon.
#
/usr/bin/X11/xterm -geom 80x40+1+1 &
/usr/bin/X11/xterm -geom 80x40+300+270 &
/usr/bin/X11/xterm -iconic &
```

```
#
# Change the screen background color.
# This can be a foreground process,
# as it completes quickly.
#
/usr/bin/X11/xsetroot -solid lightgrey
#
# Start a clock program.
#
/usr/bin/X11/oclock -geom 120x120+900+0 &
#
# Start the window manager
# as the foreground process.
#
exec /usr/bin/X11/twm
```

The first command loads user resources stored in the file **.Xresources**, which can be found in the user's home directory (the file name **.Xresources** is arbitrary). This command runs in the foreground because it completes quickly. In addition, we want to ensure that the proper environment is set up before launching any other X program.

The next three commands launch *xterm* windows. The third window is created as an icon to clean up the cluttered screen. We run these commands in the background, since we want to interact with the *xterm* windows for a long time.

The next command, *xsetroot*, changes the screen's background color to light gray. Most users don't like the default X cross-hatch background. This command runs in the foreground, as it, too, completes quickly. However, most commercial versions of UNIX include a system-dependent means for the user to change the screen background color. If your system does this, you're off the hook: your users can set this up for themselves. Hewlett-Packard systems, for example, have a VUE Style Manager that allows users to choose a solid color or a bitmap-pattern screen backdrop.

After *xsetroot*, the *oclock* command starts a clock window. Being Type-A personalities, we both like to know what time it is—all the time.

The final command in our sample **.xinitrc** file launches the window manager in the foreground. We use *exec* to launch the window manager because *exec* will overlay the shell process with the window-manager process, using system resources more efficiently. Figure 4.1 shows the result of using this **.xinitrc** file and starting X with *xinit*.

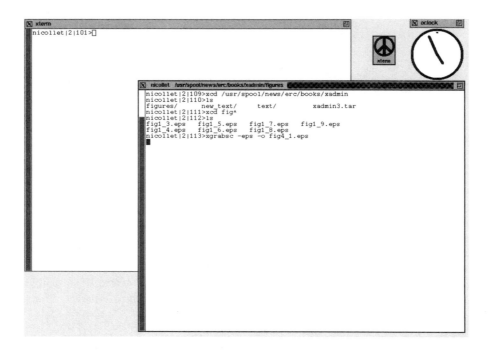

Figure 4.1   The X environment started by our example .*xinitrc* file.

If *xinit* fails to find a **.xinitrc** file, it starts the X server and one 25-line *xterm* window. To quit X, users must quit the *xterm* window by typing **Ctrl-D** or **exit**, or by using **kill** to terminate the X server's process ID. These are not very intuitive.

Starting X with Startx

As hardware prices continue to drop and standard PCs gain in performance, more and more PCs are used to run UNIX. Many of these systems will run a variant of a free X package called XFree86, which is a port of the X software to most Intel-based versions of UNIX. If your site uses UNIX-based PCs as an X station, you'll need to note how XFree86 differs from the X conventions. For starters, XFree86 uses a shell script called **startx** to initiate an X session, not *xinit*. (However, the use of **startx** is not limited to XFree86 users. It's just that XFree86 is where **startx** is used most often.)

Under the hood, **startx** passes parameters to *xinit*. Many of these parameters are based on values found in the **Xconfig** file in **/usr/bin/X11**.

Starting X on OpenWindows under Solaris 2.*x*

Sun's OpenWindows uses a script called **openwin** to start X (located, by default, in **/usr/openwin/bin**). As with most systems, it's best to go with the flow and use the SunSoft-provided scripts, customizing them as necessary. The **openwin** script acts a lot like the *startx* script covered previously.

Before running **openwin**, set the OPENWINHOME environment variable to the location of the OpenWindows directory, usually **/usr/openwin** or **/home/openwin**. The following command works for the C shell:

```
setenv OPENWINHOME  /usr/openwin
```

If running the Bourne or Korn shells, use these commands instead:

```
OPENWINHOME=/usr/openwin
export OPENWINHOME
```

TROUBLE-SHOOTING

If OPENWINHOME is set to anything other than /usr/openwin, OpenWindows may not start properly. If OpenWindows is installed into a different directory, use a symbolic link to link /usr/openwin to the alternative directory.

The **LD_LIBRARY_PATH** should point to the OpenWindows library directory, as shown in the following C shell command:

```
setenv  LD_LIBRARY_PATH  $OPENWINHOME/lib
```

In the Bourne or Korn shells, use the following commands:

```
LD_LIBRARY_PATH=$OPENWINHOME/lib
export LD_LIBRARY_PATH
```

In Solaris 2.*x* or higher, the system **.login** and **.profile** files should take care of setting OPENWINHOME and LD_LIBRARY_PATH for users. These values must be set if they are not being set otherwise.

TROUBLE-
SHOOTING

If you experience problems connecting to the OpenWindows X server, run openwin with the -noauth (no authorization) option. Otherwise, there's no need for any command-line parameters for openwin.

The **openwin** script will start X and then run the commands in **.xinitrc**, if there is such a file in the home directory. If not, **openwin** looks for a file named **.openwin-init** in the home directory and executes the commands in that file. This file is very similar to **.xinitrc**. The **.openwin-init** file is created by saving the workspace (a menu choice in *olwm*, the Open Look window manager). This allows users to restart an X session like the one they last ran—an important consideration for most users, so we suggest using the **$HOME/.openwin-init** file instead of **$HOME/.xinitrc** on OpenWindows systems. Inside the **openwin-init** file there are a number of **toolwait** commands in a format similar to:

```
toolwait xclock
```

Toolwait takes the name of an X program on the command line. **Toolwait** then starts this X program, passing any arguments to the X program, and waits until the X program starts. Once started, **toolwait** quits. This provides a more orderly start-up: There's no control over when background programs come up, as different X programs take a different amount of time to start.

There's no need to start a window manager inside the **.openwin-init file**, as the **openwin** script starts *olwm* by default. If a different window manager is desired, use the *-wm* command-line parameter to **openwin**, as in the following command:

```
openwin -wm twm
```

The above command starts the *twm* window manager instead of *olwm*.

Keyboard Problems on Sun Systems

After quitting X on a Sun workstation, users may experience a locked-up keyboard. If that's the case, run the *kbd_mode* program to reset the keyboard. The following command should do this:

```
kbd_mode -a
```

Because the keyboard will be locked up, you'll need to execute this command from another workstation and remotely login to the system with the downed keyboard.

Because we found ourselves facing too many locked-up keyboards, we customized our start-up sequence to call **openwin** and then run *kbd_mode* afterward, as shown in the following command:

```
openwin ; kbd_mode -a
```

Two other commands that help restore the Sun environment include **clear_colormap** (which gets rid of a colormap bug) and **clear** (which removes a dangling cursor rectangle). Run both of these after the **openwin** script exits.

Starting the X Environment with *Xdm*

In place of *xinit*, most modern versions of UNIX are moving toward *xdm* or a close system-specific variant. In fact, *xdm* is considered the preferred method for starting X: *xdm* provides an X-based login prompt, rather than the old-fashioned text login prompt.

Xdm, short for X Display Manager, controls an X server. It also controls user logins to a given display, which makes it very useful for X terminals. *Xdm* can manage a number of X servers, including X servers that run on X terminals. In fact, if you log on a workstation and see an X-based login screen, you're probably running *xdm*.

N O T E

As system administrator, it's important that you always remember that xdm is normally run by the root user. This means you must set up xdm—your end users cannot.

Xdm manages a collection of X displays. These displays may be local to a machine, or may include X terminals over a network. When managing displays, *xdm* provides services similar to what *init*, *getty*, and *login* do on a text-based terminal. *Xdm*, run by the root user, presents a login screen and then, after accepting a user login, starts the user's X session. When the user logs out, *xdm* reasserts control over the X display and again presents a login screen.

If running *xdm*, don't run *xinit*, since these two programs conflict.

X∂m performs the following tasks:

❈ Presents an X-based login screen that requires users to login to use the X display

❈ Launches a predetermined set of programs when the user logs in

❈ Launches a user-defined set of programs after that

X∂m first runs the system-defined environment and then any user-defined commands found in the **$HOME/.xsession** file. This allows *x∂m* to securely set up the user environment before starting the user-defined session.

The main *x∂m* configuration files are located in **/usr/lib/X11/xdm**, where there are also a number of root-owned files that control which X servers *x∂m* controls, as well as the starting environment to launch.

When users want to control their X session with *x∂m*, they must edit a **$HOME/.xsession** file instead of the **.xinitrc** file used by *xinit*. The two files are very similar. However, the **.xsession** file usually does a lot more to set up the environment than **.xinitrc**.

The **.xsession** file must be an executable file—it does not have to be a shell script, but it must have execute permission. In addition, this file will not be started by a shell, so that it will not inherit the user's shell environment. Because of this, many commands in **.xsession** files set up such an environment.

If using *xdm*, the **.xsession** file can be much the same as the **.xinitrc** file. We strongly advise copying the system **.xsession** file first and then customizing, as there are usually many system-specific customizations already in place.

Starting X Under the COSE Common Desktop Environment

The COSE Common Desktop Environment (CDE) uses a modified version of *x∂m* to control its environment. Modeled after H-P VUE, the main CDE login manager (*∂tlogin*) configuration files are located in **/etc/opt/dt** by default. Inside this directory, the configuration is very similar to that of *xdm*. Hewlett-Packard systems not running the CDE use *vuelogin*, a program much like *dtlogin*, with the configuration files stored in **/usr/vue/config**.

Connecting to Other X Displays

As we stated in Chapter 1, X is a network-transparent windowing system. You can start an X application program on one machine and interact with it on another. This makes configuring X harder, but also allows you to sit at one workstation and work on any machine on your network. This especially helps system administrators deal with a large and diverse network.

There are two main ways to connect between machines on the network: You can connect from your machine to another and you can connect from the other machine to yours. To envision this, imagine you have a very small network of only two machines: *eric* and *kevin*. Let's also say that you're sitting in front of machine *eric*, which is your main workstation.

As an administrator, though, you need to perform some maintenance on machine *kevin*. You use *rlogin* (or *telnet* or some other utility to log on to a remote host) to login to machine *kevin*. In fact, an easy way to do this from X is to run *xterm* and tell *xterm* to run *rlogin* and connect to machine *kevin*. To do this, use the following command:

```
xterm -e rlogin kevin &
```

This runs a copy of *xterm* locally (on machine *eric*). When *xterm* starts up, it normally runs your preferred shell, such as *ksh* or *csh*. With the *-e* command-line parameter, *xterm* runs a different process instead; in this case, *xterm* runs **rlogin kevin**. Put all together, this creates a new *xterm* terminal window on your display and this new window is logged in to machine *kevin*.

In addition, you can set up X programs to go the other way. Once you have a terminal window logged in to machine *kevin*, any X programs you run will display, by default, on machine *kevin*. Since you're sitting at machine *eric*, you no doubt want to display these programs at the machine at your desk. To do this, you need to set up the DISPLAY environment variable or use the *-display* command-line parameter, which every X program should understand. (These are essential for working with X terminals.)

For example, you may want to run *xload*, which displays the system CPU load, to provide a graphic picture of the CPU load on machine *kevin*. But remember that you want to display the results on machine *eric*. In the *xterm* window that's remotely logged in to machine *kevin* (which we started with the **xterm -e rlogin kevin**), you need to start *xload* and tell it to display on machine *eric*. The following command does this:

```
xload -display eric:0
```

The **eric:0** is the display name for machine *eric*, and it specifies the machine name, *eric*, and which X server, 0 (for the first X server), on machine *eric* to connect to. With this command, you're running *xload* on machine *kevin*, but displaying the results on machine *eric*.

There are some security issues involved. You may get an error when you run the command:

```
xload -display eric:0
```

If you get an error, such as *"X Toolkit Error: Can't Open display"*, you should check to see if the remote machine has access to your local display.

The DISPLAY Environment Variable

No one likes to type the *-display* command-line option for every X program started. Instead, a better way is to set an environment variable that all X programs should check. You type in the display name once, instead of every time you launch an X application. To do this, set the DISPLAY environment variable.

The DISPLAY environment variable contains the name of the default X server, usually the X server running on the workstation on your desk. This is the X server name used by most X programs, unless you explicitly state otherwise using the *-display* command-line parameter (covered above). Inside the DISPLAY environment variable, you place the same display name you would use with the *-display* command-line parameter.

For example, to set the DISPLAY environment variable to the first server on the first screen on a machine named *eric*, you can use the following command (in the C shell, *csh*):

```
setenv DISPLAY eric:0.0
```

In the Korn or Bourne shells, you'd use the following commands:

```
DISPLAY=eric:0.0
export DISPLAY
```

Setting the Display Environment Variable Automatically

Setting the DISPLAY environment variable every time you login to a remote machine is a real pain, especially if you need to connect to many other machines during a given day. To get around this, you can pass the value for your current display along to the remote machine, using *rsh*, the remote shell. *Rsh* launches a shell on the remote machine and can run an X application from that shell. (Some systems have a restricted shell and a remote shell. In these cases, the restricted shell may be named *rsh*, and the remote shell *remsh*. You want to run the remote shell program.)

The trick to passing the display name to the remote machine is to evaluate the DISPLAY environment variable locally first, as part of the command line you pass to the remote machine.

**TROUBLE-
SHOOTING**

For this trick to work, you must have set the DISPLAY environment variable to include your hostname. You cannot just use a display name of :0, which means the local machine. If you do so, this trick won't work.

For example, to run an *xterm* on a remote machine and have the *xterm* appear on your display, you can use a command like:

```
rsh kevin -n xterm -display $DISPLAY
```

This tells *rsh* to run the command

```
xterm -display $DISPLAY
```

on machine *kevin*, where $DISPLAY is the value of your local DISPLAY environment variable. Once this *xterm* is running, you can easily launch programs on the remote machine from that *xterm*, since the *xterm* has a shell on that machine which will connect up to the X server on your local machine. To successfully run this command, though, you may need to edit files like **/etc/hosts.equiv** and **.rhosts** to set the proper permissions—check your UNIX manual for details.

In addition, the shell on the remote machine may not know where the *xterm* program resides, so you may need a command like:

```
rsh kevin -n /usr/bin/X11/xterm -display $DISPLAY
```

The *xterm* program is normally placed in **/usr/bin/X11**, but it may not be on your system, especially if you're running X on a 386/486-based UNIX system. Under OpenWindows on Solaris systems, *xterm* is located in **/usr/openwin/bin**.

Using CPU Resources

When you use *rsh* to spawn a shell on the remote system, you are using a good chunk of that system's resources. First, you have a shell on that machine, and then you add in an *xterm*. There's a great debate over whether this is more or less efficient than simply using *rlogin* or *telnet* to log on to the remote machine from a locally run *xterm*. There are persuasive arguments on both sides of the issue, so use whatever method you think is best.

Stopping X

Your users probably will be very upset with you if there's no way to stop X, or if the method of stopping X is too complicated.

The key to stopping the X server is to stop the key last process in the chain of X applications. For example, if you start X using *xinit*, *xinit* is the parent process for all the X processes—when *xinit* stops, the X server will be killed. *Xinit* stops when the **.xinitrc** script ends. The **.xinitrc** script, in turn, ends when the last foreground process in the file stops. If you start X from *xinit*, though, you may want to add a command into the user's **$HOME/.login** or **$HOME/.profile** file to log the user out after exiting the X session. Otherwise, the user will simply see the UNIX prompt when X quits.

For users, then, they need to exit this key process. *Mwm*, for example, provides a menu choice for quitting.

N O T E SGI systems use *xdm* to start an X session and the program *endsession* (found in **/usr/bin/X11**) to terminate the X session. The *endsession* program clears out a property on the root window that was originally created by the program named *reaper* (also stored in **/usr/bin/X11**). Clearing this property tells *xdm* to shut down the user session and kill all the user processes. The Silicon Graphics window manager, *4Dwm* (a variant of the Motif window manager), automatically runs *endsession* when the user quits *4Dwm* using a menu choice.

Summary

This chapter covers several methods for starting X on a variety of hardware platforms. Special attention is paid to *xinit* and *xdm*, the two main methods for starting X.

Starting X is not as simple as you'd imagine. X uses a series of configuration files no matter what the startup method, and your job as system administrator involves the management of these files. Attention to detail is important; even something as simple as the order of commands in the configuration files can confuse your users.

Stopping X, on the other hand, is a relatively simple act. Most leading window managers allow users to quit X on their own, while X can be set up to quit when the last foreground process in a script file is terminated.

In the next chapter, you will learn how to set up a user account for X.

Setting User Environments

Topics covered in this chapter include:

❋ Setting all command paths to run X programs

❋ Start the X server, if necessary (when using *xinit*)

❋ Information about the basic X start-up files in user accounts

❋ Load X resources with *xrdb*, if desired, to configure the X environment

❋ Start all desired X clients to form the user's X environment, with an X start-up file

❋ Saving applications and restarting them with X session managers

❋ Differences on major UNIX platforms

Logging in to the X Environment

To start a user's X environment, you must ensure that a number of steps occur when the user logs in. These steps include:

❊ Setting all command paths to run X programs

❊ Starting the X server, if necessary (when using *xinit*)

❊ Starting all desired X clients to form the user's X environment

❊ Loading X resources with *xrdb* to configure the X environment

This chapter covers how to configure a user account to correctly start an X environment. In doing so, we use the following philosophy: First, configure the account to run X, then finesse the account to start the way you want it to. Since most UNIX systems now come preconfigured to run X, the initial step becomes much easier if you copy the system files and get things going from there, instead of rewriting all the X start-up scripts on your own.

If your system does provide a means to set a user account to launch X automatically, by all means use this method. You'll take advantage of everything your UNIX vendor has set up for you, instead of reinventing the wheel. You should then use this chapter as a guide to show you where to modify the system default files.

If you are starting from scratch, this chapter should help you get a user account set up to run an X environment.

Set All Command Paths

Most X Window executable programs are located in **/usr/bin/X11**. On Sun OpenWindows systems, you'll probably find them in **/usr/openwin/bin**, and on COSE systems, **/opt/dt/bin**. In your environment, you may have installed X in a nondefault location.

In all cases, you must edit the user start-up files, such as **.login** or **.profile**, to set the proper paths for X. For C shell users, add the following command to the user's **$HOME/.login** file:

```
set path = ( $path /usr/bin/X11 )
```

assuming that **/usr/bin/X11** is where X executables are stored.

For Bourne and Korn shell users, add the following commands to the user's **$HOME/.profile** file:

```
PATH=$PATH:/usr/bin/X11
export PATH
```

again, assuming that **/usr/bin/X11** is where X executables are stored. Otherwise, users are likely to experience *"Command not found"* errors.

Sun OpenWindows Paths

For Sun OpenWindows users, you need to define three environment variables: OPENWINHOME, PATH, and LD_LIBRARY_PATH.

OPENWINHOME specifies the top-level OpenWindows directory, usually **/usr/openwin**.

The PATH environment variable must be set to **$OPENWINHOME/bin**, where the OpenWindows executable programs are stored. Usually, this is in **/usr/openwin/bin**.

You'll also need to set the LD_LIBRARY_PATH, which controls where the system looks for shared libraries, to point to the OpenWindows library directory. If you don't set LD_LIBRARY_PATH properly, users will see errors like *"/usr/lib/libX11.so.4 not found"*.

To put this all together, the following C shell commands set all three environment variables:

```
setenv OPENWINHOME  /usr/openwin
set path = ( $path $OPENWINHOME/bin )
setenv  LD_LIBRARY_PATH  $OPENWINHOME/lib
```

In the Bourne or Korn shells, use the following:

```
OPENWINHOME=/usr/openwin
export OPENWINHOME
PATH=$PATH:$OPENWINHOME/bin
export PATH
LD_LIBRARY_PATH=$OPENWINHOME/lib
export LD_LIBRARY_PATH
```

Starting the X Server

As we stated in the last chapter, you can choose between the two basic methods for starting X: running *xinit* as the user logs in, or using *xdm*, which manages the display and presents an X-based login screen. Use whatever method you prefer, though *xdm* is considered the preferred method. If you use the *xinit* method, you need to ensure that the user's start-up shell script (**.profile** or **.login**) calls *xinit* properly to start the X server.

The best place to start the X server with *xinit* is in a shell start-up file, such as **.login** for C shell users or **.profile** for Bourne or Korn shell users. In both cases, the task is the same. You need to add code to the **.login** (or **.profile**) file to detect if the user is logging in at the system console. If not, you probably don't want to start the X server.

If the user is logged in at the console, run *xinit* with any necessary command-line parameters, as we discussed in the last chapter.

When *xinit* exits, you probably want to log the user off, as the X session will be complete.

For C shell users, you can add the following lines to the user **$HOME/.login** file:

```
setenv DISPLAY :0

set path = ( $path /usr/bin/X11 )
if ( 'tty' == "/dev/console" ) then
    xinit
    logout
    endif
```

The previous commands set the DISPLAY environment variable and the PATH, and check to see if the user is logging in at the console (as opposed to a terminal login or a login over a network link). If so, then the **.login** file starts the X server with *xinit*. When *xinit* exits, the **logout** command logs the user out. (You may want to replace the call to *xinit* with *startx*, or *openwin* or the appropriate means to start X.)

Basic X Start-Up Files

Once you have the X server started, you need to define the user's X environment. With *xdm*, the basic way is to create a **$HOME/.xsession** file. Again, users can customize this later. With *xinit*, the basic way is to create a user **$HOME/.xinitrc** file that your users can customize later.

Some vendors use their own files in place of **.xinitrc** or **.xsession**. On SGI systems, for example, you'll typically use a **$HOME/.sgisession** file in place of **.xsession**. On Sun OpenWindows systems, you'll typically use a **$HOME/.openwin-init** file instead of **.xinitrc**.

Use the appropriate file, based on your system type and the method you choose to start X.

Table 5.1 lists the basic X start-up files.

Table 5.1   Basic X start-up files.

File	Use
$HOME/.xinitrc	Starts X clients from *xinit*
$HOME/.xsession	Starts X clients from *xdm*
$HOME/.sgisession	Starts X clients on SGI systems
$HOME/.openwin-init	Starts X clients on Sun OpenWindows systems

Whatever start-up file you use, you'll need to add commands to the file to load any necessary X resources and start any desired X applications.

Configuring and Loading X Resources

X resources allow users and system administrators to customize X programs in a variety of ways. As a system administrator, it's important to note that resources allow you to enforce a consistent look and feel among your entire user base, as resources govern colors, fonts, window locations, window sizes, and even the text messages displayed by X programs.

However, X considers resources to fall under the guidance of users — remember that old canard about mechanism, not policy. X resource files are merely text files that any user can edit, provided they know enough about X to configure resource files properly. (They probably won't, as X resources can be fairly confusing.) As UNIX system administrator, you'll need to know more than the basics of resource setting: You can assume that at least some of your users will want to change their resources, and you can assume that at least some of your users will make a mess of things when they attempt to change their resources. In both cases, you'll need to read more about X resources, which we cover in greater depth in Chapter 8.

The basic means to set X resource values is through X resource files, like **$HOME/.Xdefaults**, which sets the default X resources for a user's X session. However, many systems are now moving to a scheme where the major X resources are loaded into the X server to avoid the overhead of file accesses.

Loading X Resources

The *xrdb* command loads a set of resources into a data area associated with a given screen. Usually the original resource-setting commands are stored in a file, by convention **$HOME/.Xresources**. If that's the case, you can load a set of X resources from this file with the following command:

```
xrdb -load $HOME/.Xresources
```

If the X environment already has some resources loaded, use the *-merge* command-line parameter instead of *-load*, as shown in the following command:

```
xrdb -merge $HOME/.Xresources
```

The *-merge* command-line parameter tries to merge the new resources with the old. The *-load* command-line parameter replaces any existing resources with newly loaded resources.

On Hewlett-Packard systems, the VUE environment automatically calls *xrdb* to load resource values. On such systems, you don't need to run *xrdb* yourself. If you do, though, be sure to use the *-merge* command-line parameter rather than *-load*.

Launching Applications

The second, and most important, task of the X start-up file is to start any X applications that the user wants when the X session begins. Since we covered this task in Chapter 4 (*"An Example .xinitrc File"*), we won't cover it again here in depth.

For systems that start X with *xдm*, you'll want to copy the default *xдm* session file, located in **/usr/lib/X11/xdm/Xsession**, to the user's home directory as **.xsession**. Then, edit this file to include any other commands you want to execute. (SGI systems use a file named **$HOME/.sgisession**, by default, instead of **$HOME/.xsession**.)

Starting Xterm Windows

A frequently used X application is *xterm*, which provides a terminal window to the UNIX shell. For what it does, *xterm* works well.

We find that *xterm* is easiest to use when outfitted with scrollbars (so users can view text output that scrolls past the terminal) and with the *9x15* font, which is highly readable and widely available. Neither setting is the default, but both can be set with resources or command-line options. On the command line, *-sb* tells *xterm* to use a scrollbar. The *-fn* option tells *xterm* which font to load.

The *-geom* or *-geometry* command-line parameter tells *xterm* how large to make its window. Unlike most X applications, the width and height passed to *xterm* are in characters, not pixels. To create an 80-column by 46-line *xterm* window, you'd use a *-geometry* option of:

```
xterm -geom 80x46 &
```

To put it all together, the following command line tells *xterm* to use a scrollbar, what font to use, and the number of lines and columns encompassing the window:

```
xterm -geom 80x46 -fn 9x15 -sb &
```

Window Manager Start-Up Files

Each major window manager sports a separate configuration file or files. Many window managers, such as *mwm*, have an X resource file (usually named similarly to the window manager; for instance, in the case of *mwm*, the resource file is **Mwm**), which controls aspects of the visual appearance of the window manager and the window decorations that it produces.

In addition, most window managers have a dot file controlling the window-manager menus and other, usually nonvisual, aspects of the program. *Mwm*, for example, has a **$HOME/.mwmrc** file setting the window-manager menus and keyboard equivalents.

You generally don't have to mess with these files. Once the account is defined, you may need to go back and edit the files. Again, users can edit these files directly, so don't be surprised if you must field a few requests for assistance from confused users.

Saving Application States with Session Managers

Modern X systems are more attuned to the needs of average end users, instead of being geared to the needs of power users. One such improvement is to save the state of the user's applications when the user quits X. The next time X starts, this session is magically restored.

The mechanism that manages an X user session is called a *session manager*. Session managers are usually not configured as separate programs—instead, they are part of the window manager, as is the case with the COSE CDE *dtwm* and the Hewlett-Packard *vuewm*, both of which act as combination window managers and X user session managers.

Behind the scenes, X session managers are really quite primitive. In essence, the session manager asks each X application for the command line necessary to restart the program. In theory, this command line will restart the program in its current state, but usually all you get is the proper window size, location, and font—which for most users is enough.

The session manager then stores this command line to a file and executes this command when the next X session starts, magically bringing back the application. Users love this.

**TROUBLE-
SHOOTING**

If you find that some applications won't restart, then the problem may lie with the command line that originally launched the program. For example, suppose you launch a copy of *xclock* with the following command:

```
xclock &
```

This command assumes that the user's command path is already set. This may not be the case when the session manager attempts to restart the X applications. To work best with X session managers, you should use the full path to the program.

Platform-Specific Differences

There are a few platform-specific differences among the major platforms, including Sun Solaris, IBM AIX, Hewlett-Packard HP-UX, and the COSE Common Desktop Environment.

Solaris OpenWindows User Accounts

For Sun OpenWindows systems, you need to start the X server with the *openwin* shell script, as we described in this and the previous chapters.

In addition, the default user environment is nicely configured, so most users should be happy with it. To aid the users in customizing this, though, have your users run the X applications they desire and then choose the **Save Workspace** menu choice from the *olwm* (or run the *owplaces* program). This writes the current session, in the form of UNIX commands necessary to restart the applications, to the **$HOME/.openwin-init** file. With this, you may never have to edit the **$HOME/.openwin-init** file directly.

IBM User Accounts

IBM systems use a utility called *smit* to create new user accounts. This graphical utility helps you set up a user's new account as well as the IBM Power Desktop environment. For users who don't have this environment, you should start X using the *startx* shell script (which should also, by default, start the Power Desktop environment).

Hewlett-Packard User Accounts

Hewlett-Packard systems provide a highly integrated user environment called VUE. If you use VUE, then you don't have to do much, because the basic HP-UX utilities to add a new user can configure VUE for you. Most of the VUE user configuration information is stored in the **$HOME/.vue** directory.

Once in VUE, users can configure the environment to save their current session at every logout, and restore that session the next time they login. In addition, VUE calls *xrdb* automatically to restore all X resources that were loaded in the previous session. All in all, this makes your job a lot easier.

If you have any reason to call *xrdb*, you should use the *-merge* option previously described. Also, users can use the *-merge* option at any time to extend the set of X resources loaded into the X server. VUE then saves this information and restores it the next time the user logs in if VUE is configured to save and restore the current session.

N O T E

COSE User Accounts

COSE systems act much like Hewlett-Packard VUE systems. The COSE Common Desktop Environment will save the user session (if told to do so) and restore the next time the user logs in.

Summary

This chapter covered the very basic task of configuring a user account to launch X automatically, in a fashion the user desires. This included setting up the proper configuration and resource files, as well as taking advantage of provisions like session managers and platform-specific management tools.

In the next chapter, you will learn how to explore your system's X environment through utilities like *xdpyinfo*, *xwininfo*, and *xprop*.

Configuring X

In many ways this section is the heart and soul of this book, because it covers the nitty-gritty details about properly configuring your X environment.

Before you can configure anything, however, it's good to know the existing configuration. Chapter 6 covers the many tools available for exploring your X environment (including *xdpyinfo*, *xwininfo*, and *xprop*), while recommending a UNIX administrator's toolbox, including *xlswins*, *xlsclients*, *xprop*, and *xload*.

Chapter 7 discusses the sticky issue of fonts and the Release 5 font server. Setting up font paths and the font server can be a delicate matter, with far too many things that can go wrong.

Chapter 8 covers resources, resource files, and command-line parameters. Resource files govern all aspects of X usage and appearance. Your users, if they are adventurous, will try and change their X resources; this chapter exists so you can bail them out.

Chapter 9 discusses the keyboard and key bindings, as well as various tools that allow you to assign specific characters and actions to keys. X works under an abstract model of a keyboard—necessary to accommodate a wide variety of UNIX and PC keyboards—which gives you a lot of freedom in configuring keyboards. Programs covered in this chapter include *xkeycaps* and *xmodmap*.

Chapter 10, a short chapter, covers colors and color names. As a system administrator, you won't have to do a lot of work with colors, as typically colors are governed by the window manager and applications. However, in the likely event that something goes wrong, it's good to know exactly how color is managed within X.

Chapter 11's covers bitmaps and icons. Again, there's not a lot you'll need to do with bitmaps or icons, but it's good to know what to do should the situation arise.

The section ends with a discussion of the basic security features found within the X Window System. While you shouldn't be relying on X Window to be providing security for your system—indeed, the answer to securing an X installation is to secure the *entire* environment—there are still a few handy security features found within X.

Exploring Your X Environment

Topics covered in this chapter include:

* What you can tell at a glance from an X display
* Discovering screen capabilities with *xdpyinfo*
* Tracking windows with *xwininfo*
* Setting window geometries
* Listing X properties with *xprop*
* Controlling X server parameters with *xset*
* Using *xload* to monitor the CPU load
* Killing errant programs with *xkill*

Discovering X

The ideal situation would be configuring an X environment scratch, making sure that everything was set up correctly and uniformly.

Right.

Chances are that you've inherited someone else's UNIX and X configuration, however. And if that's true, you've probably inherited someone else's set of problems and quirky arrangements.

Let's face it, users just love to tinker with their environments. They may not like the font used by *xterm*, or they may dislike the look of the standard X screen saver. As a result, they may start making undocumented changes to their X environment. And when things start going wrong, they'll turn to you for the solution.

For these situations, then, it's important to possess the tools needed to figure out exactly how an X environment is configured. When it comes to diagnostic tools of all sorts, the X Window System—either as shipped directly from the X Consortium or from a commercial vendor—is woefully lacking. There are a few basic utilities that report back on the state of an X environment, along with a few basic tools for changing these configurations.

This chapter covers the basic X tools that will aid you in exploring your X systems, mostly through our recommended UNIX administrator's toolbox based on standard and freely available X programs.

What You Can Tell at a Glance

Before we delve into the toolbox, however, we'll begin with the most basic of diagnostic tools: your eyes. Believe it or not, there's a surprising amount of information you can get from just looking at an X display. For example, you should be able to get a good idea of what window manager controls the display and most of the X applications the user executes. Take a look at Figure 6.1 and try to see what information you can get from a picture.

You should be able to tell that the window manager is some variant of the Motif window manager (in this case, Hewlett-Packard's *vuewm*). You can tell that the user is attempting to configure system fonts under some sort of X environment. You also see windows for Mosaic, an Internet navigation tool we cover in Chapter 24, and the tried-and-true *xterm* for a UNIX command-line interface.

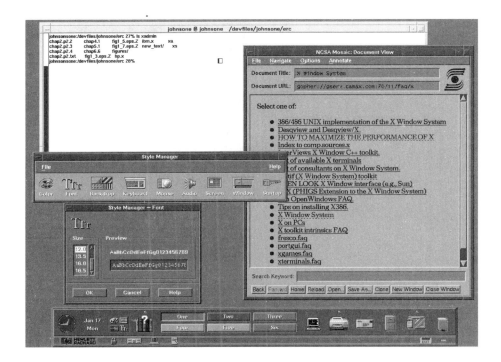

Figure 6.1   A sample X display.

And you should also see that the font used in *xterm* looks odd—proportional, not fixed width. This makes the *xterm* window look odd. The user appears to be attempting to fix the problem with the VUE style manager, but without any noticeable success. Try the same process with Figure 6.2.

In this case, you can see that the user is trying to get help from Sun's AnswerBook program. The help page describes *xset*, a program used to control many of the X server's basic settings, like font paths and screen savers. This user runs the Open Look window manager, *olwm*.

And finally, the picture in Figure 6.3 show a more traditional X display running freely available X clients.

Figure 6.2   A second X display.

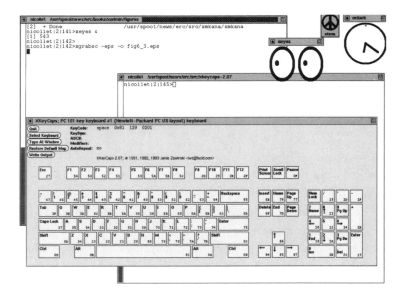

Figure 6.3   A third X display.

In Figure 6.3, you can see the *twm* window manager, as well as the CPU-cycle-eater called *xeyes*. This user runs *xkeycaps* to try to change the keyboard.

In the previous three examples, you can tell the basic environment each user runs, while noting that nothing seems terribly wrong with any of the systems. Even so, each user is trying to modify the X environment in some way.

A UNIX Administrator's Toolbox

For the rest of this chapter, we build a small toolbox of useful X utilities you should be aware of and able to use. None of the tools are really very useful on their own, but we've found them helpful when trying to track and fix problems. Table 6.1 lists a number of useful X utilities.

Table 6.1   An administrator's toolbox.

Tool	Capabilities
xdpyinfo	Screen capabilities, X extensions, available colors, and resolution
xwininfo	What windows are on the screen; location and information on any window
xlsclients	Which (well-behaved) X programs are running on a display; command line that started programs
xprop	Command line that started program; information on X properties; window-manager properties
xset	Change X server settings; control screen saver
xload	UNIX system load in graphical format
xkill	Kills errant X clients

These programs should be located in **/usr/bin/X11** or wherever your system stores X programs, such as **/usr/openwin/bin** under Sun's OpenWindows.

(There are some exceptions; for instance, *xdpyinfo* and *xprop* are stored in **/usr/contrib/bin/X11** on Hewlett-Packard systems.)

Discovering Screen Capabilities with *Xdpyinfo*

Xdpyinfo is probably the handiest of the utilities presented here. It's a rather basic tool, but it discloses a ton of information regarding your X display, including the screen resolution, the number of available colors, and any extensions to the base X protocol that this X server supports. Much of the information is worthless, unfortunately, but you can find a few gems in the dross.

Listing the Version of X

You can use *xdpyinfo* in a limited fashion to help determine which version of X you're running. Some of the initial information printed by *xdpyinfo* includes the following:

```
version number:     11.0
vendor string:    MIT X Consortium
vendor release number:    5000
```

The version number isn't very useful, as it only lists the version of the X protocol, which hasn't changed since X11 Release 1. Thus, you'll almost always see a version number of 11.0.

The vendor string tells you where the X server came from. Common vendor strings include MIT X Consortium, Hewlett-Packard Company, and Sun Microsystems, Inc.

The vendor release number tells you the vendor's private version number. This number is useful for reporting bugs, but not very useful for determining if your system is at X11 Release 4, 5, or 6, as each vendor uses its own numbering scheme. Only the X Consortium's vendor release number will tell you which release of X you're running (4, 5, or 6).

In the previous example, we can tell we're running a Release 5 X server, because the 5000 corresponds to R5. With any other vendor, such as Apple Computer or IBM, you won't be able to tell which release of X the vendor used originally to build the X server. The only means to tell this is to look in your vendor's system documentation.

X Extensions

You'll need to know what version of X you're running if you need features, such as PEX or input methods (used for internationalization), that are supported only at a certain release number or higher.

PEX is an *extension*, an optional X component. *Xdpyinfo* lists the extensions supported by a given X server. If an extension isn't listed, then it isn't supported.

The names may look weird, but they are usually easy to decipher. A common set of X extensions follows:

```
number of extensions:     6
    XTestExtension1
    SHAPE
    MIT-SHM
    X3D-PEX
    Multi-Buffering
    MIT-SUNDRY-NONSTANDARD
```

Common extensions are listed in Table 6.2.

Table 6.2   Common X extensions.

Extension	Description
Adobe-DPS-Extension	Display PostScript extension
DPSExtension	Display PostScript extension
HPExtension	Proprietary Hewlett-Packard extension
MIT-SUNDRY-NONSTANDARD	X Consortium miscellaneous extension
MIT-SHM	Shared-memory image extension
SGI-SUNDRY-NONSTANDARD	Proprietary Silicon Graphics extension
SHAPE	Nonrectangular windows
SUN_ALLPLANES	Proprietary Sun extension
SUN_DGA	Proprietary Sun extension
SunWindowGrabber	Proprietary Sun extension
X3D-PEX	PHIGS 3D extension to X

continued

Extension	Description
XTestExtension1	Testing extension
XIE	X Image Extension
XInputExtension	Input-device (such as digitizing tablets) extension
XVideo	Video extension

Color and Resolution Information

In the latter part of the information provided by *xdpyinfo*, you'll find information on the actual physical monitors currently supported by the X server. For the vast majority of systems, there will be only one screen per X server. Starting with the number of screens, you'll see information on the graphics resolution:

```
number of screens:      1
screen #0:
 dimensions:     1152x900 pixels (390x304 millimeters)
 resolution:     75x75 dots per inch
 depths (2):     1, 8
 default number of colormap cells:    256
 preallocated pixels:     black 1, white 0
 options:     backing-store YES, save-unders YES
 number of visuals:     6
 visual:
   class:      PseudoColor
   depth:      8 planes
   size of colormap:     256 entries
```

In this case, we have only one screen (surprise, surprise), with a resolution of 1152x900 pixels, which happens to be a standard resolution on Sun systems.

Don't trust the millimeter dimensions or resolution returned by *xdpyinfo*, as the X server has no true way of knowing this information. You'll often find that the Sun 16-inch and 19-inch monitors, if they both support the same pixel resolution, will both show the same screen size in millimeters. Obviously this is not correct, as a 16-inch monitor has a smaller screen display than a 19-inch monitor.

The other piece of useful information is the number of color cells. The majority of X workstations provide 256 colors (for 8-bit planes of color), but as prices drop, we're finding more and more 24-bit color systems.

Tracking All the Windows with *Xwininfo*

At first glance, it seems odd to list all the windows on an X display—after all, they are all on the screen, right? No. A number of important windows may not be visible at any given time. Window managers create a number of windows surrounding application windows, and sometimes it's useful to be able to get a listing of what the window manager is doing. That's why *xwininfo*, which presents information on windows, is useful.

In addition, *xwininfo* presents a lot of useful data about any particular window, including its size and location. You'll need this feature when you want to restart an X program and place its window at the same place with the same size. Users do this when they set up their X environment.

Xwininfo program lists information in two ways: by specific window, or for all the windows on the screen. In both cases, *xwininfo* turns the cursor into a crosshair and asks you to select the window you want information on. If you select the root window (the screen background), you'll get a listing of every window on the display. This is accomplished by running *xwininfo* with the *-tree* option. Our example involves the *oclock* application, which to the eye appears to be a single entity. However, when using *xwininfo* with the *-tree* option, you'll see the output looks something like:

```
xwininfo: Window id: 0x1c00052 (has no name)

Root window id: 0x2a (the root window) (has no name)
Parent window id: 0x2a (the root window) (has no name)
 2 children:
 0x1800007 "oclock": ("oclock" "Clock")
        120x120+0+21 +902+23
  1 child:
  0x1800008 (has no name): () 120x120+0+0 +902+23
 0x1c00053 (has no name): () 120x19+-2+-2 +900+0
  3 children:
  0x1c0005a (has no name): () 26x15+70+2 +972+4
  0x1c00057 (has no name): () 11x11+104+3 +1006+5
  0x1c00056 (has no name): () 11x11+3+3 +905+5
```

This information can help you if you need to know how big a window the window manager is placing on an application's top-level window. The true *oclock* top-level window (with a window ID of 0x1800007 in hexadecimal) is really the child of a window created by the window manager. The *oclock* application, in turn, creates one child window of its own, while the window manager needs three more windows for the titlebar and various window manager controls placed in the titlebar. This is not unusual; most applications create a huge number of windows, usually at least one for each push-button, text label, or menu. Scrollbars often use a total of six windows each, so expect to see a lot of windows listed on the display when you use the *-tree* option.

Another useful *xwininfo* option is *-id*, which allows you to specify a window ID in hexadecimal, using the C language style for formatting hexadecimal numbers (such as 0x1c0005a; the leading *0x* is used by C programmers to specify hexadecimal numbers.) For example, you can ask about window 0x1c0005a with the following command:

```
xwininfo -id 0x1c0005a
```

The *-id* command-line option can be used with *-tree*.

When would you do this? When you set up a number of X applications—for example, an *xterm* window and an *oclock* window—and then want to know the exact position and size of each window. With this information, you can create a **.xinitrc** or **.xsession** file (see Chapter 4), which starts up all the initial X client programs. (On systems that feature session managers, the system takes care of saving the state of each application and restarting the user session.)

Since all systems don't do this for users, you may need to run *xwininfo* to determine the sizes and locations of application windows. If you try *xwininfo* on a sample application, say *oclock*, the cursor changes into a crosshair shape and you'll see the following grammatically awkward prompt:

```
xwininfo: Please select the window about which you
   would like information by clicking the
   mouse in that window.
```

Move the mouse cursor over the window you're interested in and click a mouse button. Once selected, *xwininfo* prints information on the window. For example, here's the information printed for an *oclock* window:

```
xwininfo: Window id: 0x1800007 "oclock"

Absolute upper-left X:  902
Absolute upper-left Y:  23
Relative upper-left X:  0
```

```
Relative upper-left Y:  21
Width: 120
Height: 120
Depth: 8
Visual Class: PseudoColor
Border width: 0
Class: InputOutput
Colormap: 0x27 (installed)
Bit Gravity State: NorthWestGravity
Window Gravity State: NorthWestGravity
Backing Store State: NotUseful
Save Under State: no
Map State: IsViewable
Override Redirect State: no
Corners:  +902+23  -130+23  -130-757  +902-757
-geometry 120x120+900+0
```

To set up the window's geometry, we'll need the width (120) and height (120), as well as absolute position (902, 23). The position must be defined in root (or absolute) coordinates, since most window managers wrap X application windows in windows owned by the window manager. Luckily, *xwininfo* converts the relative position 0, 21 in local coordinates (local to the window's parent—owned by the window manager) to its position in global coordinates. In addition, *xwininfo* prints out the proper *-geometry* command-line parameter value needed to restart the application. To restart this *oclock* to the same size and position, you'd use a command like this:

```
oclock -geometry 120x120+900+0 &
```

The X Coordinate System

If you're not familiar with X Window coordinates and window geometry, the preceding paragraph is probably somewhat confusing, so a brief digression is in order.

The origin in X is at the upper-left-hand corner. At this point, in global coordinates, the position is 0,0. The bottom-right-hand corner then holds the largest X and Y values possible for the screen. With this, the X values increase going to the right and the Y values increase going down. (You may be used to other graphic systems that place the origin in the lower-left-hand corner.)

Knowing the coordinate system, you can then build up the window's geometry. In X terminology, a window's *geometry* is its size and position, usually in terms of global coordinates. X goes further and creates a special way to format this information, which you can use on the UNIX command line and also in X resource files. You use this information to tell X applications where to start and how large to make their windows. This special format is called the *geometry specification*.

The basic format of the geometry specification is width, height, X offset, Y offset. The exact formula is:

```
[=][Width x Height ][{+/-}XOffset{+/-}YOffset]
```

The *WidthxHeight* and *+Xoffset+Yoffset* are both optional, but if you specify the width, you must also specify the height. The same goes for the X and Y offsets.

The leading equal sign (=) is intended for backward compatibility only. Don't use it.

WARNING

In this format, a 300-pixel-wide by 200-pixel-high window would have a geometry of 300x200. In this case, we're stating nothing about the window's position. If we want to specify the window's position, we can certainly do so. For example, if we place the same window at 10 pixels to the right of the origin and 20 pixels down from the origin, we'd then have a geometry specification of 300x200+10+20.

If size is unimportant to you, but you want to ensure that the window has a particular location, you can skip the width and height part. For the example above, we'd then have a geometry specification of simply +10+20.

In the geometry specification, the width and height are normally defined in terms of pixels. Some applications, notably *xterm*, treat the width and height instead as the number of character cells, with the resulting pixel size then determined by the size of the font *xterm* uses. In this case, a normal window size would be 80x25 for 80 columns (character positions) wide and 25 lines (character positions) high, the size of a VT100 terminal in terms of character positions. Very few applications treat the width and height this way.

NOTE

Negative Positions

Negative positions in a geometry specification don't always work the way you'd expect. A negative X coordinate means to position the right edge of the window that many pixels from the right edge of the screen. In this light, we can interpret positive X coordinates to mean to position the left edge of the window x pixels from the left edge of the screen.

Similarly, a positive Y coordinate means to position the top of the window y pixels from the top of the screen. A negative Y coordinate specifies that the *bottom* of the window should be positioned a number of pixels above the *bottom* of the screen.

While this looks odd, it really serves a purpose in that users may login different X terminals, which have different screen resolutions. If the X clients that start up are spaced from the edge of the screen, it doesn't matter what the actual screen resolution is.

The Four Corners of X

For geometry specifications, X treats 0 as having a positive or negative value. This follows from the interpretation of negative positions described previously. In Table 6.3, we show the means to specify the four corners of the screen.

Table 6.3   Corners for window geometries.

Corner	X and Y offsets
Upper-left corner	+0+0
Lower-left corner	+0-0
Upper-right corner	-0+0
Lower-right corner	-0-0

Example Geometries

To help put all this together, it makes the most sense to look at a few examples, which we provide in Table 6.4.

Table 6.4   Example geometry specifications.

Geometry Specification	Meaning
300x200	A window that is 300 pixels wide by 200 pixels high
+10+20	A window placed 10 pixels from the left, 20 pixels down from the top
400x500+5+6	400x500 pixels, located at 5, 6
350x210+0+0	350x210 pixels, located at 0, 0 (the origin)

The Geometry Option

Just about every X program accepts a *-geometry* option, which can also be abbreviated as *-geom*. With this option, you pass the window geometry. To start an *oclock* window in a window that is 100x120 pixels in size and located at position 150,300 (from the origin), you'd use the following command:

```
oclock -geometry 100x120+150+300 &
```

You could abbreviate the parameter as follows:

```
oclock -geom 100x120+150+300 &
```

Listing Running Applications

There are times when you'll need to know exactly what applications are running, especially if an application window doesn't appear, and you want to determine if the application is actually running on the display. The traditional UNIX utility *ps* can't always help in this regard—remember, under X the programs on your display may actually execute on another computer across your network. Because of this, you may need to get a listing of the running X applications using *xlsclients*.

The *xlsclients* programs lists the X clients that have registered their presence in the manner required of well-behaved applications. Not all X applications are well-behaved (there are a number of criteria programmers must meet in order to make their applications well-behaved; these are irrelevant for the purposes of this discussion), but most are, at least in this regard. *Xlsclients* rarely detects the window manager, however.

The list presented by *xlsclients* looks like the following:

```
eric  hpterm -C -iconic -ls
eric  /usr/bin/X11/xterm -geom 80x42
eric  xterm -geom 80x48
eric  xterm -title kevin -n kevin \
  -geom 80x40 -e rlogin kevin
kevin xterm -geom 80x52 -bg grey96
kevin xterm
```

Listing X Properties with *Xprop*

X provides the ability for programmers to store any named set of data with any window on the screen. In X terminology, such data is stored in a property. Normally you won't have to worry about programming issues, but the key for administrators is that X applications use properties to communicate with the window manager. The application stores data into certain properties to control the window-manager decorations placed on the window, as well as the command used to restart the application. Armed with this knowledge, you can look at the properties on a window to see why the application won't restart or why the window manager still places the full titlebar when the application asked for no titlebar, and so on.

The tool that lists property data on a window is called *xprop*. You use *xprop* much like *xwininfo*, that is, you need to select the window you want information on. Most of the information you see will appear meaningless, like the following example shows:

```
WM_STATE(WM_STATE):
  window state: Normal
  icon window: 0x0
WM_PROTOCOLS(ATOM): protocols  WM_DELETE_WINDOW
WM_CLASS(STRING) = "oclock", "Clock"
WM_HINTS(WM_HINTS):
  Client accepts input or input focus: False
  Initial state is Normal State.
  bitmap id # to use for icon: 0x1800001
  bitmap id # of mask for icon: 0x1800003
WM_NORMAL_HINTS(WM_SIZE_HINTS):
```

```
user specified location: 900, 0
user specified size: 120 by 120
window gravity: NorthWest
WM_CLIENT_MACHINE(STRING) = "nicollet"
WM_COMMAND(STRING) =
  { "/usr/local/X11R5/bin/oclock",
  "-geom", "120x120+900+0" }
WM_ICON_NAME(STRING) = "oclock"
WM_NAME(STRING) = "oclock"
```

This property listing came from an *oclock* window, in keeping with our extended set of examples in this chapter.

Although the above list seems mostly meaningless, you can derive a few useful pieces of information from the property data. Table 6.5 should help you decode useful information from the property data.

Table 6.5 Decoding property information.

Property	Use
WM_CLIENT_MACHINE	UNIX network hostname where application is computing
WM_COMMAND	UNIX command used to restart application
WM_HINTS	Check if application accepts keyboard input
WM_NAME	Window name, usually displayed in titlebar
WM_PROTOCOLS	If WM_DELETE_WINDOW is set, then should quit properly on Close or Quit menu choice

With the WM_CLIENT_MACHINE property, you can tell on what machine the X application is really executing. With WM_COMMAND, you can see the UNIX command that should be called to restart the application.

TROUBLE-
SHOOTING

If an application doesn't restart and you think it should, check the WM_COMMAND property. Often you'll see that the command uses a relative path, such as just plain *oclock*, instead of the absolute path like **/usr/local/X11R5/bin/oclock**. This can create a problem if the command path isn't set up when an X session manager tries to restart the application. Because of this, you should tell your users to always type in the full absolute path for any applications they want to see restarted—assuming, of course, your system provides a session manager.

The WM_HINTS property will tell you if the application is configured to accept keyboard input or not. (Note that *oclock* will not accept keyboard input.) This is useful in trouble-shooting problems with applications that won't accept user input.

You can use the WM_PROTOCOLS property to track down applications that don't quit gracefully. If you see a WM_DELETE_WINDOW in the WM_PROTOCOLS property, then the application in question should gracefully accept a Close or Quit menu choice from the window manager's menu.

Checking and Changing X Server Settings

The X server has a lot of built-in parameters, such as the screen saver and the keyboard autorepeat rate, which you can control with the *xset* program. Table 6.7 lists all the options for *xset*.

Table 6.7   Xset options.

Option	Meaning
b off	Turns off bell
b on	Enables bell with system defaults
b *vol pitch dur*	Sets bell volume to *vol,* pitch to *pitch*, and duration to *dur*
bc	Turns on bug compatibility mode
-bc	Turns off bug compatibility mode
c vol	Set key click volume to given percentage (*vol*)
c on	Restore key click volume to system defaults
c off	Disable key click

continued

Option	Meaning
fp=*fontpath1, fontpath2,...*	Set font path to comma-delimited list of directories
fp default	Restore font path to system defaults
fp rehash	Reread font databases in current font path
+fp *fontpath1, fontpath2, ...*	Add list of font paths
-fp *fontpath1, fontpath2, ...*	Remove specified paths from font path
led #	Turns on LED 1 to 32, depending on the value of #
-led #	Turns off LED 1 to 32, depending on the value of #
m default	Restore mouse acceleration defaults
m *accel_mult/accel_div threshold*	Set mouse acceleration and threshold
m *accel_mult threshold*	Set mouse acceleration and threshold
m *accel_mult*	Set mouse acceleration
r	Enable keyboard autorepeat
-r	Disable keyboard autorepeat
s off	Turns off screen saver
s on	Turns on screen saver
s default	Turns on screen saver to default values
s blank	Sets screen saver to blank video
s noblank	Sets screen saver to display a background pattern
s *v1 v2*	Enable screen saver after *v1* seconds; change pattern after *v2* seconds

N O T E

Most of these settings are self-explanatory, so we won't waste your time explaining the obvious. Instead, we'll cover the more arcane settings made possible by the *xset* command. And always remember that nothing is guaranteed with X Window, especially the theoretical settings possible with *xset*. Don't be surprised if your system doesn't respond to *xset*.

Querying the Current Server Settings

Before changing the X server settings, it's a good idea to know what's already set up. To do this, you can use the *-q* command-line parameter to *xset*; this command will list out all the current settings that you can manipulate with *xset*. As you can tell by the following information returned by *xset*, the information can get quite verbose:

```
Keyboard Control:
 auto repeat: on  key click percent: 0
    LED mask:  00000000
 auto repeating keys:0000000000000000
                     0000000000000000
                     0000000000000000
                     0000000000000000
 bell percent: 50 bell pitch: 400
   bell duration: 100
Pointer Control:
 acceleration: 2/1  threshold: 4
Screen Saver:
 prefer blanking: yes  allow exposures: yes
 timeout: 600 cycle: 600
Colors:
 default colormap:0x27 BlackPixel: 1
    WhitePixel: 0
Font Path:
/usr/local/X11R5/lib/X11/fonts/misc/,
/usr/local/X11R5/lib/X11/fonts/75dpi/
Bug Mode: compatibility mode is disabled
```

Ring My Bell

To control the bell's volume, the most likely change you'll make to the X bell, use the following command:

```
xset b volume pitch duration
```

The volume is in percent, from 0 (off) to 100 (full volume). Set the pitch in hertz and the duration in milliseconds; both are optional. Be warned that not all systems can control the bell to such a precise level. In such cases, *xset* tries as best as it can and then punts.

Restoring Compatibility

The Release 4 X server solved many bugs in X, but in doing so broke a number of applications that depended on these bugs. For example, many very old Motif programs will crash when the user tries to adjust the size of a pane in the Motif application's window. If your users experience this, you should turn on the bug compatibility mode by using the *bc* option; to turn off bug-compatibility mode, use *-bc*. (To turn on the bug-compatibility mode, the X server must support the MIT-SUNDRY-NONSTANDARD extension. You can use *xdpyinfo* to check this.)

Click and Clack

To control the key-click volume, use the following command:

```
xset c volume
```

Set the *volume* to the percentage level you want, from 0 (off) to 100 (full on).

To restore the key-click volume to the system defaults, use:

```
xset c on
```

Changing the Autorepeat Rate

X provides for a keyboard autorepeat. When a user holds down a key, X starts repeating that keystroke, after a certain threshold. To turn on the autorepeat mode, use:

```
xset r
```

To turn off autorepeat mode, use:

```
xset -r
```

Lighting the Lights

You can use *xset* to control the LED lights on the keyboard, using the *led* and *-led* options. Usually, the LEDs display various keyboard modes, such as **Caps Lock**, **Num Lock**, and **Scroll Lock** on PC keyboards. The following command turns on the first LED:

```
xset led 1
```

In X, the LEDs are numbered from 1 to 32, although we have yet to see a keyboard with 32 LEDs. To turn off an LED, use the *-led* command-line parameter:

```
xset -led 1
```

Accelerating the Mouse

When you move the mouse (or another pointing device) a certain threshold distance in a short period of time, the cursor motion will accelerate. This means you can move the mouse cursor to the far side of the screen with a very short, but fast, motion, improving usability of the system.

This acceleration is controlled by two values: the threshold, in pixels, which is the distance the pointer must move (in a short period of time) for the acceleration to kick in, and the acceleration multiplier, which is how many times faster the mouse should move, once the threshold is crossed.

To set the acceleration multiplier and threshold, use the following command:

```
xset m accel_mult threshold
```

The *accel_mult* is the multiplier, in the number of times faster you want the mouse to move, such as 2 times. The *threshold* is the number of pixels that must be moved (quickly) for the acceleration to kick in, such as 4 pixels. In such a case, the *xset* command would be as follows:

```
xset m 2 4
```

You can also use a fraction for the multiplier, like 3/2, as in the following command:

```
xset m 3/2
```

You may skip the threshold, as the previous example also shows.

Using *xset* to Control the Screen Saver

In order to avoid monitor burn-in, the X server includes a screen-saving option. The default is that after five minutes of no user input (keyboard or mouse), the screen will go blank. Any user input, such as jiggling the mouse or pressing a key, will restore the screen. We recommend using the mouse because typing a key may do something unexpected in the program with the keyboard focus.

This option helps extend monitor life (and extend, as well, your investment in expensive monitors), but can be disconcerting to some users, who ask why the screen suddenly goes blank.

To disable this option, you can use the following command:

```
xset s off
```

To restore the screen saver, use:

```
xset s on
```

To tell the screen saver to use a pattern, such as the X Window logo (a stylized X), instead of blanking the screen, use the following command:

```
xset s noblank
```

To adjust the screen saver timeouts, use the following command:

```
xset s value1 value2
```

The first value, *value1*, is the amount of time, in seconds, before the screen saver should turn on. The default is five minutes (300 seconds). The optional *value2* is the number of seconds between changes to the background pattern (if you're using the *noblank* option).

To restore all the defaults, use:

```
xset s default
```

Monitoring the System Load

Xload is a generic tool that presents a moving graph of CPU load, as shown in Figure 6.4.

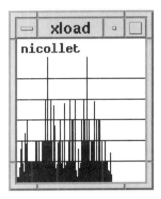

Figure 6.4 **Monitoring system load with *xload*.**

Figure 6.4 shows a heavily loaded system. A more lightly loaded system should present an *xload* graph more like the one in Figure 6.5.

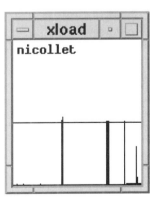

Figure 6.5 **A lightly loaded system, as shown by *xload*.**

Since it provides no scale, you shouldn't trust *xload* for an exacting picture of CPU usage, though you can get a general idea of how heavily the CPU is being utilized. With the ability to run X programs on one machine and display the output on another, you can run *xload* on a number of systems at your site and display all the results on your home workstation's display. This can help you to remotely monitor a number of systems.

You can normally run *xload* without any command-line parameters. By default, *xload* places the system's hostname as a label at the top of the graph. This is very useful when monitoring remote systems. You can also change the label with the *-label* command-line parameter:

```
xload -label "This is my label" &
```

Killing Errant X Programs

Sometimes, no matter what you do, you can't seem to stop an X program. You can use the UNIX *kill* utility once you get the proper process ID (you can use the *ps* command to track down process IDs). Tracking down the process ID may be a bit of a chore if you need to first check which machine the application is computing on. To help aid the task of killing errant X programs, you can use the *xkill* utility.

With *xkill*, you select the application to die with the mouse. *Xkill* will then destroy that application's connection to the X server. You don't need any command-line parameters:

```
xkill
```

You will then see a prompt like the following:

```
Select the window whose client you
wish to kill with button 1....
```

Summary

This chapter covers some handy X utilities:

* *xdpyinfo*, used to display screen capabilities, X extensions, available colors, and resolution

* *Xwininfo*, used to list the windows are on the screen, as well as the location and information about any window

* *Xlsclients*, which lists X programs running on a display

* *Xprop*, which lists the command line that started a program, as well as information on X and window-manager properties

* *Xset*, which changes a whole slew of X server settings

* *Xload*, which displays the UNIX system load in graphical format

* *Xkill*, which kills errant X clients

In the next chapter, you'll learn more about system configurations, as we delve into the wonders of X fonts and the font server.

Fonts and the Font Server

Topics covered in this chapter include:

* Explaining X fonts in depth
* Choosing font directories
* Font configuration files
* Font files and formats
* Font aliases
* Installing fonts
* Extending the X server's font path
* Selecting fonts
* Decoding long font names
* Setting up the font server

Fonts in X

Even in a graphical windowing system, most work performed—whether it be word processing, database management, inventory management—is text based. Consequently, displaying text is one of the major jobs of the X Window System. To enhance readability, X uses many fonts to display text in a variety of shapes, styles, and sizes. It's up to the administrator to ensure that these fonts are properly installed and configured.

In this chapter, you will learn about fonts from the point of view of the system administrator. The basic administrative tasks with X fonts include:

✳ Choosing font directories and maintaining enough disk space for all of X's fonts

✳ Installing new fonts

✳ Helping users select fonts

✳ Configuring and maintaining the font server

✳ Editing fonts and creating new fonts

Explaining X Fonts

A complete set of characters of one size of one typeface—including upper- and lower-case letters, punctuation marks, and numerals—is called a *font*. X provides two data storage sizes for the characters in fonts: 8-bit fonts and 16-bit fonts. The more common 8-bit fonts each have up to 256 characters, which is plenty for US ASCII and most Western European languages. These fonts are usually in ISO Latin-1 format, based on the international standard ISO 8859-1, which contains US ASCII (a 7-bit standard) in the lower 128 positions and a variety of extra characters needed for European languages, such as Ü, in the upper 128 positions.

While 256 characters is fine for Swedish, English, French, Greek, and Russian, it is inadequate to the needs of most Asian languages like Chinese, Japanese, and Korean. For these languages, X provides 16-bit fonts, encoded according to various national standards, such as JIS 0208-1993 for Japanese characters. For example, the font *kanji24* provides a number of Japanese characters, as shown in Figure 7.1.

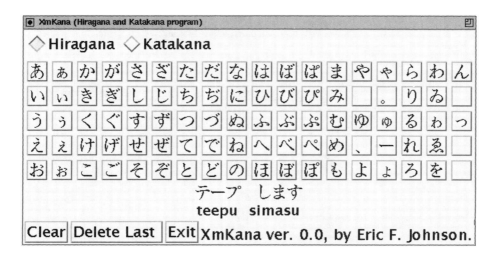

Figure 7.1   Japanese characters displayed in an X font.

Beyond storing text in fonts, you can literally store any monochrome images you want in fonts. For example, you can store mathematical symbols like α, legal marks like ©, and little icons that the publishing world refers to as dingbats. Other uses include fancy glyphs for applications, press releases from Prince, and even games. For instance, the XView programmer's toolkit uses a set of X fonts for picturing the scrollbars and pushpins used in the Open Look interface style, as shown in Figure 7.2.

Although we don't expect you to program, we mention this use for fonts because of a common error. If users try to run an Open Look program without the required *olglyph* and *olcursor* fonts, the program probably will exit with an error message. In this case, you may need to locate the proper Open Look fonts and install them. Luckily, most systems at X11 Release 5 or higher have most of these fonts installed. Even so, when faced with an Open Look program that won't run because of a missing font, you'll now know what to do.

Some games use special fonts, such as the Mahjongg tiles shown in Figure 7.3.

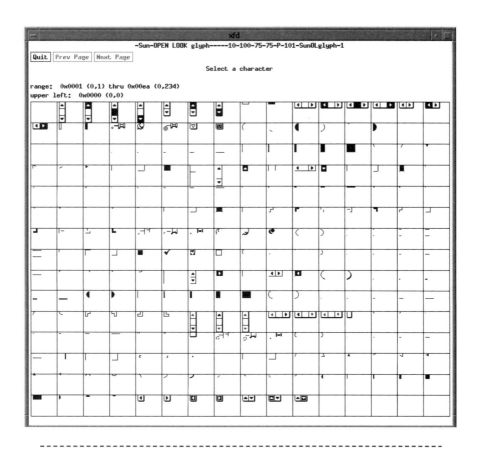

Figure 7.2   Olglyph-10, an Open Look font used for applications.

Programs for Working with Fonts

The standard X release from the X Consortium provides a number of essential tools for working with X fonts, including those listed in Table 7.1.

Table 7.1   X programs for working with fonts.

Program	Use
bdftopcf	Converts bitmap font file to binary X server font file *continued*

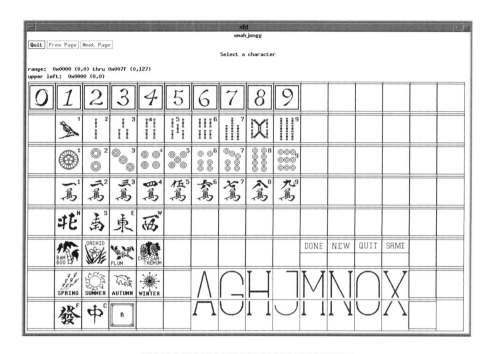

Figure 7.3   The X mahjongg font.

Program	Use
fs	Font server; can scale fonts for X server
fsinfo	Prints information on font server
fslsfonts	Lists font server fonts
fstobdf	Converts a font server scaled font to a bitmap font file
mkfontdir	Sets up a font directory
xfd	Displays characters in a font
xfed	Font editor, not part of standard X distribution
xfontsel	Allows you to choose a font graphically
xlsfonts	Lists available font names
xset	Sets font path for X server

Choosing Font Directories

X fonts take up a lot of disk space; a lot is around 14 megabytes. These fonts are stored in files, usually in a directory hierarchy under **/usr/lib/X11/fonts** (**/usr/openwin/lib/X11/fonts** under Sun's OpenWindows). You can install as many fonts as you desire. Due to different font formats, you may actually have multiple copies of the same font installed under different formats. Table 7.2 lists the most common font directories.

Table 7.2   Font directories under /usr/lib/X11/fonts.

Subdirectory	Contains
75dpi	X font files tuned for a 75-dpi display
100dpi	X font files tuned for a 100-dpi display
misc	Miscellaneous X font files
PEX	Fonts for the PEX 3D extension to X
Speedo	Scaled fonts for font server
Type1	PostScript scaled fonts for font server

The normal, or bitmapped, fonts are stored in the **75dpi**, **100dpi**, and **misc** directories.

Even though they seem to imply a certain required monitor resolution, the 75- and 100-dpi fonts are merely tuned for the given resolution. Users are free to use any of these fonts on any X screens.

N O T E

The **Speedo** and **Type1** directories hold scalable fonts used by the font. The **PEX** directory contains 3D scalable fonts used by the PEX three-dimensional extension to X.

In addition to these directories, you're free to create any font directories at any location in the file system. Part of the administrator's job is managing disk space, and X provides a lot of flexibility as to where you can store fonts. Table 7.2 lists the default locations.

Font Files

Inside the various font directories, you'll find X font files, as well as a few font-configuration files.

Most X font files are large binary files that contain the bitmap images for a single size, such as 12 point, and face, such as italic, for a single font family, such as Times. This is very different from PostScript or Speedo fonts, where a single font may be scaled to any number of sizes. Table 7.3 summarizes the various X font file formats.

Table 7.3   Font file formats.

Code	Format	Use
PCF	Portable Compiled Font	R5 binary fonts, server-neutral
BDF	Bitmap Distribution Format	ASCII format for distribution
SNF	Server Natural Format	R4 binary fonts
Speedo	Bitstream Speedo Format	Scaled format
F3	Folio	OpenWindows scaled format
Type1	PostScript Type 1	Scaled format

With X11 Release 5, most of the font files in subdirectories of **/usr/lib/X11/fonts** are binary bitmap fonts in PCF format. Unlike the older SNF format, the PCF font files are portable, in that you can use them on machines of different architectures. Prior to R5, you had to maintain a set of font files for each system and X terminal architecture, which added much to the disk requirements. Each SNF font file is a BDF font compiled into the format best suited for your particular X server. If you have an old X system, you may need to maintain SNF font files.

When you get a new font file, though, chances are the font will be in BDF format. In this format, each character is represented by an ASCII-printable bitmap. This format was developed before the PCF files, and the ASCII BDF format allowed you to exchange fonts more easily between system architectures. This ASCII format seems obsolete, but it's still widely used in exchanging fonts. The program called *bdftopcf* converts BDF font files into PCF files. You'll need to use this program when installing a new font (see the section on "Converting File Formats").

Font Configuration Files

In addition to the basic font files, each X font directory will have one or two special configuration files. The **fonts.dir** file in each font directory lists the mapping between file names for the fonts and the long font names. This is called the *font database*. The long font names are based on an X standard called the *X Logical Font Description Conventions*, or XLFD. A document describing the XLFD is included with the X Window System from the X Consortium.

As you'll discover, X font names tend to be very long. Many UNIX systems, though, limit the length and format (no spaces) of the filenames, so X provides a **fonts.dir** file to map the short filenames to the long font names. When X applications then ask for a font, the application sends a long font name to the X server.

The **fonts.dir** file is an ASCII text file. In the **fonts.dir** file, the first line just contains a number, such as 200. This is the number of fonts in the file. The program *mkfontdir* maintains this number and all the font names.

On every following line in the **fonts.dir** file, you'll find a file name, such as **courO08.pcf**, then white space, followed by the long XLFD font name, such as `-adobe-courier-medium-o-normal--11-80-100-100-m-60-iso8859-1`.

Font Aliases

Some of the X font names are very long. In addition, different systems may get fonts from different vendors, which makes for different font names. If you want a simple font, such as an 8x13 pixel fixed-width font for use with *xterm*, you may not be able to request the same font on all systems. Because of this, X provides the capability for *font aliases*. In the previous example, a font named *8x13* is available on most systems. This font name is an alias for a much longer font name. Other common font aliases are *fixed* (a fixed-width font) and *variable* (a proportional font, which is usually some version of Helvetica).

Font aliases are normally stored in files named **fonts.alias**. Each font directory, such as **/usr/lib/X11/fonts/100dpi**, should have a **fonts.alias** file if you want to use aliases for font names.

The **fonts.alias** file is a text file where each line describes a different alias. The format is first the alias, such as `lucidasans-bolditalic-8`, some white space, followed by the true long XLFD font name, such as `-b&h-lucida-bold-i-normal-sans-11-80-100-100-p-69-iso8859-1`.

Installing Fonts

To install an X font, you need to go through the following steps:

- ✳   Choose a directory for the font
- ✳   Convert the font to X server's desired format, usually PCF
- ✳   Make font database in the directory
- ✳   Add directory to X server's font path, or,
- ✳   Ask X server to reread font information from existing font path
- ✳   Verify font is installed with *xlsfonts*

Choose the Font Directory

The first step is to choose a directory to place the new font in. You can use a directory of your own, or you can place the font into an existing X font directory. Usually this latter approach is best unless you have a large number of fonts to install. If you reuse an existing font directory, we've found that the **misc** directory (usually **/usr/lib/X11/fonts/misc**), which holds miscellaneous X fonts, is often the best choice.

Converting File Formats

Once you choose the directory, you need to place the new font in the directory—in the proper format. In most cases, the new font you'll have will be in the ASCII-encoded BDF format. The next step is converting your font to the PCF format required by the X server (if you have a server at R5 or a higher release), or the SNF format used by older X servers. The programs *bdftopcf* and *bdftosnf* take care of this.

As you'd expect, *bdftopcf* converts a BDF font file to the PCF format. The output is sent to standard output, so you'll usually need to pipe the output or redirect it. The following command converts a BDF font file named **font-file.bdf** to the PCF format required by the X server and stores the resulting PCF font in the file **fontfile.pcf**:

```
bdftopcf fontfile.bdf > fontfile.pcf
```

If your system is at X11 Release 4 or older, you'll probably need to convert the ASCII BDF font file into the SNF format. Remember that each machine architecture uses a different SNF format, although it's virtually impossible to tell what the exact format is without digging into the binary SNF files.

With these older systems, you'll need to use the program *bdftosnf*, which acts much like *bdftopcf*. The following command converts a BDF font file named **fontfile.bdf** to the SNF format required by the older X server and stores the resulting SNF font in the file **fontfile.snf**:

```
bdftosnf fontfile.bdf > fontfile.snf
```

Making the Font Database in a Font Directory

Once you've converted the ASCII font file to the format required by your X server, the next step is to rebuild the **fonts.dir** file, which contains a database of the font filename to font name mapping, with the program *mkfontdir*. To run this program, you merely need to change to the font directory and issue the following command:

```
mkfontdir
```

After running *mkfontdir*, you next need to either add a new font directory to the X server's font path, or ask the X server to reread the font information from an existing font directory.

The Sun Font Database

Sun's latest version of OpenWindows uses an X server based on the X Consortium's release. Older versions of OpenWindows, up to Solaris 2.2, provided a Sun X11/NeWS server, which supported both the X and NeWS window protocols. If you have such an older system, you'll need to run different programs to install new fonts.

First, instead of running *bdftopcf* to convert the font into the proper binary format, you'll need to run the Sun program *convertfont*.

Second, instead of a **fonts.dir** file, OpenWindows used a **Families.List** file. The function of these files are similar, but you'll need to run the *bldfamily* program in place of *mkfontdir*.

With Solaris 2.3 and higher, though, you can use the standard X methods discussed in the rest of this chapter instead of the OpenWindows-specific methods.

Adding to the Font Path

If you're using your own font directory, you need to inform the X server about this directory. To do this, run the *xset* program, which we introduced in the last chapter. With *xset*, you need to use the *+fp* command-line parameter to extend the X server's list of directories where it looks for fonts, also called the font path. You can to extend the font path to include your new font directory with the following command:

```
xset +fp mydirectory
```

With this command, replace *mydirectory* with the name of your font directory.

You'll need to ensure that this *xset +fp* command gets executed each time the X server starts up. Because of this, you'll often need to place the previous command in the **.xinitrc** or **.xsession** files used by individual users. This is another reason for reusing an existing font directory.

TROUBLE-SHOOTING

If you get strange errors with *xset* when you extend the X server's font path with the +*fp* command-line parameter, the error message may not be descriptive of the real problem. If you're sure you've done everything right, then check the file permissions on the directory

you're trying to add to the X server's font path. In order for *xset* to work, it requires write access to this directory. In many systems, the font directories allow only write access for the root user. The *xset* error message, though, doesn't give you a clue if this is the problem.

Ask X Server to Reread Font Information

If you reuse an existing font directory, you merely need to ask the X server to reread the font databases from the **fonts.dir** files. To do this, you also use *xset*:

```
xset fp rehash
```

Your new font should now be available.

Verify Fonts with Xlsfonts

To check that your new font is properly installed, you can run *xlsfonts*. The *xlsfonts* program lists out the voluminous set of all fonts available to your X server. Expect pages and pages of font names in the long XLFD format.

The simplest command to use that tests for your new font is as follows:

```
xlsfonts | grep fontname
```

Replace *fontname* with your new font name, in the long XLFD format.

Modifying the Font Path

The *xset* program provides a number of command-line parameters for modifying the X server's font path. These options are summarized in Table 7.4.

Table 7.4   Modifying the X server's font path with *xset*.

Command	Meaning
xset fp=*fontpath1, fontpath2, ...*	Set font path to comma-delimited list of directories

continued

Command	Meaning
xset fp default	Restore font path to system defaults
xset fp rehash	Reread font databases in current font path
xset +fp *fontpath1, fontpath2, ...*	Add list of font paths
xset -fp *fontpath1, fontpath2, ...*	Remove specified paths from font path

With each set of font directories, you can use a single directory (see the previous examples), or a comma-delimited list of directories. In virtually all cases, you're only working with one font directory at a time, so you can use the simpler format.

Along with installing fonts, administrators often have to help users select fonts from the list of what's available.

Helping Users Select Fonts

X provides a number of tools to help select fonts, including:

✳ *xlsfonts*, which lists fonts

✳ *xfd*, which displays fonts

✳ *xfontsel*, which helps you select fonts

✳ *xterm* or other textual programs, which can display fonts as they will be used.

In addition, there's a also a tool built in to many X programs called copy and paste. X font names tend to get very long, so it really helps if you can avoid typing in the long names (a process that may be fraught with errors) and instead copy a font name from a listing. For example, the program *xlsfonts* lists the fonts that are installed with the X server. Once listed in an *xterm* window, you can select the text with the mouse, for pasting into another window.

When selecting fonts, it helps to know what fonts are actually available to select from, and that's where *xlsfonts* come in.

Listing the Available Fonts

You can list all the available fonts—quite a long list we might add—with *xlsfonts*. Just type in *xlsfonts* without any command-line parameters and you'll see a raft of output, including some of the fonts listed as follows:

```
-adobe-courier-medium-r-normal--10-100-75-75-m-60-iso8859-1
-b&h-lucida-bold-i-normal-sans-14-100-100-100-p-90-iso8859-1
-adobe-helvetica-bold-o-normal--11-80-100-100-p-60-iso8859-1
-adobe-times-bold-r-normal--11-80-100-100-p-57-iso8859-1
olglyph-10
8x13
fixed
cursor
variable
```

Expect pages of output. You may want to pipe the results to more to view the output one page at a time, as with the following command:

```
xlsfonts | more
```

Decoding the Long Font Names

Most of the output of *xlsfonts* comes in very long font names. While the names may look confusing, there's actually a rhyme and reason to the whole thing. As we stated above, these long font names are based on an X standard called the *X Logical Font Description Conventions* (XLFD). A document describing the XLFD is included with the X Window System from the X Consortium.

To help decode these long XLFD font names, we'll use two different fonts examples. These long font names appear as follows:

```
-b&h-lucidatypewriter-bold-r-normal-sans-26-190-100-100-m-
    159-iso885-1
-adobe-times-medium-i-normal--20-140-100-100-p-94-iso8859-1
```

Each part of the XLFD name is separated by a hyphen. If there are unused fields, you'll see two hyphens in a row. Table 7.5 describes the separate fields of the XLFD names.

Table 7.5   Decoding XLFD font names.

Field	Example	Description
Foundry	adobe, b&h	The company that created the font
Font family	times, lucidatypewriter	Basic font
Weight	bold, medium	How thick the letters are
Slant	i, r	Italic, roman, oblique, etc.
Set-width name	normal, condensed	Width of characters
Additional style	sans	Extra info to describe font
Pixel size	26, 20	Height, in pixels, of characters
Point size	190, 140	Height of characters in points * 10
Dots-per-inch	100-100, 75-75	Dots per inch in X and Y directions
Spacing	m, p	Spacing
Average width	94, 159	Average width in pixels * 10
Charset registry	iso885-1	Character set encoded in the font

NOTE Various fields in XLFD font names may have spaces. This complicates your efforts to build UNIX command lines, which may interpret the space as starting another command-line parameter. For this reason, it's always best to surround font names in quotes when used on the command line.

The slant field uses one or two letters to describe the slant of the font. Most X fonts use *r* for roman (normal) and *i* for italic. The full list appears in Table 7.6.

Table 7.6   The font slant field.

Code	Meaning
i	italic

continued

Code	Meaning
o	oblique
r	roman
ri	reverse italic
ro	reverse oblique
ot	other
any number	scaled font (new in R6)

The oddly named set-width field describes the width of the characters. Examples include *condensed*, *semicondensed*, *narrow*, *normal*, and *double wide*. Most are *normal*, though.

The additional style field allows the font designer to place any extra information needed to describe the font's style, usually something like *sans* for a sans-serif font. Most font names leave this space blank (where you'll see two hyphens in a row). A zero pixel height field usually signifies a scalable font. The point size is 10 times the real size in terms of *points* (1/72 of an inch). Thus, a point size of 190 means a 19-point font.

The spacing field tells you if the font has a fixed width or is proportional. Generally, proportional fonts look better. However, some programs, such as *xterm*, expect a fixed-width font. Table 7.7 lists the values for the spacing field.

Table 7.7   The font spacing field.

Spacing	Meaning
c	char cell/monospaced, e.g., suitable for using with *xterm*
m	monospaced
p	proportional
any number	scaled font (new in R6)

Officially, programs like *xterm* require a true character-cell font, identified with a *c*. We've found that any monospaced font, identified by *m*, also works well.

NOTE

The average width is also ten times the average width in pixels. The inflation allows for floating-point numbers to be encoded as integers—9.4 becomes 94.

The character set tells what encoding is used for the characters in the font. The vast majority of X fonts are encoded using ISO 8859-1 (often called Latin-1), which is a superset of US ASCII. Other character sets include ISO 8859-2 for other European languages like Czech and Hungarian, and JIS 0208-1983 for Japanese Kanji. Some vendors, like Hewlett-Packard, support their own supersets of ASCII. In H-P's case, this superset is called HP-Roman-8, and Hewlett-Packard provides a number of Roman-8-encoded fonts with their systems. You typically won't find these fonts on other vendors' systems.

Viewing Fonts

The standard X release from the X Consortium provides two main programs for viewing fonts, *xfontsel* and *xfd*. Of the two, *xfontsel* is better for users to select fonts because *xfontsel* helps you build up the long font names, as shown in Figure 7.4.

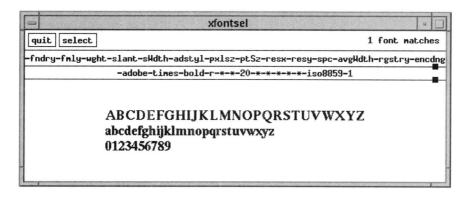

Figure 7.4   Using *xfontsel* to select a Times font.

With *xfontsel*, you start out with a blank XLFD font name and gradually narrow down the field to what you want (from the list of available fonts, of course). You can choose each field in the XLFD format separately. For example, you can start out and choose *times* for the font family field. Once you do this, all the other fields present menus based on appropriate values for Times fonts.

As you can see, *xfontsel* is very good for allowing users to select and view a font interactively. Once chosen, they can click over the *select* button and then the long XLFD name is prepared for pasting into another window.

The *xfd* program, short for X font displayer, displays a whole font at once, or as much of it as possible for the really big Asian fonts. As Figure 7.5 shows, *xfd* tries to display a page at a time of large Kanji fonts.

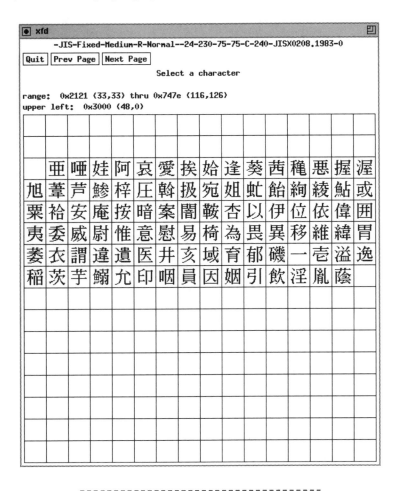

Figure 7.5   Using *xfd* to display a font.

What makes *xfd* useful is that it shows the whole font at once, which is very useful, especially for European characters like *é* or *æ*.

Unlike *xfontsel*, which requires no command-line parameters, you need to pass *xfd* the name of the font to display, using the *-fn* or *-font* command-line parameter. The following command instructs *xfd* to display the font named *fixed*:

```
xfd -fn fixed
```

You can also use the *-font* variant:

```
xfd -font fixed
```

Setting Up the Font Server

In addition to the normal set of bitmap fonts, X provides a font server, which can produce scaled fonts on demand. New with X11 Release 5, the font server was designed to provide complete compatibility with older systems, so X applications didn't have to change at all to take advantage of the font server. This is great, but it presents a great limitation. To maintain compatibility, X doesn't really provide scalable fonts. Instead, X still limits you to bitmap fonts at a single size. The trick is simple: The X server remains essentially unchanged. When the user requests a font, the X server checks its font path for the font. The font server becomes part of the font path and then scales the necessary font to the asked-for size. Once scaled, the font server provides this scaled font—as a bitmap—to the X server. The X server still deals in old bitmap fonts.

This means that the font server doesn't really give X applications dynamically scalable fonts. Instead, the font server really just adds in a much bigger set of bitmap fonts without all the associated bitmap font files.

Even so, the font server is a handy means to extend the set of available X fonts and to provide some standardization at your site. You can do this by running one copy of the font server and having it serve fonts to a number of X workstations over a network link. A single font server can easily serve machines of different architectures in a multivendor site.

You'll need to perform the following tasks to get the font server set up properly:

❊ Set up font server configuration file

❊ Choose a TCP/IP port number

❊ Start font server

❊ Verify the font server is operational

❊ Change X server's font path to include the font server

❊ Verify that the font server is providing scaled fonts to the X server

Much of the font-server documentation that came with X11 Release 5 is simply incorrect. The R6 documentation is much better. The techniques that we outline as follows, though, have worked for us, even though these techniques diverge from the official documentation. We obviously tried to get the documented techniques to work, and we failed miserably.

WARNING

The font server is unforgiving. Generally, any discrepancy or mistake causes the font server to die a flaming death. You may need a lot of patience getting this started.

Setting Up the Font-Server Configuration File

The first step in working with the font server is creating the proper configuration file. This file tells the font server what it needs to know, including where the scalable fonts are located and other configuration values. This file is an ASCII text file, and you'll normally find it in **/usr/lib/X11/fs** (where *fs* is short for font server).

In this file, you set a number of values. The syntax is simple: name the variable to set, place an equal sign (=), and then place in the new value for the variable. For example, the following sets the error file, used to log errors, to the file named **/usr/local/X11R5/lib/X11/FSERRORS**:

```
error-file = /usr/local/X11R5/lib/X11/FSERRORS
```

In the configuration file, you can set the following values, as shown in Table 7.8.

Table 7.8   Font server configuration file values.

Value	Use
alternate-servers	List of alternate servers
catalogue	List of font path entries for font server to use
client-limit	Number of clients served by font server, used to control resources
clone-self	Whether font server should clone itself when it reaches *client-limit*
default-point-size	Default point size, times 10, for unspecified fonts
default-resolutions	List of default resolutions, e.g., 75 or 100
error-file	File name for logging errors
port	TCP/IP port number, usually set to 7000
use-syslog	Whether to use *syslog* for errors, usually turned off

Table 7.8 becomes clearer when you see a working example configuration file:

```
#
# Eric and Kevin's sample font
# server configuration file.
#
# Use default TCP/IP port.
port = 7000

# Limit font server to 10 clients.
client-limit = 10

# Start up new server when it reaches limit.
clone-self = on

# Where to look for scalable fonts.
# You'll want to change the directories!
catalogue = /usr/local/X11R5/lib/X11/fonts/Speedo,
    /usr/local/X11R5/lib/X11/fonts/misc
```

```
# The misc directory holds bitmap fonts.

# Default point size, times 10.
default-point-size = 120

# Support 100 and 75 dpi by default.
default-resolutions = 75,75,100,100

# Don't use syslog
use-syslog = off

# Where to log errors
error-file = FSERRORS

# end of fs config file.
```

This configuration file tells the font server where our scalable fonts are located—in the **Speedo** directory for Bitstream Speedo format fonts. Note the custom installation (in **/usr/local/X11R5**). Lines that begin with a # character are treated as comments. For most of the values, we merely accepted the defaults.

Any Port Number in a Storm

In the previous configuration file, we choose 7000 as the port number for the font server to use. Why 7000? That's the default, and we try to stick with defaults wherever possible. By choosing 7000 for the font server, we're telling the font server to listen for clients—usually just the X server—on port 7000. X application programs, except for a few font-server query programs, generally never even know that a font server is running.

You're free, of course, to choose whatever port number you want. If you're not well versed in the innards of TCP/IP, you may just want to stick with 7000. The key to all this is that once you choose a port number you must tell the X server and the font server to communicate, so they'll both need to use the same port number.

Starting the Font Server

Once you've filled in the configuration file and chosen a TCP/IP port number, you can start the font server. The font server is usually a program named *fs* and stored in **/usr/bin/X11**.

When you start the font server, you must use the *-config* command-line parameter to tell it the name of your configuration file, such as in the following command:

```
fs -config ./config &
```

Start it in the background. If the font server detects any problems, especially with your configuration file, it will crash.

Verifying the Font Server is Running

If it appears that the font server is now running, you should verify this. (If it appears we're rather gun-shy about the font server, it's with good reason. We had lots of problems getting it going.) To verify that the font server is actually running, you can use the *fsinfo* utility program. *Fsinfo* prints out general information about the font server.

To run *fsinfo*, you need to know the hostname and TCP/IP port number where the font server is running, and then pass this information on the command line. For example, if the hostname is *eric* and you used the default TCP/IP port number of 7000, the *fsinfo* command would be the following:

```
fsinfo -server eric:7000
```

Here's some sample output of *fsinfo*:

```
name of server: eric:7000
version number: 1
vendor string: MIT X Consortium
vendor release number: 5000
maximum request size: 16384 longwords (65536 bytes)
number of catalogues: 1
        all
Number of alternate servers: 0
number of extensions: 0
```

You can replace *-server hostname:7000* if you properly set up the FONT-SERVER environment variable. Set this environment variable to the same value you need to type in with the *-server* command-line parameter. Using this previous example, the following C shell command sets up the FONTSERVER environment variable:

```
setenv FONTSERVER eric:7000
```

Another program that comes with the font server is *fslsfonts*, which lists the fonts supported by the font server. Using the same example configuration, the following command starts up *fslsfonts*:

```
fslsfonts -server eric:7000
```

Output from *fslsfonts* looks like the following:

```
-bitstream-charter-bold-i-normal--0-0-0-0-p-0-iso8859-1
-bitstream-charter-bold-r-normal--0-0-0-0-p-0-iso8859-1
-bitstream-charter-medium-i-normal--0-0-0-0-p-0-iso8859-1
-bitstream-charter-medium-r-normal--0-0-0-0-p-0-iso8859-1
-bitstream-courier-bold-r-normal--0-0-0-0-m-0-iso8859-1
-bitstream-courier-medium-r-normal--0-0-0-0-m-0-iso8859-1
```

Note all the zeros. These are values you can fill in.

After starting and verifying the font server, the next step is to configure the X server to recognize the font server and use the scalable fonts.

Adding the Font Server to the X Server's Font Path

We need to extend the X server's font path to include somehow the font server that we've just started. The basic mechanism is easy—we just use *xset* with the *+fp* command-line parameter. The basic syntax is:

```
xset +fp tcp/hostname:portnumber
```

Note the odd *tcp/* syntax. This tells the X server that this is not a directory.

You'll need to replace the *hostname* with your font server's hostname and the *portnumber* with your chosen TCP/IP port number. Using the same example, the following command extends the X server's font path to include the font server:

```
xset +fp tcp/eric:7000
```

If your *xset* command is not properly set up, or if your X server doesn't support a font server, you'll get a cryptic error message from *xset*, such as the following:

```
X Error of failed request: BadValue (integer parameter
out of range for operation)
   Major opcode of failed request: 51 (X_SetFontPath)
   Value in failed request: 0x0
   Serial number of failed request: 4
   Current serial number in output stream: 6
```

This message doesn't tell much, except that the *xset* command failed. This usually means you mistyped something. But it could mean that your X server doesn't support a font server.

Verifying the Font Server Serves Fonts to the X Server

Once you've tried to get the font server up and running, you'll want to ensure that everything, indeed, is working. The best way to do this is to run *xlsfonts* and look for fonts with zeros in the size fields, such as:

```
-bitstream-charter-bold-i-normal--0-0-0-0-p-0-iso8859-1
```

These fonts are usually scaled. The trick is filling in the zeros with the values you desire, and the font server should create a font to match. It doesn't always work this way, but so long as you type in reasonable values it should work fine.

Editing Fonts

There's no standard for editing X fonts. In fact, most of the existing X fonts were translated from another font format. But, there's at least one free program to edit fonts: *xfed*, which is short for X font editor.

We should mention that it's far easier to edit an existing font than it is to create a new font. That's why you'll probably want to find an existing font that's close to what you want, copy the font file, and edit your new font. In addition to copying an existing font, you can use the font server to scale a font for you and then edit the resulting bitmap font. The program *fstobdf* extracts a font from the font server into the common BDF font format.

Be careful, though, of copyright issues. Many of the X fonts were donated by big-time font vendors like Bitstream and Adobe. These vendors donated the fonts under certain conditions and probably won't be pleased if you violate those conditions. In addition, we assume that you want to ensure that your computer system remains entirely legal, to follow the law and avoid any hassles with vendors.

Summary

Almost all computing tasks—even those encountered by users of a graphical user interface—rely on text and, by extension, on fonts. The basic administrative tasks with X fonts include:

❊ Choosing font directories and maintaining enough disk space for all of X's fonts

❊ Installing new fonts

❊ Helping users select fonts

❊ Configuring and maintaining the font server

❊ Editing fonts and creating new fonts

In the next chapter, you will learn about X resources and resource files.

Resources and Resource Files

Topics covered in this chapter include:

* ❋ Resource files
* ❋ Installing resource files
* ❋ Application default files
* ❋ Resource-file locations
* ❋ Host-based resources
* ❋ Application resources
* ❋ Environment variables
* ❋ The *-xrm* command-line parameter

X Resources

X uses the term *resources* in many ways, but the most common way refers to an attribute of an application, such as a color or font, that users can change. When users change these values, they typically type in a new value into an ASCII text file, called a resource file, and then rerun the application to make the new value take effect.

Newer environments, such as the COSE desktop, allow users to change colors and fonts on the fly with a graphical interface. For the most part, however, customizing X applications involves editing the aforementioned X resource files.

Resource files form one of the greatest benefits of X—most applications are highly configurable—but also one of its major weaknesses. Unless resource files are installed properly, many applications don't work well at all, while the resource-editing syntax is a bear to learn.

As an administrator, you won't have to edit many resource files. However, each X application comes with a default resource file, usually called an application defaults file. You'll need to install this file in a common location, such as **/usr/lib/X11/app-defaults**, a directory where only you can install files. Users can then create their own X resource files in their own directories and use these resource files to override the system default ones.

As an administrator, you'll also need to ensure that the user environments get set up properly. After discussing where to install resource files, we provide an overview of the wide variety of locations where users can place these files and the environment variables that change the equation.

Installing X Resource Files

Each X application typically comes with a resource file intended for use as a system default. Usually, these resource files are located in **/usr/lib/X11/app-defaults**, but you can place them anywhere. Normally, users won't have permission to change files in **/usr/lib/X11/app-defaults**, so you'll need to log in as the root user to install these files.

Installing a resource file involves copying the file into the proper directory. So long as the file has the proper name, it should be read when the X application starts up.

If you want, you can customize this default resource file for your site. For example, if you want most X applications to use the same font, or if you want to change the keyboard mapping for an application, you may want to edit the application defaults resource file.

Naming the Application Defaults Files

The name of the application defaults file should be the application's class name. Sounds simple, right? Unfortunately, it isn't. You somehow need to determine the class name for each application, and sometimes this isn't easy.

To provide an example, the class name for the *xterm* application is XTerm. Therefore, the application defaults file in **/usr/lib/X11/app-defaults** should be named **XTerm**. How do you know this? Most class names start with an uppercase letter. If the first letter is an X, many applications, like *xterm*, make the second letter uppercase as well.

A common way to determine this class name is to use *xprop*, which you read about in Chapter 6, and look for the WM_CLASS property. This property should have two names, the application name, such as *xterm*, and the class name, such as XTerm.

Application Default Files for Free Applications

Many free X applications use a common naming scheme for naming the application defaults file. This usually involves adding an *.ad* (for application defaults) to the class name. Using our *xterm* example, the application defaults resource file would be named **XTerm.ad**. You then need to copy this file to **/usr/lib/X11/app-defaults** and give it the new name **XTerm**. Many applications follow this convention.

Places to Store X Resource Files

Users may place X resource files in many locations in your system. There's a number of common locations, such as **/usr/lib/X11/app-defaults** for class resource files. True to the X Window tradition, you can liberally customize this. Internationalization, for example, adds complexity to many of the standard resource file locations.

Due to the incredible ability to customize resource file locations, there's a strong likelihood of conflicts in resource-setting commands. Because of this, X defines a precedence for resolving conflicting definitions. We show this precedence in Table 8.1.

Table 8.1   Decoding X resource file locations.

Resource Type	Locations
Command-line	**-xrm, -bg, -geometry**, etc.
User host resources	XENVIRONMENT or **$HOME/.Xdefaults-hostname**
User server resources	RESOURCE_MANAGER/SCREEN_RESOURCES or **$HOME/.Xdefaults**
Application resources	XUSERFILESEARCHPATH, XAPPLRESDIR, or **HOME**
Application defaults	XFILESEARCHPATH or **/usr/lib/X11/app-defaults**

Table 8.1 represents many different locations to remember. Because of this, we strongly advise you not to use the X environment variables unless you really need to. These environment variables often serve only to complicate matters. They become useful in very specialized circumstances. Avoid them unless you really need them. Even so, this material is useful, since your users may not heed this advice.

User Host-Based Resources and Environment Variables

The XENVIRONMENT environment variable can hold the full pathname of a resource file. For example, if you create a user resource file named **MyResources** in the **/users/eric** directory, then you should set the XENVIRONMENT environment variable to **/users/eric/MyResources**.

In the UNIX C shell, you can use the following command:

```
setenv XENVIRONMENT /users/eric/MyResources
```

While XENVIRONMENT points to a file, the XAPPLRESDIR environment variable points to a directory in which to look for files. The search-path environment variables, such as XUSERFILESEARCHPATH, point to a colon-delimited list of paths.

If the XENVIRONMENT environment variable is not set, then X applications will look for a file named **.Xdefaults-*hostname*** in your home directory, where ***hostname*** is the network hostname for the system.

Most users don't set up host-based resources. Use host-based resources when you have a situation where users log into the same home directory from a number of machines and want to customize their X resources (particularly font sizes) on a per-machine basis.

N O T E

User X Server-Based Resources

User resource files contain resource-setting commands for anything they'd like to set. While class resource files just apply to one application class, user resource files apply to any application under X.

Inside one of these user resource files, though, you place the same resource-setting commands. The only difference is that these commands can apply to all application classes (that is, to all applications), so you need to be very specific on which application resources you choose to set. Use these files with care.

The traditional grab-bag X resource file is a file named **.Xdefaults** and stored in a user's home directory. This user resource file applies to all X programs. In fact, most users probably already have a file named **.Xdefaults** in their home directories. In addition to all these files, there's two properties that may be present on the root window, RESOURCE_MANAGER and SCREEN_RESOURCES. These properties, if present, override the **.Xdefaults** file.

Usually users will run the *xrdb* program to load up the resource-setting commands in an X resource file into this RESOURCE_MANAGER property. In many cases, the data for *xrdb* comes from the **.Xdefaults** file, which negates the difference between the file and the property (except that changes to the file won't be automatically loaded into the RESOURCE_MANAGER property).

Newer X environments, such as the Hewlett-Packard VUE or the COSE common desktop, automatically use *xrdb* to restore the resource settings of the user's previous session. This is quite handy. If your system has this ability, users may never need to edit resource files directly and they may never have to worry about the multitude of locations for X resource files.

The key is that if the RESOURCE_MANAGER property is set, it overrides any *.Xdefaults* file in the user's home directory.

Application Resources

After looking for user resource files, X applications typically next search for application class resource files set up by the user. These files are the same as the application defaults files we discussed at the beginning of this chapter, except that the user can install these files in a number of user-owned directories. The default location for these application class resource files is the user's home directory.

The search for application resources checks the XUSERFILESEARCHPATH environment variable. If XUSERFILE-SEARCHPATH isn't set, the next directory checked is the one specified by XAPPLRESDIR. If neither XUSERFILESEARCHPATH or XAPPLRESDIR is set, the application checks the user's home directory.

The XUSERFILESEARCHPATH Environment Variable

The XUSERFILESEARCHPATH environment variable holds a colon-delimited search path. Inside this search path, you can use a number of substitutions, which are expanded at run time. For example, %N in the search path is substituted with the application's class name, such as XTerm.

Most of the substitutions work for internationalizing X resource files, as shown in Table 8.3.

Table 8.3   Path substitution in X search paths.

Substitute	With
%C	Special customization, such as *-color* or *-mono*; new in R5

continued

Substitute	With
%L	Full locale, such as *fr_CA.iso8859-1* for French in Canada or *ja_JP.EUC* for Japanese in Japan
%l	Language part of locale, such as *fr*
%t	Territory part of locale, such as *CA*
%c	Codeset part of locale, such as *iso8859-1*
%N	Application's class name
%S	Suffix, such as *.bm* for bitmap files
%T	File type, usually *app-defaults*

These substitutions also apply to the XFILESEARCHPATH environment variable.

In X11 Release 5, the default XFILESEARCHPATH is set to:

```
base/%L/%N%C: \
base/%l/%N%C: \
base/%N%C:   \
base/%L/%N: \
base/%l/%N: \
base/%N
```

The *base* is set to the value of the XAPPLRESDIR environment variable or the user's home directory, if XAPPLRESDIR isn't set. If XFILESEARCH-PATH is set to anything other than the defaults listed previously, then XAPPLRESDIR is ignored.

Application Defaults

The application defaults resource files are simply class resource files, but they are stored in system locations such as **/usr/lib/X11/app-defaults**, the default location for these files. Normally, regular users don't have permission to change these files as they are meant to apply system-wide and are usually set up by system administrators.

The application defaults are looked for in the XFILESEARCHPATH search path or in **/usr/lib/X11/app-defaults**, if XFILESEARCHPATH isn't set. Some versions of X, notably on Sun systems, modify this default to be **$OPENWINHOME/lib/app-defaults**.

The XFILESEARCHPATH Environment Variable

XFILESEARCHPATH holds a colon-separated list of directory paths. Each directory is searched in order to find the application defaults (class resource) file. For example, on a Sun OpenWindows system, you may want to set XFILESEARCHPATH to:

```
setenv XFILESEARCHPATH \
    /usr/lib/X11/%T/%N:$OPENWINHOME/lib/%T/%N
```

With X11 Release 5, the default for XFILESEARCHPATH is set to:

```
/usr/lib/X11/%L/%T/%N%C:\
/usr/lib/X11/%l/%T/%N%C:\
/usr/lib/X11/%T/%N%C:    \
/usr/lib/X11/%L/%T/%N:   \
/usr/lib/X11/%l/%T/%N:   \
/usr/lib/X11/%T/%N
```

We summarize these resource file environment variables in Table 8.4.

Table 8.4   Resource file environment variables.

Environment Variable	Example
XAPPLRESDIR	/users/eric
XENVIRONMENT	/users/eric/MyResources
XFILESEARCHPATH	/usr/lib/X11/%L/%T/%N%C:/usr/lib/X11/%T/%N
XUSERFILESEARCHPATH	$HOME/%L/%N%C:$HOME/%N

WARNING

Again, we urge you to tell users to stay away from the X environment variables unless they absolutely can't avoid it.

X Application Command-Line Parameters

In addition to resource files, you change many resources in an application from the command line. With X applications, there's a common set of command-line parameters that users can pass to set resource values and change the behavior of the application. Table 8.5 summarizes the common command-line parameters.

Table 8.5   Common command-line parameters.

Option	Use
-bg background_color	Set background color
-display display_name	Specify X server to connect to
-fg foreground_color	Set foreground color
-geometry WidthxHeightXY	Set window size and location
-iconic	Starts application as icon
-name application_name	Sets instance (not class) name
-title window_title	Sets window title for titlebar
-xnllanguage language	Sets locale for international applications
-xrm X_resource_manager_string	Used to set any other resources

Most of these command-line parameters are self-explanatory. The two odd command-line parameters are *-geometry*, which we covered in Chapter 6, and *-xrm*, which we cover as follows.

Using the *-xrm* Command-Line Parameter

The *-xrm* command-line parameter allows users to pass a resource-setting command to an application without editing a resource file. You can also use the *-xrm* command-line parameter to override settings in a resource file.

You follow the *-xrm* with a value resource-setting command. Usually, you'll need to enclose this command in quotes, because most resource-setting commands have embedded spaces.

For example, to set the font resource for the *xterm* program, you can use the following command:

```
xterm -xrm "*font: lucidasanstypewriter-12"
```

This sets the value of the font resource to `lucidasanstypewriter-12`. Of course, with the font, it's much easier to use the *-fn* command-line parameter, with its simpler syntax. However, you may find a need for the *-xrm* command-line parameter for more obscure resources.

Summary

This short chapter covers the idea of resources and the ideal locations for resource files. In the next chapter, we cover keyboards and keyboard mappings.

The Keyboard, Keys, and Key Bindings

Topics covered in this chapter include:

* ✳ Keyboards and X
* ✳ Key bindings
* ✳ The Meta key
* ✳ KeySyms
* ✳ Using *xmodmap* to change a keyboard setting
* ✳ Determining KeySyms with *xev*
* ✳ Using *xkeycaps* as a front end to *xmodmap*

The Problem with Keyboards

The main problems with UNIX keyboards is that far too many are completely different. Each system vendor, with a few notable exceptions, provides their own keyboard—or many keyboards, as is the case with Sun systems.

To attempt to deal with this plethora of keyboards in a generic fashion, the designers of X created a set of generic keys, called *KeySyms*. The generic KeySym, such as *A* for an uppercase letter "A", are the same on all X systems. It is then up to the X server to handle the mapping between the low-level, hardware-dependent codes actually sent by the keyboard—called *keycodes*—to the generic KeySyms.

For example, the X server maps the 82nd key code on a PC-style keyboard to the **Page Up** key, which X calls the Prior KeySym.

X provides KeySyms for **Escape**, **Return**, function keys like **F3**, and all the keys on the numeric keypad. In general, the idea is that if your key has a specific symbol (called *glyph* in X terminology), the key will act as you expect. The left arrow key, for example, may have any odd number for its key code, but the X server translates that to the Left KeySym. (It's then up to individual X programs to use the left arrow in an intelligent manner.)

Most of the common QWERTY keys are located in similar positions on most keyboards, but the special-purpose keys vary greatly. Many similar keys are gathered under common names. For example, **Page Down**, **PgDn**, and **Next** all share the same keysym, Next.

Luckily, most UNIX vendors are moving toward PC-style keyboards. Not that the PC keyboard is so great, but at least it's reasonably consistent.

Important Keys

There are a few important keys in X, and the most important is the Meta key. Most X programs use an **Alt**-key combination to provide short-cuts, such as **Alt-E** to pull down the Edit menu in Motif programs.

Unfortunately, not all UNIX keyboards sport keys labeled **Alt**. On some keyboards, this key is labeled **Extend Char**, or even presented with just a diamond glyph. To handle this wide variance, the designers of X invented the concept of the Meta key—which would act as a modifying key much as **Alt** is used. On Intel-based PCs, SGI Iris workstations, and IBM RS/6000s, the Meta key is indeed labeled **Alt**. When you see any reference to the Meta key, you'll know that this key is really mapped to another key on your system.

Modifying Key Mappings with Xmodmap

The most common keyboard problems we face are of our own making. As users of UNIX systems, we get used to finding certain keys, like **Escape** and Tilde (~), in the same places. Unfortunately, in a multivendor environment, these keys may be located all over the keyboard—even on keyboards from the same vendor. Occasionally (far too often, in fact), we need to modify the keyboard configuration to make a new keyboard more in line with what we're used to.

Because the X server maintains the mapping between the proprietary keycodes and the generic keysyms in a mapping table, you can modify this table. This, in effect, changes the logical definition of keys. This ability comes in handy when you want to swap the **Caps Lock** and **Control** keys.

Many newer PC-style keyboards place the **Caps Lock** key above the **Shift** key and the **Control** key below. For many users, this is fine. But for us, raised on older keyboards with the **Control** key above the **Shift** key, this represents a problem.

Luckily, you can indeed change this with X. The conventional solution is to use *xmodmap*, a cryptic utility that allows you to modify the keyboard (and mouse) mapping. The *xmodmap* program takes a rather involved syntax, and generally you'll need to fill in a temporary text file with a set of *xmodmap* commands. In this text file, for example, you could place the commands to swap the **Caps Lock** and **Control** keys.

In the *xmodmap* syntax, you first need to remove the **Caps Lock** and **Control** keys from the list of locking keys and control modifiers. The following *xmodmap* commands do that:

```
remove lock = Caps_Lock
remove control = Control_L
```

Caps_Lock and *Control_L* are the keysym names for the **Caps Lock** key and the left (sometimes only) **Control** key. Then you need to add new *lock* and *control* modifiers, as follows:

```
add lock = Control_L
add control = Caps_Lock
```

Putting this together, you have the following *xmodmap* file:

```
remove lock = Caps_Lock
remove control = Control_L
add lock = Control_L
add control = Caps_Lock
```

Once this is set up, you can pass this file to *xmodmap* on the UNIX command line:

```
xmodmap filename
```

where *filename* is the name of your file.

Finding the Current State of the Modifier Keys

If you use *xmodmap* without any filename or other parameters, *xmodmap* returns with the current modifier key settings, shown as follows under SunSoft's Solaris 2.3 (with a Type 5 PC keyboard):

```
shift   Shift_L (0x6a),  Shift_R (0x75)
lock    Caps_Lock (0x7e)
control Control_L (0x53)
mod1    Meta_L (0x7f),  Meta_R (0x81)
mod2    Mode_switch (0x14)
mod3    Num_Lock (0x69)
mod4    Alt_L (0x1a)
mod5    F13 (0x20),  F18 (0x50),  F20 (0x68)
```

With this listing, it isn't very difficult to change modifier keys such as the **Caps Lock**, as they are clearly delineated. However, finding regular keys can be a pain, as you need to know the KeySym. Of course, it isn't always easy to guess the KeySyms for arbitrary keys on the keyboard, particularly for the numeric keypad and function keys.

In this situation, use *xev* to list the KeySyms. *Xev* places a window on the display and then prints out all events received by the window. (This results in voluminous output.) In this case, you'll type into the window, and *xev* will tell you what keys it thinks you're typing. Since there's no way to log this process, you must type a key into the *xev* window and write down the resulting keysym—a tedious process at best.

For example, if you type what you think should be the Meta key on your keyboard and X doesn't seem to respond, try using xev to discover the Meta key that X uses. Many keyboards supply a number of Meta keys, usually right and left Meta keys (X supports up to five Meta keys). Below, we pressed the left Meta key on an SGI Iris keyboard:

```
KeyPress event, serial 13, synthetic NO,
    window 0x3400001,root 0x29, subw 0x0, time
    1133486580, (103,58), root:(295,250),
    state 0x0, keycode 91 (keysym 0xffe9, Alt_L),
    same_screen YES,XLookupString gives 0
    characters:""
```

Providing a Friendlier Front End to *Xmodmap*

Tracking down the right KeySym isn't the only problem with *xmodmap*. As a means to change the keyboard mapping, *xmodmap* isn't considered a friendly interface. That's why a free utility called *xkeycaps* is so popular. *Xkeycaps* presents a graphical picture of the keyboard, as shown in Figure 9.1, and then allows you to change the keyboard mapping using the mouse. *Xkeycaps* then outputs a file suitable for use with *xmodmap*.

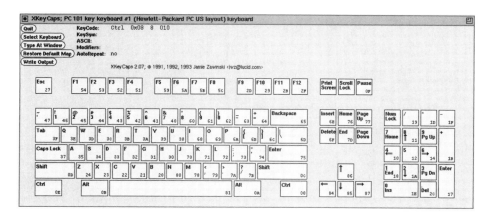

Figure 9.1   Using *xkeycaps* to change key definitions.

With *xkeycaps*, you see a virtual keyboard—a picture of your current keyboard in all its glory. You can use this keyboard picture alone to help figure out how X interprets your present keyboard.

You can also use the graphical representation of the keyboard to modify the key definitions, as a friendly front-end to *xmodmap*. In fact, once you've made some changes to *xkeycaps*'s virtual keyboard, the program automatically generates a file suitable for use with *xmodmap* to implement those changes.

Using *Xkeycaps* to Change Keys

A common keyboard problem with older Hewlett-Packard keyboards is mistaking the **Reset/Break** key for the **Escape** key, since Hewlett-Packard placed the **Reset/Break** key where many other keyboards place the **Escape** key. (The actual **Escape** key is located just beneath the **Caps Lock** key.) To change this, you can use *xmodmap* to map the **Reset/Break** key to generate the same KeySyms as the **Escape** key.

Without *xkeycaps*, you first need to figure out either the keycode or the KeySym for the **Reset/Break** key. For this, you can run *xev* and then type the **Reset/Break** key into the *xev* window. Once you've figured out the keycode or KeySym, you need to generate the *xmodmap* syntax to map this key to the **Escape** key. In the case of the Hewlett-Packard keyboard, you can type the following into a text file:

```
keycode 0x0F = Escape
```

You can then pass this text file to *xmodmap*:

```
xmodmap filename
```

where *filename* is the name of your file.

With *xkeycaps*, though, all you need to do is move the mouse over the **Escape** key and call up the key menu by pressing the rightmost mouse button. From this menu, you want to duplicate the **Escape** key. You then select the **Reset/Break** key. You've now taken care of all the syntax. A single mouse click tells *xkeycaps* to write out the data in *xmodmap* format. You can then pass this data to *xmodmap* and you're done.

As a front end to *xmodmap*, *xkeycaps* sends the *xmodmap* data to standard output, so, for best results, you'll need to redirect this output to a file. For example, you can use the following command to start *xkeycaps*:

```
xkeycaps > modmap.data
```

Once in *xkeycaps*, you can use the graphical interface to set up the keyboard configuration you want on the virtual keyboard. Be sure to select the button to write the output to the file. When you're done with *xkeycaps*, you'll need to pass the filename to *xmodmap*:

```
xmodmap modmap.data
```

This will then configure your keyboard for whatever changes you made during your *xkeycaps* session.

Problems with Xkeycaps

Xkeycaps doesn't always pick the proper keyboard. You'll often have to select the keyboard type from an internal list of about 35 common keyboard types. For example, the default Hewlett-Packard keyboard is the old-style, not the PC-style keyboard. If you're using the newer PC-style keyboard, you'll need to select the HP 700/RX X-terminal keyboard from the scrolled list presented by *xkeycaps*. You can also pass the keyboard type with the *-keyboard* command-line parameter.

Summary

This chapter briefly covers *xmodmap*, *xev*, and *xkeycaps*, three tools that you can use to change keyboard layouts. In the next chapter, you'll learn about colors and color names.

Colors and Color Names

Topics covered in this chapter include:

* ❋ X and color
* ❋ Setting colors from the command line
* ❋ Listing the available colors
* ❋ The X color database
* ❋ Adding to the X color database
* ❋ Using RGB values for color specifications
* ❋ Displaying the default colormap
* ❋ Setting the screen background color

Coloring Between the Lines

Like fonts, color is one of those areas that users love to change. Because of this, X provides a list of hundreds of colors and their associated numeric values. These colors include everything that you'd expect, such as *red*, *orange*, and *brown*, but also add in quite a few colors you've probably never heard of, such as *old lace*, *papaya whip*, and *misty rose*.

Under the hood, X defines all colors in terms of their red, green, and blue (or RGB) components. Most users, though, would prefer to set colors based on more realistic names, such as *lime green*, *maroon*, or *goldenrod*, or with a graphical color-chooser program.

That's where the X color database comes in. The color database is the massive list of the aforementioned colors. You can then use these colors on the command line or in resource files to control applications.

The most common use of these color names is setting colors from the command line.

Setting Colors on the Command Line

Most X applications accept *-bg* and *-fg* command-line parameters. The *-bg* command-line parameter sets the background color. The *-fg* command-line parameter sets the foreground color, usually the color used to draw text.

For example, to start *xterm* with a foreground (text) color of pink and a background color of brown (which is surprisingly readable), you'd use the following command:

```
xterm -fg pink -bg brown &
```

Listing the Available Colors

You can list the set of available colors from the color database with the *showrgb* command:

```
showrgb | more
```

We always pipe the output to *more*, as there are over 700 colors on a typical system.

Many systems don't ship the *showrgb* program, but don't worry. All this program does is print out the contents of the **rgb.txt** file, an ASCII text file normally located in **/usr/lib/X11**. You can use *more* (or *cat* or your favorite program to list the contents of a file) on the **rgb.txt** file.

Whether you use the *showrgb* program or list the **rgb.txt** by hand, you'll see hundreds of entries like the following:

```
50 191 193   aquamarine
255 114 86   coral
126 126 126  gray
255 182 193  light pink
250 240 230  linen
143 0 82     maroon
255 0 255    magenta
```

The first three numbers are the red, green, and blue values, respectively. What follows is the color name that users can type in.

The Color Database Files

The **rgb.txt** file presents the source data for the color database. The actual color database files are **rgb.dir** and **rgb.pag**, also usually stored in **/usr/lib/X11**.

A program named *rgb* that is available only with the X sources (and typically not in **/usr/bin/X11**) converts the **rgb.txt** file into the UNIX dbm database format, resulting in the two files **rgb.dir** and **rgb.pag**. The **rgb** program, the only possible tool for altering the color database, is usually stored in **mit/rgb** in the source directory (presuming you have the X source code, of course). This directory also has the master copy of **rgb.txt**.

To add a new color name to the color database, you must edit the **rgb.txt** file in **mit/rgb** and then add in your new entries. Place color names one to a line.

Once you're done editing the file, you can run *make* to rebuild the **rgb.dir** and **rgb.pag** files. You'll then need to copy all three files (**rgb.txt**, **rgb.dir**, and **rgb.pag**) to **/usr/lib/X11**, or wherever these files are stored on your system.

Using RGB Numbers for Color Values Directly

If the color name format doesn't appeal to you or your users, there's another form for specifying color values: setting the RGB numbers directly. This syntax is simple: *#RedGreenBlue*, where you replace *Red*, *Green*, and *Blue* with the color values, in hexadecimal. You must use the same number of digits for the red, green, and blue values. For example, red would be: #FF0000; or, you could use more digits: #FFFF00000000.

FFFF is full on, and *0000* is full off for a color. This format is valid through X11 Release 5. However, Release 5 supersedes this #rgb format with a newer format: *rgb:Red/Green/Blue*. For example, rgb:FFFF/0/0.

Setting the Screen Background

One common use of these color names is to set the color of the root window—and by extension, changing the screen's background color. To do this, we use the *xsetroot* program. However, a number of virtual window managers, such as *olvwm*, *vuewm*, and *tvtwm*, create a number of screen-sized windows on top of the root window, obscuring any colors changed by *xsetroot*. (If *xsetroot* doesn't seem to work for you, this is the likely case.)

To set the root window's background color, use the *-solid* command-line parameter, as shown in the following command:

```
xsetroot -solid maroon
```

The *-solid* parameter tells *xsetroot* to use a solid color, rather than a bitmap. The *-bitmap* parameter tells *xsetroot* to set the root-window background to a monochrome bitmap image, stored in a bitmap file. You can also pass the *-fg* and *-bg* parameters to color the bitmap. The following command creates a green and black root-window background with the bitmap file named *radura.xbm*:

```
xsetroot -bitmap radura.xbm -bg green -fg black
```

Showing the Color Cells

There are a number of programs that display the contents of the default colormap on an X system. For example, *xshowcmap* displays the currently allocated color cells, as shown in Figure 10.1.

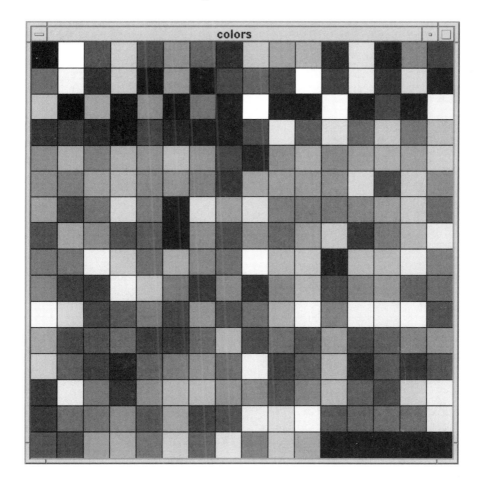

Figure 10.1   Displaying the current colormap with *xshowcmap*.

Similar programs include *xcolormap* and *xcmap*.

Summary

This chapter contains a brief description of color under the X Window System, explaining how to set up colors and display the contents of the default colormap. In the next chapter, we cover bitmap and icons.

Bitmaps, Icons, and Screen Dumps

--- --- --- --- --- --- --- --- --- --- --- ---

Topics covered in this chapter include:

* Using bitmaps
* Using the *bitmap* program
* Using icons
* Using bitmaps as a screen background
* Setting up icons with *xterm*
* Capturing screen images
* Printing screen images
* Converting *xwd*-format files
* Using *xgrabsc* and *xgrab*
* Magnifying portions of the screen with *xmag*

Pop Icons

A *bitmap* is an image made up of color or monochrome dots. Bitmaps are extremely popular in graphical software and are used to liven up interfaces. In many cases, a picture is indeed worth a thousand words and more clearly aids users.

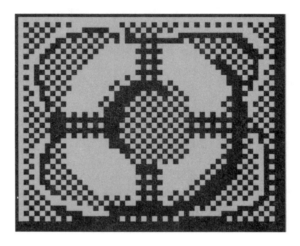

Figure 11.1   A bitmap.

In the X Window System, you'll see a lot of bitmaps, especially those used for icons. An *icon* is a small pictorial representation of a program's window. Most users think of icons as representing applications so the user can work with other software, eliminating the inevitable screen clutter that occurs with multiple windows. At any given time, most X displays show one or two icons, as shown in Figure 11.2.

Figure 11.2   Some program icons.

Some window managers, such as *mwm*, provide a means to keep icons inside an icon box, as shown in Figure 11.3.

Figure 11.3   Mwm's icon box.

In theory, X allows only for monochrome icons, but some window managers, such as the COSE common desktop, allow programs to set up colored icons.

Creating Your Own Icons and Bitmaps

There may be times when you want to create you own bitmaps, either for use as a screen background or as an icon (both instances are covered later in this section). Most applications hardcode the icons into the program executable.

If this is the case, you don't need to edit or create your own icons. But some programs, like *xterm*, don't define their own icons. In this case, you can set up an icon if the window manager allows it. You can create your own bitmaps with a number of X-based tools, including the *bitmap* program depicted in Figure 11.4.

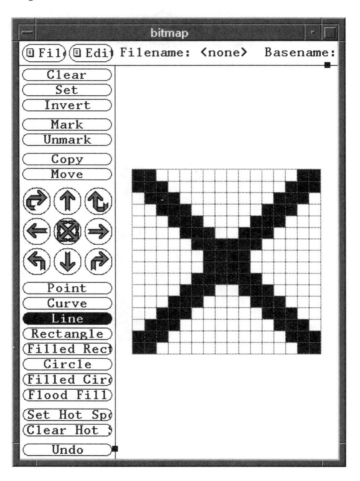

Figure 11.4   The bitmap program.

The *bitmap* program creates images in an ASCII format, usually called the bitmap file format. This file format stores all the image data in a snippet of C language program code, such as the following:

```
#define X_width 16
#define X_height 16
static char X_bits[] = {
0x03, 0xc0, 0x07, 0xe0, 0x0e, 0x70,
0x1c, 0x38, 0x38, 0x1c, 0x70, 0x0e,
0xe0, 0x07, 0xc0, 0x03, 0xc0, 0x03,
0xe0, 0x07, 0x70, 0x0e, 0x38, 0x1c,
0x1c, 0x38, 0x0e, 0x70, 0x07, 0xe0,
0x03, 0xc0};
```

When you display the above source code with a program like *bitmap*, you'll see the image shown in Figure 11.5. The bitmaps themselves are just ASCII text files; these files end with a suffix of **.xbm**.

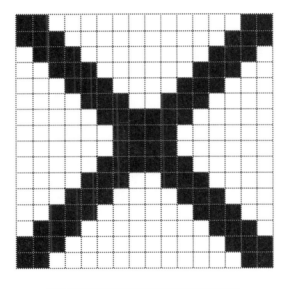

Figure 11.5   A sample bitmap.

Changing the Screen Background to a Bitmap

In the last chapter, we described how to use the *xsetroot* program to set the screen background to a solid color, using the *-solid* command-line parameter. The same mechanism works for setting up bitmaps as screen backgrounds, using the *-bitmap* command-line parameter:

```
xsetroot -bitmap filename
```

where *filename* is the name of the monochrome bitmap file.

By default, the bitmap is replicated over the screen background (the root window) in black and white. You can use the *-fg* and *-bg* command-line parameters to modify this as well.

The following command displays a bitmap (contained in the file *mybitmap.xbm*) with a green foreground color and a yellow background color (not a particularly pleasing combination):

```
xsetroot -fg green \
    -bg yellow \
    -bitmap mybitmap.xbm
```

Changing Xterm Icons

The *xterm* program doesn't set up any icon at all, so any *xterm* icon must be provided by the window manager. *Mwm* provides a default icon (shown in Figure 11.6) for any X program that has no icon.

Figure 11.6   The *mwm* default icon.

If you or your users prefer a different icon, you need to convince the window manager to use a specific icon for *xterm*. You can do this with most window managers, but the process is different for each window manager.

For *mwm* (and close variants like *vuewm*, *4Dwm*, and *∂twm*), you can set the window manager's *iconImage* resource. Add the following line to your **.Xdefaults** file or *Mwm* class-resource file:

```
Mwm*xterm*iconImage: /u/erc/bitmaps/mybitmap.xbm
```

where *mybitmap.xbm* is the arbitrary name of a bitmap file. This sets the *iconImage* resource for all instances of the *xterm* program (that is, all programs with the resource name *xterm*) to use the bitmap image stored in **/users/erc/bitmaps/mybitmap.xbm**. The *iconImage* resource expects a file name for a monochrome bitmap in the ASCII bitmap file format (the same format as is used by the *bitmap* program).

For *mwm* variants, like Hewlett-Packard's *vuewm*, use the window manager's proper resource class name in place of *Mwm*. In the case of *vuewm*, this is *Vuewm*, as found in the following resource command:

```
Vuewm*xterm*iconImage: /u/erc/bitmaps/mybitmap.xbm
```

Editing Color Icons

In addition to the *bitmap* program, there are a number of programs that allow you to edit bitmaps, including Sun's *iconedit*, Hewlett-Packard's *vueicon*, and the COSE common desktop's *dticon*. Each of these programs provides a much more sophisticated editing interface than plain old *bitmap*. The *vueicon* program is shown in Figure 11.7.

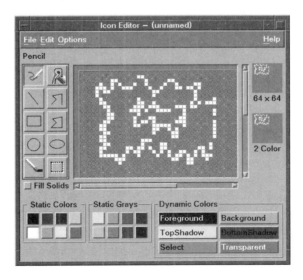

Figure 11.7   The *vueicon* program.

There are also free programs like *pixmap* and *xpaint*. We show *xpaint* in Figure 11.8.

Figure 11.8 *Xpaint* in action.

The *pixmap* program edits files in the XPM (short for *X PixMap*) format. The *xpaint* program supports a number of formats.

Capturing and Displaying Screen Images

There are times when you want to capture (a process sometimes referred to as capturing a *screen dump*) and print the contents of a screen. For instance, when you finally get around to creating the documentation for your system—and we all know what a high priority *that* is—it would be nice to include some screen captures to show new users exactly what to expect.

The basic X configuration includes a number of programs for capturing and displaying screen images, as listed in Table 11.1. In addition, many commercial software packages, such as *FrameMaker*, allow you to capture parts of the screen for inclusion into a document.

Table 11.1   X programs for capturing and printing screen images.

Program	Used For
xdpr	Captures screen dump and prints picture
xmag	Magnifies the bits on part of the display
xpr	Prints out a captured screen image
xwd	Dumps (captures) a screen image
xwud	Undumps or displays a captured screen image

Using *Xwd* to Dump a Window's Contents

The *xwd* program forms the basic X screen capture program. Primitive at best, *xwd* dumps the contents of a window to an *xwd*-formatted image file. You can specify the window ID from the command line or choose the window interactively with the mouse.

The *-out filename* command-line parameter specifies the name of the output file, instead of standard output. The standard-output option can be used if you want to pipe the output of *xwd* to another program, such as *xpr*.

The following command allows you to interactively select a window and output the screen image of that window to a file named **screen1.xwd**:

```
xwd -out screen1.xwd
```

With *xwd*, you choose the window to dump with the mouse or pass the *-id* command-line parameter, along with a window ID, such as:

```
xwd -id 0x2000ab
```

You can select the root window using the *-root* command-line parameter. The other key command-line parameters include *-frame*, which includes the window frame or border, and *-nobdrs*, which doesn't include the window border.

Unfortunately, the output format is an odd X-only format used only by *xwd* and a few select other programs. However, there are a number of programs you can use to convert *xwd*-formatted files; we cover one of the most useful software packages in "Converting Bitmap File Formats," which follows shortly.

Printing Screen Images with *Xpr*

Xpr prints screen images captured with *xwd*. As with most printing programs, there's a plethora of options, which we describe in Table 11.2.

Table 11.2 Command-line parameters for *xpr*.

Parameter	Meaning
-device *device*	Specifies output device, such as "ps" for PostScript
-gray *number*	Use a number of 2, 3, or 4 for dithering
-header *string*	Sends *string* as the image header
-landscape	Specifies landscape mode for the paper (default)
-output *filename*	Sends output to *filename* rather than standard output
-portrait	Specifies portrait mode for the paper
-scale *value*	Scales each pixel to *ValuexValue* pixel grids

In most cases, you'll use the *-output* command-line parameter or pipe the output to your printer device.

The *-device* command-line parameter controls the formatting. Since the vast majority of UNIX sites use a PostScript printer, you'll almost always use *-device ps*. (If your system doesn't have a PostScript printer, check the *xpr* online manual pages to see a list of the devices supported on your system. For example, Hewlett-Packard systems tend to support most H-P printers in addition to the default set.)

To put this all together, the following command dithers a screen dump, adds a header, and prints to **lp**, which is assumed to be a PostScript printer.

```
xpr -device ps -gray 3 \
    -header "Nice Screen Dump" \
    -portrait screen1.xwd | lp
```

Undumping a Screen Image with *Xwud*

Xwud (short for X Window Un-Dump) displays an image captured with *xwd*. The *xwud* program makes a new window that is an image of the captured window and displays this image in the same location as the window was originally captured. Generally, you'll need to use the *-in* command-line parameter, which specifies the input filename:

```
xwud -in screen1.xwd
```

Converting Bitmap File Formats

Many of the X screen-capture utilities use the odd *xwd* file format, which is not widely supported even within the X Window world. To get around this problem, you may need to run software to convert an *xwd*-formatted image to a more common format, such as Encapsulated PostScript (EPS), Tagged Image File Format (TIFF), or Graphics Image File (GIF). The most useful conversion software of this type is called PBM (for the Portable BitMap package), which can be found in both UNIX and DOS versions. Called *pbmplus* (there's a scaled-down DOS version called *PBMLITE*), this package contains a huge set of programs to convert just about every image type.

PBM does this by first converting an image (such as an *xwd*-formatted file) into a neutral PBM format with one program, and then running a second program to convert the neutral image to the target format (such as TIFF, EPS, or PICT).

PBM is not part of the standard X software. See Chapter 17 for more on how to obtain PBM and other free X programs.

N O T E

Using *Xgrabsc* to Capture Screen Images

In addition to the standard X programs, we've discovered a very handy screen-capture program that supports more popular graphics formats, like EPS and PostScript.

Xgrabsc allows you to capture any rectangular area on the screen, instead of limiting you to entire window boundaries. You can capture the image of a dialog box along with a program's main window, for example.

In addition, there's a front end to *xgrabsc*, called *xgrab*, that presents a friendlier interface than using the command line, as shown in Figure 11.9.

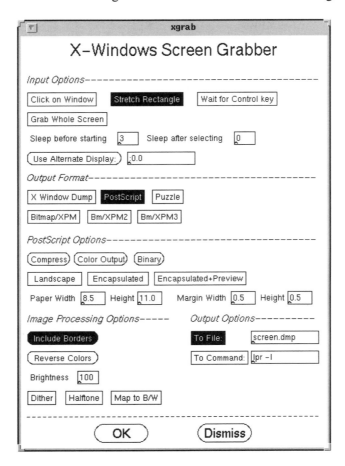

Figure 11.9   Using the *xgrab* front end to *xgrabsc*.

Unfortunately, though, *xgrabsc* does not come with the standard X sources from the X Consortium. (We did, though, include a version on the CD-ROM that accompanies this book.)

Magnifying Images with Xmag

Xmag, as the name implies, magnifies images on the screen. We often find it handy to magnify an image and then capture the magnified image, instead of the small original.

To magnify an image, *xmag* creates a window where each pixel in the source image is represented by a number of pixels, making the original image bigger, as shown in Figure 11.10.

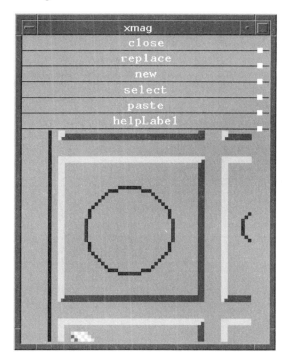

Figure 11.10   Using *xmag* to magnify an image.

When you run *xmag*, the program prompts you to select an area to magnify. The *-source* command-line parameter allows you to change the default 64-by-64-pixel geometry for the size of the area to be magnified.

The following command magnifies a 150-by-200 pixel area of the screen:

```
xmag -source 150x200 &
```

Summary

In this chapter you learned the various tools for creating and editing bitmaps, as well as the many tools used to capture, print, and manipulate screen images, including:

- ❋ *bitmap*, a program used to edit and create bitmaps
- ❋ *xwd*, used to capture a screen or portions of a screen and save to file
- ❋ *xpr*, used to print images captured by *xwd*
- ❋ *xwud*, which displays an image created by *xwd*
- ❋ *xgrab* and *xgrabsc*, which captures the screen or portions thereof and saves it to common file formats
- ❋ *xmag*, which magnifies a portion of the screen so it can be captured more clearly

In the next chapter, we shift our focus to more administrative tasks, beginning with the hot topic of security and X.

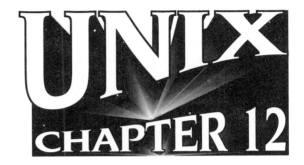

Security and X

Topics covered in this chapter include:

* Security—and the lack of it
* Workstation security issues
* Host-based security with *xhost*
* Using *xauth* for security
* The three main *xauth* security methods
* Using the **.Xauthority** file
* *Xauth* command-line parameters
* Using a screen-locking program
* Securing *xterm* with the keyboard-locking program

An Overview of Security in X (There Isn't Any)

From the beginning, X was designed to make interaction between networked computers go smoothly. As such, security wasn't a big issue; the problem was connecting computers, not creating barriers between them. This lack of security within X is still the case.

That said, there are a number of things you can do to improve your system security. The fundamental problem with X is basic: everything you see on your display travels from X applications to the X server over a network link. In the other direction, every key pressed travels from the X server to these applications over the same network link. And, as we all know, clever users can monitor these network links.

As X-based workstations and terminals become the norm, it's easy to forget about this fact and lull yourself into a false sense of security—you did after all, login to your system, which is protected by a password.

Security Issues for System Administrators

The most commonly used X program, especially for system administrators, is *xterm* (or one of many variants), which provides an interface to the UNIX shell. With a command-line shell interface, you'll no doubt type in a lot of commands, especially the **su** command, to temporarily change to the root user.

Watch out, though. When you type in **su**, you typically next enter the root user password, which could be picked up by another user, as the characters in this password are sent—unencrypted—over the network from the X server to the *xterm* window.

Another danger: any program that sends events to your windows, rather than merely snooping the events. Many X programs, including *xterm*, won't accept synthetic events—events sent from another X application—by default. (To check whether your *xterm* windows can receive synthetic X events, check the *allowSendEvents* resource. You normally want to set this to *False*.) If not configured this way, a malicious user could send in a command like:

```
/bin/rm -r /*
```

With this command sent to one of your windows, it could cause some damage.

If a user has access to your X display, that user could place a number of fake windows on top of all your windows and intercept all X events, as you wouldn't know the difference between these windows and your real windows.

Other Workstation Security Issues

In industrial-automation applications or perhaps an air-traffic-control system, a malicious user could modify X colormaps to convert danger areas, say, in red, to an all-clear color, say green or blue. No application should depend on color alone to convey information, especially if there are safety issues involved.

Also, X is the cause of security problems on other windowing systems. In many versions of SunOS, for instance, a user can access the Sun workstation graphics frame buffer (usually **/dev/fb**) directly, allowing them to present false windows. These windows could ask for your password and do other not-so-nice tricks.

In addition, some workstations now sport microphones or even video cameras. Not only is Big Brother listening and watching, but clever users may be as well, should they gain access to the UNIX device files for these peripherals.

What You Can Do to Secure Your X System

All is not lost. There are a number of things you can do to enhance security at your site. X provides two main security systems: the simple host-based system (using the program *xhost*) and a more secure authorization system (based on *xauth*). However, none of these security schemes are really secure. The real answer is to fully secure your UNIX environment, instead of just trying to secure X.

Simple Host-Based Security with *Xhost*

The simplest means to provide some measure (albeit not much) of security is to use the *xhost* program. With *xhost*, you can enable or disable access to your X server from other hosts, on a hostname-by-hostname basis. For example, if you're sitting at a workstation named *eric* and you want to disable access to your X display to any program running on a machine named *kevin*, you'd use the following *xhost* command:

```
xhost -kevin
```

This command disables any program running on machine *kevin* from connecting to your X display. You must enter *xhost* commands at the display's console. That is, the above *xhost* command must be run from machine *eric* (the machine used for the previous example).

Each X server maintains a list of hosts that are allowed access. You can use *xhost*, then, to add or subtract from this list. Any program running on a "trusted" host can then access your X display. The only way to disable access is to disable an entire host. You can also disable all hosts—except for the one the X server runs on—with this method.

To enhance security, many modern versions of UNIX, such as Hewlett-Packard's HP-UX, turn off all foreign host access by default. In this case, if you want to allow access from a particular workstation, you need to use the + command-line parameter to *xhost*. For example, to allow programs running on machine *kevin* to access your X display, you'd use the following command:

```
xhost +kevin
```

To enable access from all hosts to your workstation, you can use the following command:

```
xhost +
```

WARNING

Using the *xhost* **+ command means that any workstation on the network can access your display. Watch out!**

Setting Up a Default Xhost Database

You can set up a default list of trusted hosts. The file **/etc/X0.hosts** contains the default list of the hosts with access to display 0 on a given host. (Most workstations have only one X display, display 0.) You can create one of these

files for every X server on a given computer. The filename is
/etc/Xnumber.hosts, where *number* is the display (X server) *number* (starting
at 0). The *xhost* program can override the entries in this file.

Using the X Authority Package
for Stronger Security

If the *xhost*-based approach isn't enough for you, you can try the more detailed
authorization scheme associated with the program *xauth*. This scheme uses
special protocols, by default MIT-MAGIC-COOKIE-1, to limit access to the
X server. Under this scheme, client programs must send the proper (encrypt-
ed) code—called a *magic cookie*—to the X server for it to accept the connection.
The X server then maintains a list of valid cookie values.

The base Release 5 of the X Window System provides for three stronger
security systems based on the *xauth* program and the magic-cookie concept,
as listed in Table 12.1. X11 Release 6 adds Kerberos-based security, which
can be used to enhance your site's security. Kerberos covers much more than
merely X, however, and is beyond the scope of this book.

Table 12.1 *Xauth* security methods.

Method	Security Level
MIT-MAGIC-COOKIE-1	Shared plain-text cookies.
XDM-AUTHORIZATION-1	Secure DES-based private-keys.
SUN-DES-1	Based on Sun's secure RPC system.

Magic Cookies

With the MIT-MAGIC-COOKIE-1 method, each X application sends a
128-bit cookie to the X server. The cookie value sent by the application must
match the cookie stored in the X server, otherwise the application is not
allowed to connect to the X server.

With this method, each user has a **.Xauthority** file in the user's home directory. (This means that anyone who can gain access to this file can connect to the

X server.) You can also use the XAUTHORITY environment variable. The XAUTHORITY environment variable should name an alternate cookie file.

If you set up the X Display Manager, then *xdm* stores a cookie value in the **.Xauthority** file in each user's home directory, or in the file named by the XAUTHORITY environment variable. If you don't use *xdm*, you must set up this cookie value with the *xauth* program.

Once a magic cookie value is stored in a user's home directory, X programs must access this file to get the cookie value. If a program doesn't have access to the user's **$HOME/.Xauthority** file, then that program cannot get the magic cookie value and cannot connect to the X server.

By default, the .Xauthority file has permissions of -rw-------, which means that only the user can access the file. Anyone who can log in as this user can access this file.

WARNING

The magic cookie value used with the MIT-MAGIC-COOKIE-1 is sent over the network with no encryption. This means that other software may intercept the cookie value and snoop into its contents. This scheme is slightly better than the *xhost* method, which allows any program on a given host to connect to your display, but it still is by no means secure.

Sending an Encrypted Cookie

The XDM-AUTHORIZATION-1 method, available only in the United States (due to U.S. export laws), works much like the MIT-MAGIC-COOKIE-1 method, but the XDM-AUTHORIZATION-1 encrypts the magic cookie value before sending it out over a network. In this case, the magic cookie value has two parts: a 56-bit DES encryption key and a 64-bit random value, used to authenticate the user. In addition to this data, programs using XDM-AUTHORIZATION-1 also encrypt their TCP/IP address and port number, as well as the system time (in seconds, since the start of the UNIX world — midnight on Jan. 1, 1970). The XDM-AUTHORIZATION-1 method is useful for systems where you cannot assure network security.

Sun Extensions

Users of Sun systems can opt for the SUN-DES-1 X authorization method. This method depends on Sun's Secure RPC (remote procedure call) mechanism. To use SUN-DES-1, you must first set up Secure RPC and a set of public and private keys. The advantage of the SUN-DES-1 method is that it doesn't store all the secure information in the user's **$HOME/.Xauthority** file.

Setting Up Your X Server to Use the *.Xauthority* File

Setting up the X server to use this security mechanism is easy, depending on how you start the X server. If you use the *xdm* program to provide an X-based login screen and then start the X server, all you need to do is tell *xdm* to use the authorization scheme, which we cover below, since *xdm* will start the X server with the **-auth $HOME/.Xauthority** command-line parameter.

Turning on X Security with *Xdm*

The **xdm-config** file (normally located in **/usr/lib/X11/xdm**) controls how *xdm* acts and tells *xdm* the name of most of the other configuration files. It also sets up security.

This file is an X resource file, and it controls a number of resources for the *DisplayManager* class (*xdm*). To turn on X security for display 0 on a given system, place the following line in your **xdm-config** file:

```
DisplayManager._0.authorize: true
```

The *_0* is the default display name, :0, translated to the X resource-file language. Since a colon has a special meaning in resource files, :0 becomes _0.

You can turn on authorization for all X servers controlled by a given *xdm* program with the following:

```
DisplayManager*authorize:    true
```

For some reason, it is very common to turn on authorization for display 0 and leave it off for all other displays. To do this, you place the following two X resources in the **xdm-config** file:

```
DisplayManager._0.authorize: true
DisplayManager*authorize:    false
```

Once you do this, *xdm* will automatically write out a **.Xauthority** file every time the user logs in.

You can also set the authority scheme used by *xdm*. For example, to use XDM-AUTHORIZATION-1, add the following resource command to the **xdm-config** file:

```
DisplayManager*authName: XDM-AUTHORIZATION-1
```

You can use the *authName* resource to set more than one method:

```
DisplayManager*authName: \
   XDM-AUTHORIZATION-1  MIT-MAGIC-COOKIE-1
```

The *xdm* treats the *authName* resource as a list, in order, of which security methods to try.

When you edit the xdm-config file, xdm may already be running. You can set xdm to automatically rescan the *xdm-config* file (see Chapter 14 for how to do this) or you can send the HUP (hang-up) signal to *xdm* with the following:

```
kill -HUP process_id_number
```

Set *process_id_number* to the process ID for the *xdm* program. You can get this number by running the ps command and look for *xdm*'s entry in the process table. On System V-based systems, use ps -ef. On Berkeley-based UNIX systems, use ps -aux.

Turning on X Security with *Xinit*

If you start the X server with *xinit*, you need to jump through a few more hoops to get things going, as *xinit* won't automatically write out the **.Xauthority** file like *xdm* does.

With *xinit*, then, you need to use the *xauth* program to add entries to the **.Xauthority** file. The following commands, executed before calling *xinit*, should do the trick:

```
xauth add `hostname`/unix:0 . random-number
xauth add `hostname`:0 . random-number
```

The above commands add X authority entries for the display names of unix:0 (a common default display name) and *hostname*:0. The *random-number* is a random (and presumably hard-to-guess) number that you must create. To help you create this random number, you can write a C program using the rand() or random() functions, or use the perl or ksh scripting languages, whichever you prefer. This random number must have an even number of digits. The period (.) tells *xauth* to use the MIT-MAGIC-COOKIE-1 protocol (see below).

To verify your entries, you can run:

```
xauth list
```

This command should return a list of all the displays in the **.Xauthority** file:

```
DISPLAY NAME PROTOCOL NAME         DISPLAY KEY
============ =============         ===========
unix:0       MIT-MAGIC-COOKIE-1    6666
nicollet:0   MIT-MAGIC-COOKIE-1    6666
```

Once you add the entries to the **.Xauthority** file, use the following command to start the X server:

```
xinit — /usr/bin/X11/X -auth $HOME/.Xauthority
```

Using the *Xauth* Program

The *xauth* program is surprisingly complicated and supports a host of commands and command-line parameters. With *xauth*, you pass the command-line parameters first and then a set of *xauth* commands. Table 12.2 lists the command-line parameters, and Table 12.3 lists the commands.

Table 12.2   *Xauth* command-line parameters.

Command-Line Parameter	Meaning
-b	Break any locks (used to clean up after crashes)

continued

Command-Line Parameter	Meaning
-f *authfile*	Names authority file (defaults to **.Xauthority**)
-i	Ignore locks from *xdm* or another *xauth*
-q	Don't print status messages (quiet mode)
-v	Print status messages (verbose mode)

Table 12.3 lists the commands you can pass to *xauth*. You can also place the commands in script files (see the **source** command).

Table 12.3 *Xauth* **commands.**

Command	Meaning
add *display protocol hexkey*	Add an entry for the given display; a period (.) is shorthand for a protocol of MIT-MAGIC-COOKIE-1
extract *filename display...*	Extract entries for *display* and write to *filename*; - means stdout
nextract *filename display...*	Extract entries for *display* and write to *filename*, using numeric format; - means stdout
list *display...*	List all entries for a given *display*
nlist *display...*	List all entries for a given *display* using numeric output
merge *filename...*	Merge in entries from *filename*; - means stdin
nmerge *filename...*	Merge in entries from *filename* using numeric format; - means stdin
remove *display...*	Remove all entries for *display*
source *filename*	Treat filename as a script of *xauth* commands
info	Print info on authority file
exit	Exit and save authority file

continued

Command	Meaning
quit	Exit and don't save authority file
help	List of all *xauth* commands
help *string*	List of all *xauth* commands starting with *string*
?	Print short help message

The *xauth* program supports both a textual format and a numeric format for all its data.

Propagating the .Xauthority File to Other Systems with Xauth

A very common use of *xauth* is to pass the information needed to login one display to another. The following command extracts all X authority entries for the current display and passes them on over the network to another program, merging in these entries with the authority file on the target machine (identified by *hostname*):

```
xauth extract - $DISPLAY | \
    rsh hostname xauth merge -
```

Some systems, such as Hewlett-Packard workstations, define **rsh** as the *restricted* shell and **remsh** as the *remote* shell, In this case, you want the remote shell program.

Locking the Screen While You're Away

In addition to controlling server access, there are a few other issues you should be aware of. The first issue is simple. If you went away from your X terminal or workstation, some other user could just walk up and access the world from your account, with your privileges and access. To solve this, of course, you can log out each time you get up. This isn't always convenient, as you may be in the middle of important work when you're called away from your desk. In addition, starting up X applications takes some time, which makes this an inconvenient form of security.

To solve this, you can run a screen-locking program, which places a window over the whole screen and locks your display until you return. While you're gone, all the X programs on your display remain as they were, so you won't have to terminate important work or restart any application. When you return, the authentication is based on your password.

There are a number of X screen-locking programs. Some vendor-based systems, like Hewlett-Packard's VUE and the COSE common desktop, come with their own. Other systems use *xlock*, *xnlock*, or *sunlock* (on Sun systems).

Securing *Xterm* for Sensitive Operations

When you type passwords into an *xterm* window, you can enhance your security by using the secure keyboard mode. This mode, enabled by an *xterm* menu choice (hold down the **Control** key while pressing the leftmost mouse button to see this menu), grabs the keyboard from all other X applications.

The secure keyboard mode ensures that no other X application can get the keyboard events directed at the *xterm* window. In normal circumstances, another application might ask for keyboard events from your *xterm* windows or try to grab the keyboard itself. (Of course, the keystrokes still go out over the network, so that another program could snoop on them.)

Only one application at a time can grab the keyboard. When you successfully invoke the secure keyboard mode, *xterm* will swap its foreground and background colors. If *xterm* couldn't invoke the secure keyboard mode, it beeps. It's often best to invoke this mode before you see a password prompt.

 Since only one application at a time can secure the keyboard, it's best to enable this mode, type in a password, and then disable it. Otherwise, the rest of your display will be bereft of keys.

N O T E

Summary

This chapter covers the rudimentary security measures found within the X Window System. There are two main security tools: *xhost* (used for securing a workstation) and *xauth* (used for securing a server). Neither method is foolproof, but they work better than nothing. However, the bottom line is clear: The key to successful network security is to take steps necessary to make the entire *network* secure, not merely the X Window portion of it.

In the next chapter, you will review X terminals, which are optimized to run X over the network.

X Terminals

This section covers an entirely new hardware industry created through the X Window System: X terminals. X terminals are basically smart graphics terminals that hold the X server software. As with all aspects of X, there are many options associated with X terminals; this makes configuration and maintenance issues rather interesting, to say the least.

Chapter 13 provides an overview of X terminals and discusses what you can expect from an X terminal in terms of features and performance. Chapter 14 concentrates on the tricky and involved process of configuring X terminals.

What is an X Terminal?

Topics covered in this chapter include:

- ❊ What are X terminals?
- ❊ X terminals versus workstations
- ❊ X terminal accessories
- ❊ Local window managers
- ❊ X terminals and RAM
- ❊ Booting X terminals
- ❊ Fonts and X terminals
- ❊ Serial-line support for X

What's So Special About X Terminals?

This chapter presents a brief overview of X terminals. The next chapter covers the complex chore of configuring X terminals. Chapter 15 extends the discussion to covering software that turns PCs into X terminals.

Before we get too far into using and configuring X terminals, however, we should cover a little more about what an X terminal really is. An X terminal is a smart graphics terminal—but it provides thousands of options and requires a little configuration on both the host and terminal sides.

As we described in Chapter 1, the X Window System builds upon a client–server architecture. The X server is a separate process that controls a display: a keyboard, pointing device (usually a mouse) and a monitor (or more than one monitor). X applications, or clients, then connect to the X server over a network or interprocess communications link. Each workstation on the network runs a server.

However, an X terminal occupies a slightly different role on the network. In theory, an X terminal relies on a server on the network for *all* of its computing power (although this is happening less frequently, as we'll see later in this chapter). With an X terminal, you just place the X server into one box and all X clients must be run remotely.

With the X terminal architecture, you're explicitly placing a great burden on your UNIX hosts, as each and every X application displayed on the X terminal must run on the host, consuming host resources. Remember that few X programs clock in at anything less than a megabyte in size. X certainly isn't known for efficient use of disk or memory space.

Because of this, your X terminal will sometimes include what are called local clients—application programs that run in the X terminal. This blurs the line that separate X terminals from workstations, of course. However, in real-world terms, local clients are very handy; if you can place some of the computing load onto the X terminal, then you need to place less power in the host.

When you use local clients, your X terminal looks more and more like a multitasking workstation. In fact, newer X terminals may offer small local disks to hold fonts, and some even support using the disk as swap space. You can set up other X terminals to use the host disk for swap, which makes these X terminals look suspiciously like diskless UNIX workstations. Some vendors, like Sun, even sell an X terminal that you can upgrade to a full UNIX workstation, blurring the lines even further.

With all this, you might wonder exactly what makes X terminals so special. X terminals are typically easier to maintain, install, secure, and backup than full-blown UNIX workstations. Accounting departments love X terminals, because in theory the per-seat cost of computing is much lower for an X terminal than for a full-fledged workstation.

In the final analysis of whether or not to purchase X terminals, however, a lot depends on how users work at your site. Depending on use, X terminals may provide a performance advantage or a severe loss. Before deciding on buying X terminals, you should thoroughly test out X terminals in *your* environment.

Before you rush out and send us electronic mail asking for a formula that determines X-terminal performance on a network, let us warn you: *NO such formula exists*. Network workloads differ greatly, and the only way to evaluate X-terminal performance on your network is to throw X terminals on your network and see what happens.

X Terminal Add-Ons

In addition to the usual suspects, you can get quite a variance in X terminal add-ons. This is where the vendors distinguish themselves from the competition. You'll find a wide variety of extra features, some more useful than others:

❊ Audio

❊ Local printer support

❊ Serial-line support, such as XRemote or LBX

❊ Local window manager

❊ Other local applications

❊ Remote configuration

❊ Remote upgrading

❊ Optional backing store

❊ Support for font server

❊ Ability to use swap space on host

❊ Local disks

Local Window Managers and RAM

By providing a local window manager, you free up a number of resources in your host computer, as window managers tend to be very large programs. You also improve performance by cutting down the traffic on the network; mundane operations, such as moving or resizing windows, will occur locally.

Of course, the more you place into the X terminal, the more local X terminal resources you need, such as RAM. Other RAM-eating features of X terminals include support for a number of common X extensions, such as the PEX three-dimensional extension to X and the X Imaging Extension (XIE). Both place a large demand on X server resources, especially memory.

Booting X Terminals

There are a number of means for booting an X terminal. The simplest method occurs when the X terminal has the X server software in ROM or PROM memory and can boot itself locally. The disadvantage to this method becomes apparent when you have to install 1,000 to 10,000 PROMs when upgrading your entire site's set of X terminals. (Newer X terminals place server software in flash memory, which can be updated over the network, giving you the best of both possible worlds.) A number of X terminals will boot up by downloading code from a host. Usually you're limited in what kind of host can act as the boot server.

Once configured, the X terminal can use network protocols such as *bootp* (the boot protocol) or *tftp* (trivial file transfer protocol). If you use this kind of setup, you should be able to upgrade a whole number of X terminals by merely replacing the boot software on the host. This simplifies upgrading quite a bit and saves you the task of physically traveling to each X terminal (they may be distributed over a large campus).

X Terminals and Networking

Each X terminal sits at a separate network TCP/IP address and has a separate hostname (used to generate the terminal's display name). When dealing with TCP/IP addresses, you'll need to have (or decide on) the following pieces of information:

❈　The IP address for the X terminal

❈　The hostname for the X terminal

❈　The subnet address mask

❈　The network's broadcast address

❈　The IP address of the host to boot from, if your X terminal boots from a host

❈　The network name–server address, if you use one

You'll typically type this information into a menu-driven X terminal configuration program, which is, sadly, different on each brand of X terminal.

As part of this process, you have to tell the X terminal what IP address it has. Each Ethernet device has a unique hardwired hardware address. The X terminal must convert this hardwired address into an IP address. Sometimes you'll type this into the X terminal, and it will be stored in some sort of non-volatile storage on the X terminal. Other times, you'll use *bootp* or *rarp* (reverse address resolution protocol). If this sounds completely arcane to you, see Appendix A for a list of networking administration books.

Logging in to X Terminals

Since the X terminal runs the X server and perhaps a few local client programs, users need to log in to a UNIX host from their X terminal. And, of course, you'll want password protection on the whole thing.

To do so, you need to set up *xdm*, the X Display Manager. This program manages one or more X servers and controls the user's access through an X-based login screen. The *xdm* program is in turn based on the X Display Manager Control Protocol, or XDMCP, which you will learn in depth from the next chapter.

X Terminals and Fonts

Each X terminal needs to know where it can find font files. Many X terminals come with a few fonts built into the terminal. Since X comes with a huge number of fonts (stored in very large files), you'll likely want to download the fonts from some host.

This is where Release 5 and higher versions of X come in handy, as you can share the PCF font files between X servers and terminals of most any architecture. Many X terminals support NFS (network file system) or *tftp* access to get at these font files.

Serial-Line Support

As of this writing, X terminal vendors Tektronix and NCD both offer a form of serial-line support for their X terminals. This allows you to access your host environment from a modem line, allowing workers to telecommute from home, for example.

This isn't always a smooth process, as the X architecture assumes a fast network link is in place. Even with 9600- or 14400-bps modems, you're likely to face uncomfortable delays.

X11 Release 6 adds Low-Bandwidth X, or LBX. This generalizes the Tektronix and NCD proprietary serial-line protocols. We expect LBX to evolve over the next few years, with each evolution adding in improved performance.

Summary

In this chapter, you were introduced to the notion of X terminals and how they can fit into your computing scheme.

In the next chapter, you will learn about *xdm*, which manages the login process on an X terminal.

Configuring X Terminals

Topics covered in this chapter include:

* Configuring X terminals
* Using the X Display Manager (*x∂m*)
* Configuring *x∂m*
* Setting up the **xdm-config** file
* Starting *x∂m*
* Killing *x∂m*
* Using *x∂m*
* Choosing a host to login
* Configuring *x∂m* on COSE, Sun, and Hewlett-Packard platforms

Configuring X Terminals

X terminals rely on the kindness—or rather, computing power—of others to accomplish anything, as a user at an X terminal must login another computer over the network. An X terminal, then, is basically a window onto a UNIX host. The host also holds all user data files.

Since an X terminal has no local user directories, your role as system administrator involves mechanisms that:

❊ Allow users to login

❊ Authenticate the logins with passwords and usernames

❊ Choose (or let the users choose) which UNIX host to login

❊ Start the X applications that make up the user's X session

And, of course, you always must set up user accounts on whatever systems hosting the X session.

An Overview of the X Display Manager

The X Display Manager, or *xdm*, controls an X session on a given display. Here we run into a case—more common than you might think—where the same word in X terminology has more than one meaning. In this instance, a session managed by *xdm* isn't the same thing as a session managed by a session manager, which we discussed in previous chapters.

Xdm presents a login window for user authentication, where users can enter their username and password. After a user successfully logs in, *xdm* starts an X session. A session in this case lasts as long as the controlling process does. In the traditional UNIX terminal world, this process is the user's login shell. *Xdm* sets up a similar session in the X world. When the session is over, *xdm* resets the X terminal and again displays the login screen.

Xdm, therefore, acts a lot like the traditional UNIX programs *init*, *getty*, and *login*. The main difference is that *xdm* works with X Window, either from an X terminal or from a UNIX workstation's console. In both cases, most of the configuration is the same: *xdm* runs on the UNIX system and displays on the remote computer (an X terminal or a UNIX workstation's console, or both—one system's *xдm* can control a number of X displays).

X terminals communicate with *xдm* using the *X Display Manager Control Protocol*, or XDMCP. Just about every X terminal supports this protocol. This is how the X terminal and *xдm* connect. XDMCP makes your X terminals act much like character terminals. If you cycle power on a character terminal, the user often gets logged out. The same goes for X terminals with XDMCP.

In addition, XDMCP provides for a chooser interface, which allows the user to choose one of a number of hosts to log in to. This is very useful for large sites, where users may login from the same X terminals to machines set up for different departments. (However, many X terminals have a built-in mechanism to choose a host, so you won't often worry about the *xдm* chooser.)

Configuring Xdm

To get *xдm* going, you must:

❋   Edit a set of *xдm* configuration files
❋   Choose which X displays (local and remote) that *xдm* manages
❋   Set up the login welcome message
❋   Set up the basic user session
❋   Start *xдm*, or restart it if it is already running

On a standard X environment, you should find the following files in the *xдm* configuration directory, usually **/usr/lib/X11/xdm**, as listed in Table 14.1.

Table 14.1   Xdm files located in /usr/lib/X11/xdm.

File	Common Use
xdm-config	Configures *xdm*
xdm-errors	Default error log file
xdm-pid	Holds *xdm* process ID number
Xlogin	Controls login screen background

continued

File	Common Use
Xaccess	List of X servers to accept XDMCP queries from
Xreset	Run as **root** after session terminates
Xresources	Holds resources for login widget
Xservers	List the displays (including X terminals) that *xdm* should manage
Xsession	Starts user session, including **$HOME/.xsession**
Xsession-remote	Remote (X terminal) version of **Xsession**
Xstartup	Run as **root** before session starts; after user enters password
Xstartup-remote	Remote (X terminal) version of **Xstartup**
GiveConsole	Gives ownership of console back to **root**
TakeConsole	Takes ownership of console for user

Other common locations for the *xdm* configuration directory are listed in Table 14.2.

Table 14.2   Common platform-specific locations for the xdm configuration directory.

Location	System
/usr/openwin/lib/xdm	Sun OpenWindows
/usr/vue/config	Hewlett-Packard VUE
/etc/opt/dt	COSE common desktop
/usr/lpp/X11/lib/X11/xdm	IBM AIX (but linked to **/usr/lib/X11/xdm**)

Most UNIX systems, such as those from Silicon Graphics, Sun Microsystems, and Hewlett-Packard, come with customized versions of *xdm*. Because of this, it's a very good idea to start with what your system vendor has already set up and then make only the necessary changes to these vendor-supplied files, rather than starting from scratch. There's too many things that can go wrong when you try to configure *xdm*, so it's best to go slowly and make as few changes as possible to the vendor-supplied *xdm* configuration files.

The Xdm-Config File

The **xdm-config** file controls how *xdm* acts and tells *xdm* the name of most of the other configuration files. This is where you can change defaults. A sample **xdm-config** file follows, but if your system already has an **xdm-config** file, by all means use that.

```
DisplayManager.servers:       \
        /usr/lib/X11/xdm/Xservers
DisplayManager.pidFile:       \
        /usr/lib/X11/xdm/xdm-pid
DisplayManager.errorLogFile:  \
        /usr/lib/X11/xdm/xdm-errors
DisplayManager*resources:     \
        /usr/lib/X11/xdm/Xresources
DisplayManager*session:       \
        /usr/lib/X11/xdm/Xsession
DisplayManager*reset:         \
        /usr/lib/X11/xdm/Xreset
DisplayManager*startup:       \
        /usr/lib/X11/xdm/Xstartup
DisplayManager*accessFile:    \
        /usr/lib/X11/xdm/Xaccess
DisplayManager._0.startup:    \
        /usr/lib/X11/xdm/GiveConsole
DisplayManager._0.reset:      \
        /usr/lib/X11/xdm/TakeConsole
DisplayManager._0.setup:      \
        /usr/lib/X11/xdm/Xsetup_0

DisplayManager._0.authorize:  true
DisplayManager*authorize:     false
```

The _0 is the default display name, :0, translated to the X resource-file language. Since a colon has a special meaning in resource files, the :0 becomes _0.

N O T E

Much of the **xdm-config** file contains the names of other files to use. These files then control various aspects of *xdm*. You have two levels of customization available: telling *xдm* to look at files other than the default set and editing any of the files that **xdm-config** references. If you really want to live dangerously, you can add an extra level of customization by using the *-config* command-line parameter to *xдm* to tell it to use a different file instead of **xdm-config**.

Some administrators prefer to leave the original files alone and customize copies. Whatever your style, you should create backup copies of the files in the *xдm* configuration directory before changing anything.

Setting Up X Terminals to Manage

The first file listed in the sample **xdm-config** is the **Xservers** file, which lists each of the other displays you want *xдm* to manage.

For example, to have *xдm* manage the workstation's local console, you'd place the following entry in the **Xservers** file:

```
:0 local /usr/bin/X11/X :0
```

(Many system vendors ship a customized version of *xдm*. In this case, the exact syntax listed above, which is from the Release 5 version of *xдm*, may not be appropriate. When in doubt, copy the syntax of existing entries in the **Xservers** file.)

The first part lists the X display name, with :0 as a shorthand for the local display. The word *local* also specifies that the X server is located on the same machine as *xдm*. For nonlocal displays, the following entry format usually suffices:

```
kevin:0  foreign
```

This lists a display name of *kevin:0* for a nonlocal X terminal. If you add the above entry to the **Xservers** file, *xдm* also manages the display *kevin:0*. This is how you get *xдm* to manage X terminals.

Setting Up Servers To Manage With Xaccess

With X11 Release 4 and higher, X terminals can use XDMCP query messages to find a copy of *xдm* willing to manager their displays. With Release 5 and higher, *xдm* uses the **Xaccess** file to control which X servers it should listen to and how to handle those queries.

XDMCP allows X terminals three types of queries:

1. *Direct*, where the terminal sends a message to a particular host.
2. *Indirect*, a rarely used option that allows one UNIX host to pass off a query to another host.
3. *Broadcast*, where the X terminal asks for all the hosts on the network that support *xdm*. Broadcast queries work with the chooser (discussed in "An Overview of the X Display Manager," earlier in this chapter).

With these XDMCP queries, the X terminal manages to connect to *xdm* running on some host. The **Xaccess** file, then, allows you to control which X terminals *xdm* accepts XDMCP query messages from. Luckily, you can use wildcards (**.eric.com*) in the **Xaccess** file to allow all X terminals with network names ending in *eric.com* to connect to *xdm*.

To disable machines, use a leading exclamation point (!). For example, to disallow an X terminal with a network name of *kevin*, you'd use *!kevin* in the **Xaccess** file. The default *Xaccess* file contains a wildcard (***), which allows *xdm* to respond to all X terminals that query via XDMCP.

Be careful with the Xaccess file. You do not want multiple copies of xdm on different hosts all trying to manage the same X terminals. Watch out for duplicate entries in Xaccess files on different hosts.

TROUBLE-
SHOOTING

Convincing Xdm to Reread Configuration Files

If you change the **Xservers** or **Xaccess** files, *xdm* will not reread this file until it starts again. There are two ways to work around this.

1. The easiest method is setting the *xdm DisplayManager.autoRescan* resource to *true* in the **xdm-config** file. In this case, *xdm* automatically rereads any changed configuration files.
2. A more direct method is sending *xdm* the HUP (hang up) signal, SIGHUP. The UNIX **kill** program can send the SIGHUP signal using the *-HUP* command-line parameter:

```
kill -HUP process_id_number
```

where *process_id_number* is the process ID for the *xdm* program. You can get this number by running the **ps** command and looking for *xdm*'s entry in the process table. Or you can read the **xdm-pid** file, which contains the process ID for *xdm*.

Checking for Errors

Xdm-errors contains any error messages generated by *xdm*. If you're having problems, check here first. If your system is at Release 5 or higher, then you should also look in the user's **$HOME/.xsession-errors** file for *xdm* error messages.

Creating a Login Message

The next step is to create a suitable login message for the users. You're usually limited to one line of text for this login message, so be terse. To set up this message, edit the X resource file for the *xdm* login widget, which asks the user to enter a username and password. The default name for this resource file is **Xresources**.

The most common change in this file is the greeting resource:

```
xlogin*greeting:  Eric and Kevin's X System
```

You can also adjust the colors and fonts used by the login widget from this file.

Setting Up a Basic User Session

The **Xsession** file controls the user's X session. Normally, this executes the user's **$HOME/.xsession** file, if it exists. If not, **Xsession** typically starts a window manager and an *xterm* window. In many cases, the systemwide **Xsession** file starts a window manager for the user, so the user's **.xsession** file doesn't have to. A sample **Xsession** file, configured for the C shell, appears below:

```
#!/bin/csh -f

set xsession=$HOME/.xsession
set xinitrc=$HOME/.xinitrc
```

```
if ( -f $xsession ) then
  if ( -x $xsession ) then
    exec $xsession
  else
    exec /bin/sh $xsession
  endif
else if ( -f $xinitrc ) then
  if ( -x $xinitrc ) then
    exec $xinitrc
  else
    exec /bin/sh $xinitrc
  endif
else
  twm &
  exec xterm 80x24+10+10
endif
```

Starting Xdm

Once you've configured *xdm*, the next step is actually starting the program. You'll want to start *xdm* from the *init* program by placing the *xdm* command (**/usr/bin/X11/xdm**) at the end of **/etc/rc** or other system startup files, or in the **/etc/inittab** file. *Xdm* also supports a number of command-line parameters, as shown in Table 14.3.

Table 14.3   Xdm command-line parameters.

Parameter	Use
-config *configfile*	Tells *xdm* to use *configfile* rather than **/usr/lib/X11/xdm/xdm-config**
-error *errorfile*	Tells *xdm* to use *errorfile* rather than **/usr/lib/X11/xdm/xdm-errors**
-daemon	Runs *xdm* as a daemon in the background (see next page)
-nodaemon	Makes *xdm* run in synchronous mode; useful for debugging
-debug *level*	Sets debugging level number (only positive numbers)

The *-daemon* command-line parameter sets the *DisplayManager.daemonMode* resource to *True*. You'll want to use this option. The *-nodaemon* parameter sets the *DisplayManager.daemonMode* resource to *False*.

When you set the debugging level to a nonzero number, *xdm* prints out lots of worthless debugging information. *Xdm* also sets the *DisplayManager.daemonMode* resource to *False*, like the *-nodaemon* command-line parameter.

Once a user logs in, *xdm* writes the authority key into the user's **$HOME/.Xauthority** file, if the *authorize* resource is set to *true* for that X display.

Killing *Xdm*

If *xdm* operates incorrectly, you may need to kill it. To do so, send it the SIGTERM signal using the **kill** command, just as you use the SIGHUP signal:

```
kill -TERM process_id_number
```

where *process_id_number* is the process ID for the *xdm* program. You can get this from the **ps** command or from the **xdm-pid** file.

Xdm in Action

When you start *xdm*, it examines the **Xservers** and **Xaccess** files to see which X servers it should manage. To each of these X servers (normally the workstation console or X terminals), *xdm* sends a login widget. This widget asks the user to enter a username and password. Once authenticated, *xdm* executes the **Xstartup** script. **Xstartup** is run by **root** (so be careful) after the user is authenticated, but before the user session starts. You will probably not need anything here, but you may mount directories or something similar.

Starting with X11 Release 5, the default startup file for the local workstation console is **GiveConsole**. This script changes ownership of the workstation console to the user.

Next, *xdm* executes the **Xsession** script, which should execute the user's **$HOME/.xsession** script. If **$HOME/.xsession** doesn't exist, *xdm* looks for a **$HOME/.Xresources** file and loads the resource commands in that file with *xrdb*, launching a window manager and an *xterm* window.

When the user exits the X session and essentially logs out, *xdm* executes the **Xreset** script, running this script as **root** after a user session terminates, but before the display is closed. There is often nothing in this file.

Starting with X11 Release 5, the default reset file for the local workstation console is **TakeConsole**. This script changes ownership of the workstation console back from the user to the **root** user.

After all the scripts are run, *xdm* presents a login widget on the X server, starting a new cycle.

Choosing Which Host to Login

If your system is spread out across a large site, you may want to set up the XDMCP chooser if your X-terminal vendor doesn't provide an equivalent. The chooser presents a scrolled list of hosts. With this, the user can select which host to login. To do this, the X terminal needs to use the broadcast mode, and *xdm* must be willing to accept such messages.

To set up the *xdm* chooser to work for any host, add the following lines to your **Xaccess** file:

```
# Any indirect host can get a chooser
*    CHOOSER BROADCAST
```

This presents a chooser window on any X terminal that asks for it. The hosts presented in the list are any and all that respond to the broadcast message. By default, the actual program that presents the scrolled list of hosts is **/usr/lib/X11/xdm/chooser**.

To control the list of hosts the user sees, you can use the following:

```
*    CHOOSER eric kevin sam joe
```

Any X terminal that sends a message gets a chooser window that displays the following hosts: *eric*, *kevin*, *sam*, and *joe*.

Configuring Dtlogin on COSE Common Desktop Systems

COSE CDE systems use a program named *dtlogin* instead of *xdm*. However, *dtlogin* works very much like *xdm* and shares many of the same configuration files. These files are located in **/etc/opt/dt** by default.

One important exception is that the CDE equivalent of **xdm-config** is **Xconfig**. In it, you set the *Dtlogin* resources, rather than the *DisplayManager* resources you set for *xdm*. The individual resource names are much the same, though.

Each of the COSE platforms acts slightly differently, but the process is very similar. In most cases, you'll perform very little configuration to get *dtlogin* set up for a workstation's console. You'll do more work to set up an X terminal to use the COSE common desktop. For X terminals, you can configure the **Xaccess** or **Xservers** files much as for *xdm*.

Once you configure *dtlogin*, you can start the program using the *-daemon* command-line parameter:

```
/opt/dt/bin/dtlogin -daemon
```

The **Xsession** script runs the *dthello* program, normally stored in **/opt/dt/bin**, to present a message of the day once the user has logged in. The common desktop session manager is *dtsession* (also normally stored in **/opt/dt/bin**).

Configuring *Xdm* on Sun Systems

Sun's OpenWindows (version 3.0 and higher) provides a customized version of *xdm*, so you should follow the examples in the Sun *xdm* configuration directory, normally **/usr/openwin/lib/xdm**.

Configuring *Xdm* on Hewlett-Packard's VUE

Under Hewlett-Packard's VUE, use the *vuelogin* program (located in **/usr/vue/bin**) rather than *xдm*. Also, the configuration directory will be **/usr/vue/config** instead of **/usr/lib/X11/xdm**. Other than that, *vuelogin* acts very much like *xдm*.

One exception is that the H-P equivalent of **xdm-config** is **Xconfig** (shades of COSE). The purpose of both files are much the same, but the H-P system uses the *Vuelogin* resources rather than the *DisplayManager* resources. Hewlett-Packard also adds a failsafe login, which is very useful if you've messed up your configuration files.

Summary

An X terminal relies on a remote host for its computing power, which means the terminal must set up a session that manages communications between the terminal and the host.

The X Window tool for this is the X Display Manager, or *xдm*. *Xдm* acts a lot like the traditional UNIX programs *init*, *getty*, and *login*. The main difference is that *xдm* works with X Window, either from an X terminal or from a UNIX workstation's console. In both cases, most of the configuration is the same: *xдm* runs on the UNIX system and displays on the remote computer (an X terminal or a UNIX workstation's console, or both—one system's *xдm* can control a number of X displays).

This chapter goes into the various mechanisms needed to set up a computing session managed by *xдm*. It also covers the equivalents to *xдm* on COSE, Sun Microsystems, and Hewlett-Packard systems.

PC Connectivity

With ever-dropping prices and ever-increasing performance, personal computers become more and more attractive for working with the X Window System—even with such a demanding system as X. In this section, we discuss issues for upgrading your PCs for use with X.

In Chapter 15, we show how to turn an Intel-based PC or into an X terminal through the use of X-server software. There are two ways to go with X-server software, and we discuss both ways, using *DESQview/X* and *HCL-eXceed/W* as our examples.

In Chapter 16, we cover XFree86, a very useful implementation of X Window UNIX-based PCs. Although virtually every UNIX-based PC ships with X, these X implementations tend to be out of date and limited when it comes to PC-peripheral support. Both of these issues are successfully confronted by XFree86, which makes it such a great tool.

Turning DOS-Based PCs into X Terminals

Topics covered in this chapter include:

* X Window on DOS-based PCs
* PC configurations
* *DESQview/X* and *HCL-eXceed/W*
* Configuring *eXceed/W*
* *DESQview/X* and the Motif and Open Look window managers
* Advantages and disadvantages of *DESQview/X*
* Software development with *DESQview/X*
* IBM OS/2 and X Window

X and the Ubiquitous PC

Though we'd like to see $12,000 Sun workstations on the desk of every user, reality—in the form of budgets—dictates that some discretion is warranted when it comes to expenditures.

This, of course, is the entire rationale for the existence of X terminals, which we've covered in the last two chapters. The same rationale has lead to the creation of similar market: stock personal computers configured to run X-server software.

Let's face it: PCs are everywhere. They constitute the most popular computing platform. A decked-out PC can be bought for less than $2,000 these days—even with a network card and a decent monitor—and to ignore the incredible affordability of the PC today is foolish. Plus, there's a lot of useful DOS and *Windows* software that have no parallel in the UNIX world.

This doesn't mean that we're advising you to sell off all of your UNIX workstations and switch completely to DOS. A PC with an X server will never run X as efficiently as a decent workstation. However, there are probably many of your users who could get by with a PC and X server, especially if their need to access a remote host is infrequent. For a corporation with a large installed base of PCs, upgrading the PCs to run X can be a more cost-effective method of incorporating X Window, especially if these PCs are already networked. For a company that doesn't necessarily have a long-term commitment to X, PCs can easily be converted to a networking system that doesn't involve X Window.

X-server software comes in two forms: Where the X server runs all the time and is an integral component of the operating system (as is the case with *DESQview/X*), or where the X server can be called by the operating system at any time to connect with a remote host (such as *HCL-eXceed*, in all of its various forms). Both approaches have their advantages and disadvantages, but both require (basically) the same hardware:

❋ 80386-based PC or better

❋ 160MB of hard-disk space

❋ EGA graphics or better

❋ 8MB of RAM

❋   Networking card

❋   Network operating system

These are the minimum requirements, obviously. As with everything in the computer world, the more hardware horsepower you have, the better. If you're looking at some serious network and graphics usage, we suggest the following PC configuration:

❋   i486-based PC or better

❋   200MB of hard-disk space

❋   SuperVGA graphics or better

❋   12MB of RAM

❋   Networking card

❋   Network operating system

Why do you need a separate network operating system when working with a PC X server—after all, isn't X a networking protocol? Yes, it is. However, X is designed to work with the underlying network protocol at all times, never independently of it. When *DESQview/X* opens a connection to a remote host, it needs the network operating system to actually make the request in the form of **telnet**, **rsh**, or **rexec**. In the vast majority of cases, the network operating system will use a TCP/IP transport to make the connection. Since there's no dominant network operating system (as we'll see when we discuss the individual packages), packages like *DESQview/X* and *HCL-eXceed* must support a wide variety of network operating systems—which makes your job a little more complicated, unless you decide from the beginning to use only one network operating system for the rest of your administrative life. You will learn in this text what networking operating systems are supported; then it's up to you to apply this information productively.

There's also one benefit to having the separate network operating system: It allows you to more easily identify sources of problems when troubleshooting. For instance, the vast majority of questions in the Quarterdeck Forum on CompuServe—where *DESQview/X* users can turn to for assistance—actually have to do with errors with the network operating systems, not with *DESQview/X*. Once you have the network operating system configured properly, you're not likely to encounter huge problems with the PC X server (except in the area of graphics cards, as you'll see when you read through the "DESQview/X" section later in this chapter), as the network-OS installation ensures that the proper interrupts for PC peripherals (such as a mouse) and network card are correct. Simply, the troubleshooting process is made simpler when you can eliminate the operating system.

When configuring a PC X server, it's important to remember that the same issues present when configuring an X terminal are there when configuring a PC X terminal. In most cases, the same configuration issues covered in depth in Chapter 14 will also be important when configuring a PC X terminal. Unfortunately, the actual configuration mechanisms are different among PC X servers, and we don't have the space to discuss all of the ins and outs of each package.

In this chapter, we'll cover both types of PC X servers, as they present different challenges to the UNIX system administrator.

NOTE Under no circumstances should you assume that these are the only two PC X-server products available. We're focusing on *DESQview/X* and *HCL-eXceed* because they control a significant portion of the marketplace, and also because we're the most familiar with them. In Appendix A you'll find a complete list of PC X vendors.

HCL-eXceed

HCL-eXceed, from Hummingbird Communications Ltd., comes in DOS, *Windows*, Windows NT and OS/2 forms. For the purposes of illustration, we'll discuss the *Windows* version, though all four work similarly.

To the user, *eXceed/W* appears just like any other *Windows* application: with its own set of application icons, as shown in Figure 15.1.

As you can tell by the illustration, there's nothing exceptional or "different" about the *eXceed* setup. That is part of the point: for the user, using X or a remote computing session should seem like a natural process.

HCL-eXceed/W, while comprising an X server, should be thought of as an independent application within *Windows*. Unless a user explicitly runs *eXceed* (or you, as UNIX system administrator, place it in the *Windows* StartUp folder so it launches every time *Windows* is launched), *eXceed* isn't doing anything. From an administrative viewpoint, this reduces network traffic; unless a connection is needed, it isn't automatic.

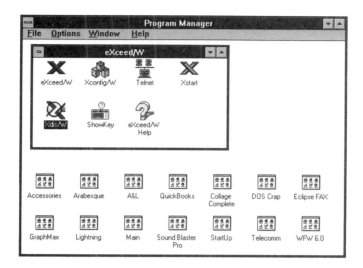

Figure 15.1   HCL-eXceed/W in a typical *Windows* environment.

As mentioned earlier, *eXceed* relies on a network operating system for its functionality; without the network OS, *eXceed* can't do a whole lot. Supported network transports for the version of *eXceed/W* installed on our systems is illustrated in Figure 15.2.

As you can tell by Figure 15.2, *eXceed/W* supports pretty much every major PC TCP/IP package.

Configuring eXceed/W

The majority of this book has been devoted to configuring X for your particular network. With *eXceed/W*, configuration details are still governed by the **Xconfig** file (the equivalent of **xdm-config**, as discussed in Chapter 14; generally, any form of X running on a PC uses an **Xconfig** file)—the difference being that Hummingbird has placed a friendlier front end to the process, as shown in Figure 15.3.

This dialog-box-driven system makes system configuration simpler. For instance, *eXceed/W* supports the XDMCP queries for X terminals discussed in Chapter 14 (direct, indirect, and broadcast). However, instead of using the **Xaccess** file to determine the mode, *eXceed/W* puts the choice in the form of a dialog box, as shown in Figure 15.4.

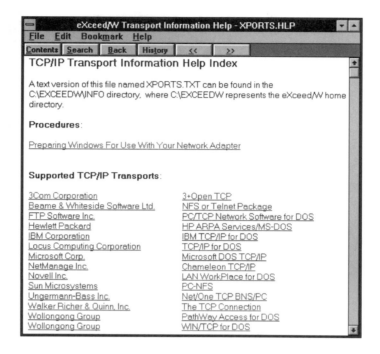

Figure 15.2   Supported transports in *eXceed/W*.

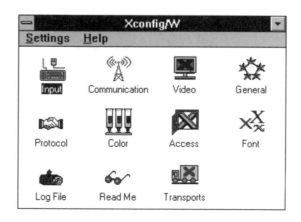

Figure 15.3   Xconfig/W.

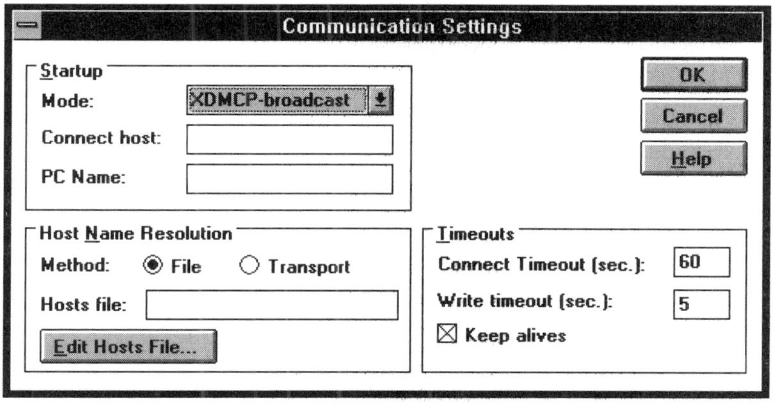

Figure 15.4   Communication settings under Xconfig/W.

HCL-eXceed/W also supports the MIT-MAGIC-COOKIE-1 client-authorization scheme discussed in Chapter 12.

Similarly, *eXceed/W* puts a friendly front end on font and color configurations, as shown in Figures 15.5 and 15.6.

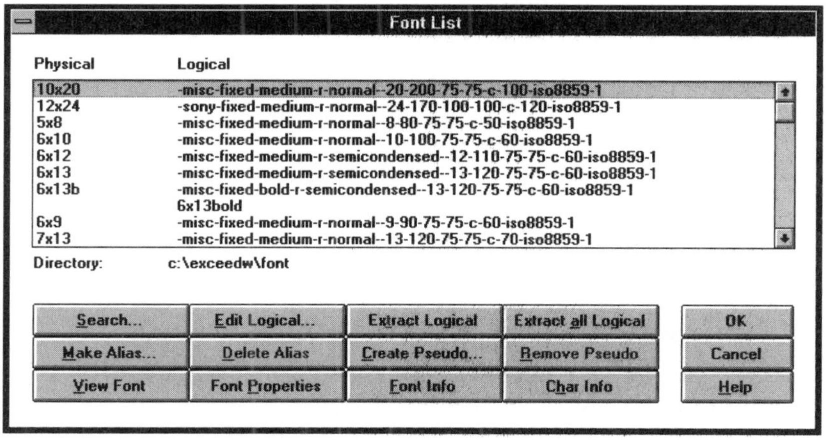

Figure 15.5   The Font List dialog box.

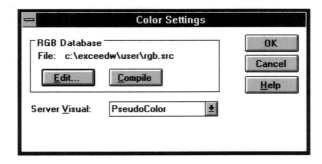

Figure 15.6   The Color Settings dialog box.

Configuration Issues

If you're not familiar with the *Windows* environment, you may want to play with it for a while before making configuration decisions—as there are many decisions to make in the configuration process.

For instance, *eXceed/W* allows you to choose whether to use *Windows* or a remote window manager as the window manager. If you choose the former, each X client is displayed in its own window under *Windows*, which essentially sets up *Windows* as the window manager. If you choose the latter, all X clients are displayed in a single *eXceed* window, putting the remote window manager (or a remote *xterm*) in charge. (If you're smart, you'll go with *Windows* as the window manager: It allows you to cut and paste between windows, and it cuts down on the network traffic.)

Xstart

As far as automation for users goes, *eXceed/W* includes a handy utility called *Xstart*, which automates an X session for the user. This utility specifies the login mechanism (**rsh** or **rexec**) and login information (user ID, password, host), as well as any command-line instructions. You can also assign icons (a few are supplied with *eXceed/W*) to Xstart files, and these files can be distributed over the network. For instance, if you want to give a department access to a Sequent UNIX server running Oracle, you can copy the same Xstart file to their machines, along with the appropriate icon.

DESQview/X

Going the opposite direction is *DESQview/X*, which uses the multitasking DESQview technology to run an X server, DOS, and *Windows* simultaneously.

There are certain advantages to this approach. The tighter integration between operating system and X server allows for both greater stability and less traffic on the network: *DESQview/X* tends to be more stable than *Windows* (it has been our experiences that *Windows* and networking do not make a very good combination), and running a local window manager will cut down on the number of network requests. However, in the case of *DESQview/X*, the merging does add a level of complexity above and beyond the daunting level of complexity already posed by UNIX and X. When everything is said and done, *DESQview/X* is still basically a DOS-based environment, and as such has to deal with the limitations of DOS, including memory management.

In line with its DOS roots, *DESQview/X* makes extensive use of menus, rather than icons. For instance, when a user starts *DESQview/X*, the first thing displayed will be the *DESQview/X* Menu, as shown in Figure 15.7.

Figure 15.7   The DESQview/X Menu.

This menu, essentially, is used to create windows. As with *HCL-eXceed*, everything is contained in a window. The *DESQview/X* equivalent of an *xterm* window is the DOS Window. For instance, the attributes associated with the default DESQview/X window manager are actually controlled by a separate DOS process, DESQview/X Setup, which is run upon installation and then can be altered at any point afterwards. The portion of Setup that controls the window manager is shown in Figure 15.8, in a typical *DESQview/X* menu.

Figure 15.8   The Window Manager Options menu.

And, as with *eXceed*, many of the configuration details connected with *DESQview/X* are contained in dialog boxes. Figure 15.9, for instance, shows a dialog box used for the installation of a remote application.

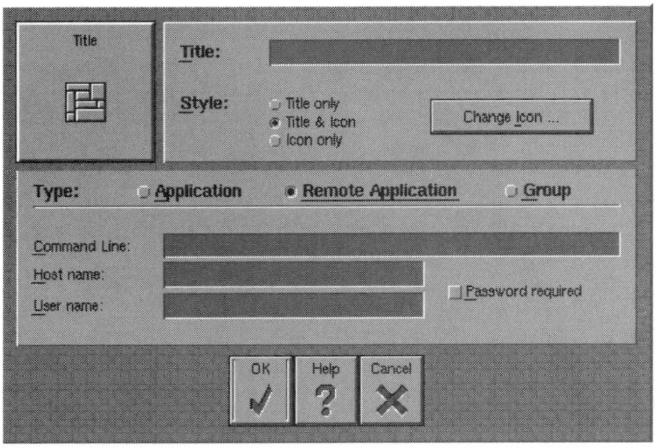

Figure 15.9   Installing a remote application.

As you can see, the installation of a remote application requires a command line, hostname, and username. It does not automatically assume that a password is needed, although if one is needed another dialog box will pop up after connection to the remote application.

Window Managers

In addition to the default *DESQview/X* window manager (which, surprisingly enough, eats up only 100K of RAM), Quarterdeck also offers versions of the Motif and Open Look window managers adapted for the *DESQview/X* environment. This gives you much more flexibility than is found in other PC X environments, which require either a remote window manager or the use of a local software tool acting as window manager (remember—*eXceed/W* allows use of *Windows* as the local window manager). Users won't be able to tell the difference between the *DESQview/X* version of the Open Look window manager and the Open Look window manager running on a Sun workstation, as you can tell from Figure 15.10, which shows *DESQview/X* running the Open Look window manager.

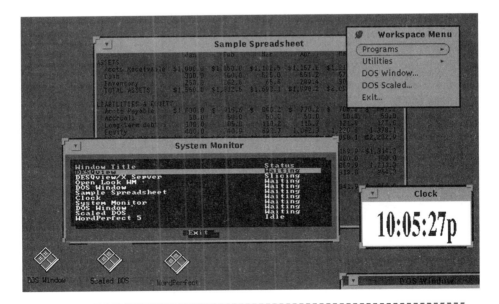

Figure 15.10   DESQview/X running the Open Look window manager.

However, you'll find that the *DESQview/X* Motif and Open Look window managers have configuration mechanisms that work slightly differently than the configuration mechanisms on a Sun or another workstation. Still, the underlying concepts are similar, so you should have no problems moving between the two.

Advantages to DESQview/X

If your users are on the advanced side and more comfortable and accustomed to working with the X Window environment, they'll definitely prefer the *DESQview/X* environment to the *eXceed* environment. The capabilities of *eXceed* are quite limited: It runs an X server and allows remote communications—and that's about it.

However, *DESQview/X* is configured more as a complete X Window environment. Many popular X Window utilities ship with *DESQview/X*, including several throughout the course of this book, such as *xset*, *xmodmap*, *xlsfonts*, and *xev* (shown in Figure 15.11). As a system administrator, you may feel more comfortable with the presence of such familiar utilities; while *Windows* configuration is not the most complicated task on the face of the earth, there's no reason to tackle both UNIX/X and *Windows* configuration when you can simplify things and stick to X configuration.

Figure 15.11 *Xev* **in action under DESQview/X.**

Plus, *DESQview/X* includes a nifty network version of Blackjack. Imagine your boss's surprise when you set up his PC to be the *DESQview/X* Blackjack server!

Drawbacks to DESQview/X

Because *DESQview/X* is a self-contained environment, it must do a lot of interacting with various hardware components in a manner unlike that of *eXceed/W*. For instance, *Windows* manages many grungy levels of configurations, such as graphics cards and mice. With *DESQview/X*, such configuration is tackled directly by *DESQview/X*.

This leads to some unfortunate situations. Many advanced graphics cards aren't directly supported by *DESQview/X*; instead, specific chipsets are supported, and if your graphics card's chipset isn't directly and explicitly supported, you're out of luck if you want a high-resolution (1,024-by-768) display. (And, unfortunately, we know that X is more difficult to use on lower-resolution displays.) With *eXceed*, however, you're in fine shape, as most high-resolution graphics cards ship with their own *Windows* drivers.

Similarly, *Windows* inherently recognizes most popular mice, but with *DESQview/X* you must install the mouse drivers in DOS and then hope *DESQview/X* recognizes it (which, however, we acknowledge will happen most of the time).

If you're dealing with a motley set of DOS-based PCs filled with off-brand graphics cards and mice already configured for *Windows*, you might want to consider going with *eXceed/W* instead of *DESQview/X*, if only to avoid the inevitable configuration problems.

And, unfortunately, Quarterdeck tends to nickel-and-dime people when it comes to functionality and support. To run *DESQview/X* on a UNIX network, for instance, you'll need *DESQview/X* and network software *as well as* a Quarterdeck package called DESQview/X to Other X Systems Network Manager. Support is rather stingy—90 days following the first contact to Quarterdeck—unless you pay extra for extended service plans.

Software Development

You can run your applications within *DESQview/X* from a remote machine, or else you can take advantage of the local X server to run X applications. However, be warned that software development for *DESQview/X* is slightly more complex than in the average X environment. You'll need to use DOS extenders to ensure that fat and happy X applications deal adequately with the memory-management schemes used to *DESQview/X*, and your choice of development tools is limited to those from GNU or small third-party developers.

Other Microcomputer Operating Systems and X

Of course, Microsoft doesn't have a monopoly on microcomputer operating systems (despite what some would have us believe, however). X-server support is also available on IBM's OS/2, a popular microcomputer operating system.

We are not OS/2 users, so we're not experts on X Window implementations. As mentioned earlier, Hummingbird Communications Ltd. has released an OS/2 version of *eXceed*, though it hit the market as this book was in the final stages of preparation.

IBM also supports the X Window System, as well as Motif, within its TCP/IP 2.0 for OS/2 software, released in August 1993. This allows OS/2 machines running TCP/IP to open OS/2 windows containing X clients, as well as hosting X clients across the network. While X Window can be purchased separately from IBM (Motif, indeed, is a separate option), it's fairly worthless without TCP/IP for OS/2. The software is available in both user and programmer versions.

In addition, someone has ported the X library to OS/2, which allows X clients to run in full-screen mode. If you're up for a little work, you can recompile X applications for use under OS/2. The files can be found in the CompuServe IBM Developers Forum 2, under the filenames **Xlib01.zip** and **Xlib02.zip**. (No, we have not tested these files, so don't ask us for advice.)

Summary

Using X on DOS-based PCs poses some of the same challenges involved when installing X terminals on your network. In this chapter, you examined two popular DOS PC X server packages—*DESQview/X* and *HCL-eXceed/W*—and point out the pros and cons of going with X on PCs, as well as comparing the two directly. We also briefly cover X Window on OS/2.

In the next chapter, you will examine XFree86, a great implementation of X for PCs running UNIX.

Running XFree86 on UNIX PCs

Topics covered in this chapter include:

* ❋ X and UNIX PCs
* ❋ What is XFree86?
* ❋ Installing XFree86
* ❋ Configuring XFree86
* ❋ XFree86 and PC graphics cards
* ❋ Using SuperProbe to determine graphics-card configurations
* ❋ Troubleshooting XFree86
* ❋ Acquiring XFree86

Running X on UNIX PC with XFree86

In addition to turning your PC into an X terminal, you can get the whole she-bang by running a multitasking operating system on your PC. The main way to do this is to run one of many versions of UNIX for the Intel architecture.

These versions of UNIX provide full-fledged operating systems and can even turn a PC into a credible workstation. PC hardware is getting faster and faster, cheaper and cheaper. With this, more and more companies use PCs for running UNIX. As a UNIX system administrator, there's the obvious advantage of using UNIX on PCs instead of installing X-server software or X terminals: You're already familiar with the UNIX operating system, so there's no need to master DOS or X terminal software.

When shopping for UNIX on the PC, you'll discover that virtually every UNIX vendor—ranging from the big names like Santa Cruz Operation (SCO), SunSoft, and Novell to smaller operations like Linux—offers the X Window System, either as a central part of the offering to an optional add-on. Many of these offerings do not provide a recent version of X-server software, nor do they support the latest in PC graphics cards. These are crucial purchase decisions. Many of the *xdm* configuration options, for example, come only with at least X11 Release 5 or later. (R4 is still prevalent in the marketplace, unfortunately.) If your PC vendor is still at a previous release, then you won't be able to take advantage of these features. In addition, the price of PC graphics cards has fallen to the point where a $200 card provides high-resolution performance that is almost mandatory for efficient X usage.

With these limitations, you're left with some hard choices for your X installation. You can port the X source code to your version of UNIX and graphics hardware, but this is a very difficult and time-consuming task. You can purchase a number of third-party X packages.

Or you can use XFree86, a freely distributable version of the X Window System ported to just about every version of UNIX running on the Intel hardware (listed in Table 16.1). XFree86 provides an X server, standard X applications, programming libraries, and fonts for a full-blown X Window System on your UNIX-based PC.

XFree86 also supports a good number of the latest PC graphics cards, so now an under-$200 graphics card provides a decent level of performance with XFree86. In addition, XFree86 has dramatically improved in quality in the latest releases.

Table 16.1   PC versions of UNIX supported by XFree86.

UNIX Version	Vendor Versions
SVR3.2	AT&T, SCO, Interactive/SunSoft
SVR4.0	ESIX, Microport, Dell, UHC, Consensys, MST, ISC, AT&T, NCR
SVR4.2	Consensys, Novell
Berkeley UNIX	FreeBSD, NetBSD, BSD/386
Others	Mach, Linux, Minix-386, Amoeba

N O T E

As with all free software, XFree86 changes rapidly. Be sure to check for the latest version of XFree86 and read its installation notes and documentation. These notes should cover all the current UNIX systems and graphics cards supported by XFree86.

Due to the changing nature of this software, this book can only provide an overview of the process of installing XFree86. Look in the documentation with your version of XFree86 to see exactly how to set it up on your systems.

XFree86 supports most PC graphics cards, including some fairly obscure cards, with the glaring exception of popular Diamond cards. To get going with XFree86, you'll need to:

❋   Install XFree86 in the proper directories
❋   Configure XFree86 for your graphics hardware
❋   Start up the X server

In addition, you may need to:

❋   Obtain XFree86 in source-code or binary format, if you don't have it already
❋   Compile the sources (if you don't opt for a binary version)

Installing XFree86

Since XFree86 is not standard software, the designers chose a top-level directory that won't conflict with existing installations. Typically, all XFree86 files are stored underneath the **/usr/X386** top-level directory. (Some operating systems, particularly Mach and Amoeba, use different default directories. Consult your XFree86 documentation for these out-of-the-mainstream PC operating systems.)

If you don't like the default choice of **/usr/X386** for the top-level XFree86 directory, you can choose another top-level location. If you do so, you must make sure that each user has the XWINHOME environment variable set to this new directory.

In addition, a number of XFree86 versions have hard-coded shared library paths to **/usr/X386**. Therefore, you'll need to set up symbolic links between all the files in your new **lib/X11/shlib** directory to **/usr/X386/lib/X11/shlib**, so the XFree86 shared libraries will be in the expected location. Watch out, as this may vary on different versions of UNIX for the PC.

Under the **/usr/X386** directory, the directory structure mimics much of the standard X release. For example, the **bin** subdirectory contains all the standard X programs. The **lib** subdirectory contains the programming libraries and configuration files. In general, these directories follow the standard X model, as shown in Table 16.2.

Table 16.2 XFree86 directories under /usr/X386.

Directory	Use
bin	Executable programs, including X server
include	Programming header files
lib	Program libraries
lib/X11	Configuration files, RGB, and error message databases
lib/X11/app-defaults	Application default X resource files
lib/X11/fonts	Font files

continued

Directory	Use
lib/X11/etc	Additional support files
man	Online manual pages

In the binary program directory, typically **/usr/X386/bin**, you'll find all the standard X programs like *xterm*.

The **lib/X11/etc** directory is not commonly found on other X systems. You'll use the files in these directory a lot as you configure XFree86 for your graphics hardware.

Unpacking the Distribution

Normally, you'll find that you need to unpack a number of files that make up the XFree86 distribution by concatenating all the files for a given area (such as the **bin** files), pipe the result to the GNU uncompression program *gunzip*, and then pipe that to *tar*, to extract the actual files.

Depending in what form you acquire the XFree86 distribution, you'll likely find that you have a set of split compressed *tar* files. For any given XFree86 release, though, this set of files may change, so consult the documentation that comes with XFree86 for the most up-to-date information.

Configuring XFree86 for Your Graphics Hardware

Once you've installed all the XFree86 files, the next step is to configure the software for your graphics hardware. Due to the vast array of PC graphics cards, you may find this task daunting, especially if you're not aware of everything that resides in your PC systems.

Of all the configuration, though, the most essential file is the **Xconfig** file, used to control its initial setup. This file should describe your system's mouse, keyboard, and graphics card.

When the X server starts up with *startx* (see Chapter 4 for more on *startx*), it first looks for the **Xconfig** file to tell it how to start the X server. The locations searched for the Xconfig file are (in order) **$HOME/Xconfig**, **/etc/Xconfig**, **/usr/X386/lib/X11/Xconfig.hostname**, and

/usr/X386/lib/X11/Xconfig. In most cases, you'll want to set up the proper values in the **/usr/X386/lib/X11/Xconfig** file.

The first part of the **Xconfig** file lists the font path and where to locate the RGB database. This part should be rather easy to decipher, especially if you use the default settings, for example:

```
RGBPath "/usr/local/X11R5/lib/X11/rgb"

FontPath "/usr/local/X11R5/lib/X11/fonts/misc/,
   /usr/local/X11R5/lib/X11/fonts/75dpi/"
```

The next section defines any keyboard options, as our example shows:

```
Keyboard
  AutoRepeat 500 5
# Xleds      1 2 3
  ServerNumLock
  DontZap
```

We usually turn off the *Xleds* option, using the # as a comment marker, so that the keyboard lights work normally. With the *DontZap* option, users won't be able to type **Ctrl-Alt-Backspace** to kill the X server

After the keyboard options comes the mouse configuration. This is very important, because the X server needs to know how to properly access the mouse. PCs, notorious for sporting hardware differences, have a number of means to access a mouse, such as through a serial port or via a special adapter card.

Typical mouse drivers, sometimes tied to offerings from specific vendors, include Logitech (including several different models, including MouseMan), Microsoft, and PS/2. The following shows a Logitech mouse on the first serial port on a PC:

```
Logitech     "/dev/tty00"
  BaudRate    9600
  SampleRate  150
```

The */dev/tty00* indicates the first serial port. The actual device file may differ on your systems.

The mouse configuration also supports an *Emulate3Buttons* option, allowing a two-button mouse to simulate a three-button mouse when the user presses both mouse buttons simultaneously to activate the pretend third button. This is very useful, as many X programs work under the mistaken assumption that all mice have three buttons.

The next section of the **Xconfig** file is the trickiest. In this section, you must properly configure your graphics card. To be honest, we've never thought that determining clock rates for graphics cards was simple, but for XFree86 to operate properly, you need to configure a surprising amount of hardware-specific, low-level information for your graphics card.

Luckily, XFree86 offers some help in this regard. First, there's a database of popular PC graphics cards, each listed with all the proper information for your **Xconfig** file, in the **lib/X11/etc/modeDB.txt** file. If you're lucky, you should be able to copy an entry from this file for your **Xconfig** file. This entry will contain a number of dot clocks, a set of video timing numbers that describe different modes for your graphics card. These different modes correspond to different screen resolutions.

If you're not lucky, you have two main options: You can determine the timing information yourself or run a neat-o program called SuperProbe. SuperProbe tries to determine your graphics hardware and will present the information necessary for the **Xconfig** file.

If SuperProbe doesn't work, there's a handy tutorial on video modes and timing information in **/usr/X386/lib/X11/etc/VideoModes.doc**. And if after all of this fails, you should do what you should have done in the first place: dig out the documentation—if your system shipped with documentation for the graphics card. This is usually the time where UNIX system administrators start cursing the names of the people who bought the corporate PCs from NoName Clones because they were 2 percent cheaper. Most low-priced clone vendors don't ship adequate system documentation, quite honestly, when it comes to *peripherals du jour*—especially graphics cards.

If you're lucky to find the documentation somewhere in the corporate archives, you'll soon discover that you will learn more than you ever hoped about video circuitry. For example, you'll need to know your monitor's sync frequency ranges in both horizontal and vertical directions. Since most PC monitors are of the multisyncing variety, your monitor probably supports a number of frequencies. You'll also need to discover the frequency bandwidth supported by video card.

Using SuperProbe to Determine Hardware Characteristics

SuperProbe searches for known memory addresses and registers for EISA or ISA graphics cards. SuperProbe supports a number of command-line parameters, most of which are useful only if you really know what's inside your PCs. We list some of the more useful parameters in Table 16.3.

Table 16.3   SuperProbe command-line parameters.

Parameter	Use
-verbose	Prints out lots of information
-no16	Tells program to only look for 8-bit graphics cards
-bios base_address	Sets base BIOS address
-excl ports...	Exclude the given ports (comma-delimited list)

Unless you're a PC hardware guru or have one at hand, the base address for the graphics BIOS sounds like a foreign langauge. The default address is C0000 (in hexidecimal, which is normally typed in as 0xC000, with the leading *0x* indicating the number is in hexidecimal notation). Many graphics cards come with information booklets that describe such esoteric information.

Depending on the hardware you have configured, the SuperProbe program may lock up your system. Therefore, if you know for sure that the PC does not have a 16-bit graphics card, then use the *-no16* command-line parameter. If you know the port address for your disk controller, use the *-excl* command-line parameter to exclude that address.

Choosing the Proper X Server

After you fill in all the values in the **Xconfig** file, you'll need to ensure that the proper X server executable program gets linked to the program X.

XFree86 provides a number of different X server executable programs, each aimed at a different segment of the PC graphics hardware. You need to choose the appropriate X server program (listed in Table 16.4) and then link this to a file named **X** in the **/usr/X386/bin** directory.

Table 16.4   X server programs for XFree86.

Server File	Use
XF86_SVGA	8-bit color SuperVGA X server
XF86_Mono	Monochrome X server
XF86_S3	Accelerated S3 X server
XF86_Mach8	Accelerated Mach8 X server
XF86_Mach32	Accelerated Mach32 X server
XF86_8514	Accelerated 8514/A X server

For example, if you have a standard SuperVGA graphics card, you should link the file **XF86_SVGA** to **X**, as shown in the following command:

```
ln XF86_SVGA X
```

Setting Up XFree86 Environment Variables

The next step is to configure any necessary environment variables. You may need to do this if you've set up a nonstandard installation, such as not using **/usr/X386** for the top-level directory. XFree86 supports a number of environment variables, including the ones shown in Table 16.5.

Table 16.5   XFree86 environment variables.

Variable	Use
XLOCAL	Describes local connection means
XCONFIG	Specifies an alternate **Xconfig** file
XWINHOME	Names a nondefault (not **/usr/X386**) top-level directory

Starting XFree86

With XFree86 all configured, the next step is to start up the X server. As you'd expect, XFree86 supports both the *xinit* and *xdm* methods of starting the X server. If you use *xinit*, you should use the *startx* program provided, which checks the **Xconfig** file and then calls *xinit*.

N O T E

Be sure to add **/usr/X386/bin** (or wherever you stored the XFree86 executable program files) to your users' command path.

Some useful command-line parameters are listed in Table 16.6. Usually, though, you can just type in *startx* and away you go.

Table 16.6. XFree86 command-line parameters.

Parameter	Use
-showconfig	Print out list of graphics drivers configured
-xconfig *filename*	Use *filename* instead of **Xconfig**
-verbose	Print out extra information
-quiet	Don't print extra information

Troubleshooting XFree86

If you face troubles with XFree86, the first thing to do is verify that the information in the **Xconfig** file is correct. To help with this, you can use the SuperProbe program described above. You may even have to pull apart the PC's cover and determine exactly what kind of hardware is *really* installed in the machine.

If the X server has started and things appear locked up, you can try a keyboard combination to kill the X server. Typing **Ctrl-Alt-Backspace** (hold down all three keys at once) should kill the X server, unless you used the *DontZap* option in the **Xconfig** file.

You can also use key combinations to make the X server switch to the next graphics mode in the **Xconfig** file. This is useful if the X server starts at a low resolution and you want to jump to a higher resolution, assuming your graphics hardware supports such a mode, of course.

Ctrl-Alt-Plus (the **+** key on the numeric keypad) should change the current video mode to the next video mode configured in the **Xconfig** file. **Ctrl-**

Alt-Minus (the – key on the numeric keypad) should change back to the previous video mode.

Building XFree86 from Source Code

There are two main ways you can get XFree86: as a binary distribution for a particular operating system, such as UNIX System V Release 3.2, or in source form. Up to now, we've covered the binary version.

The source version is really a set of patches against the X11 Release 5 source tree. To use this, you must have at least X11R5 with R5's patches 1-25 installed. You can then apply the XFree86 patches to the X server software and compile the ddx (device-dependent X server) code for the Intel platform.

Obtaining XFree86

XFree86 source distribution is compressed to a little over one megabyte of disk space. The binary distributions, specific to a particular type of UNIX, weigh in with more than 30 megabytes each. With this large size, you should exercise restraint when picking up files via anonymous FTP on the Internet. Try to avoid cross-ocean network communication, as this can be very expensive for the sponsoring organizations. For example, the machine named *ftp.physics.su.oz.au* is located in Australia and *ftp.prz.tu-berlin.de* is located in Germany. Users in North America should stick to a closer location, such as the machine named *ftp.x.org*, which is located in Massachusetts.

Table 16.7 lists some common locations for obtaining the source-code distribution.

Table 16.7   Where to get XFree86 source code on the Internet.

Machine Name	Directory
ftp.x.org	/contrib/XFree86
ftp.physics.su.oz.au	/XFree86

continued

Machine Name	Directory
ftp.win.tue.nl	/pub/XFree86
ftp.prz.tu-berlin.de	/pub/pc/src/XFree86

If you want the binaries for your system, you need to obtain them from a particular site, as most FTP sites don't provide more than one set of binaries. We list some common sites in Table 16.8.

Table 16.8   Where to get prebuilt XFree86 binaries on the Internet.

Version	Machine Name	Directory
FreeBSD	*XFree86.cdrom.com*	**/pub/XFree86/FreeBSD/XFree86-2.0**
FreeBSD	*gil.physik.rwth-aachen.de*	**/pub/XFree86**
Linux	*tsx-11.mit.edu*	**/pub/linux/packages/X11**
Linux	*ftp.unipi.it*	**/pub/linux/XFree86_2.0**
Mach386	*ftp.cs.uwm.edu*	**/i386**
NetBSD	*agate.berkeley.edu*	**/pub/NetBSD/ports**
NetBSD	*sun-lamp.cs.berkeley.edu*	**/pub/NetBSD/ports**
NetBSD	*ftp.cs.mcgill.ca*	**/pub/NetBSD/XFree86**
SCO	*stasi.bradley.edu*	**/pub/XFree86/sco**
SCO	*ftp.physics.su.oz.au*	**/XFree86/SCO**
SVR3/ISC	*blancmange.ma.utexas.edu*	**/pub/ISC**
SVR3/ISC	*ftp.prz.tu-berlin.de*	**/pub/pc/isc/XFree86**
SVR4	*ftp.physics.su.oz.au*	**/XFree86/SVR4**
SVR4	*ftp.win.tue.nl*	**/pub/XFree86/SVR4**
SVR4	*ftp.tcp.com*	**/pub/SVR4/XFree86**
SVR4	*stasi.bradley.edu*	**/pub/XFree86/SVR4**

You can also purchase XFree86 on CD-ROM (see Chapter 17 for more information). Normally, this just has the source code, but a number of CD-ROM vendors, such as Prime Time Freeware, offer binary distributions on CD-ROM.

Summary

This chapter covers XFree86, a freely available implementation of X Window for PCs running UNIX. While most UNIX vendors do offer X Window in their PC UNIX implementations, most do not offer an up-to-date version of X. This chapter covers configuration details associated with XFfree86, as well as information about acquiring it in source-code or binary format.

In the next chapter, you will review different methods for acquiring X Window as a whole.

Free X Programs and What to Do with Them

In a sense, most X programs you're already running are free, as you can get the sources to the entire X Window System. There are also a huge number of free X programs available, many of which prove handy for UNIX system administrators.

This section concentrates on such programs: how to get them, how to build them, and what to do with them. Even if you keep up with freeware X programs, chances are you'll discover a new program or two, along with some useful techniques for building and installing these programs.

Chapter 17 starts off the section by covering where to find the sources to the X Window System as well as most free X programs. We include almost all of the freeware mentioned in this section on the accompanying CD-ROM. If your system doesn't have a CD-ROM, we also provide information on where to pick up this freeware via the Internet, where you can pick these up using anonymous FTP.

Once you get the source code for an X application, you'll find the information in Chapter 18 useful, as we go over how to compile, link, and install X programs, including configuring an evil program called *imake*.

Starting with Chapter 19, we describe a number of free X tools of use to the system administrator. Chapter 19 covers administration tools to monitor the system load on a number of UNIX systems, view disk space usage, convert font files between various font-file formats, and edit font files.

Chapter 20 covers how to build graphical X front-ends for text-based applications and a number of tools to help in that process.

Chapter 21 returns to security issues and examines a number of tools that lock a user's screen while they walk away.

Chapter 22 covers some low-level tools to help you debug problems in errant X applications. We've never liked doing this, but these tools have proven themselves essential in our work.

Chapter 23 provides a grab-bag of sorts. In it, we cover a wide array of useful and fun X programs that really didn't fit into any large category. This includes reading documentation on-line, new and innovative ways to keep track of the time, and a handy audio CD player that turns your expensive UNIX workstations into the equivalent of a $100 CD player.

Finally, Chapter 24 covers X tools for information access, especially over the Internet. Even if you're not on the Internet, you can take advantage of some of these tools for your local network.

Obtaining X and
Other Free X Sources

Topics covered in this chapter include:

* Free X software
* Acquiring X
* X on the Internet
* Mail servers
* The xstuff mail archive
* Contributed X software
* X on CD-ROM
* Usenet news groups
* Patches and X

A Sampling of Free X Software

One of the greatest joys about the X Window System is that X is free, in the form of source code from the X Consortium. Because of this, there's a huge amount of free software for X, some of it quite good and some even essential. (And that's saying a lot coming from picky people like us.) You'll find that much of it will be useful in your everyday administrative chores—which is why we included it on the CD-ROM accompanying this book. We list some interesting free programs in Table 17.1.

Table 17.1   A sampling of free X software on the accompanying CD-ROM.

Program or Package	Description	Primary Author
calctool	X calculator	Rich Burridge
mosaic	Internet information browser	Marc Andreessen
PBM+	Image conversion utilities	Jef Poskanzer
Tcl/Tk	Tool command language and X toolkit	John Ousterhout
Wcl	Widget creation library	David E. Smyth
workman	XView Music CD player	Steven Grimm
xgen	Front-end to text programs	Kurt Buehler
xgrabsc	Screen capture program	Bruce Schuchardt
xlock	Screen locker	Patrick Naughton
xmon	X protocol debugging tool, based on *xscope*	Greg McFarlane
xscope	X protocol debugging tool	James L. Peterson
XFree86	X server for 386/486 UNIX	David Wexelblat
xmahjongg	One of the better Mah-Jongg games	Jeff S. Young
xsol	Solitaire game	Jon Brinkmann

There's a host of X-based calculator programs. *Xcalc* comes with the X release from the X Consortium. Hewlett-Packard systems come with *xhpcalc*, which presents an RPN calculator based on common H-P models. *Calctool* is for those of us who don't think in RPN, but want more than what *xcalc* offers (if you have the COSE common desktop, its calculator is also a far cry better than *xcalc*).

To capture screen images from X, we find two tools essential: *xgrabsc* to capture the images and PBM+ to convert the images to whatever format you need. PBM+ comes with a host of programs to convert images to and from common formats like PCX, GIF, TIFF, and Encapsulated PostScript. *Xgrabsc* allows you to capture rectangular areas of the screen and dump the resulting image into a file.

Tcl, the Tool Command Language (pronounced *tickle*), provides a scripting language and a C library that you can use to embed this scripting language into your applications, providing an instant command language into your programs. We cover it in Chapter 20.

If you work at a site where you're concerned about security, the *xlock* program may help. This program locks your screen while you're away so that others can't access it. When you return, *xlock* requires you to correctly enter your password to unlock the screen. See Chapter 21 for more on *xlock* and related programs.

Even if your site isn't on the Internet, you'll find that tools like *gopher*, *xgopher*, and *mosaic* are great network-based information browsers. See Chapter 24 for more on those.

Sometimes X programs generate strange errors that are hard to track down, especially if you don't have the source code to the X application. In that case, *xmon* or *xscope* come in very handy. Both these programs act as a proxy X server, intercepting every X packet sent to and from the X server, and printing out selected packets. See Chapter 22 for more on *xscope* and *xmon*.

On a lighter note, you can use the *workman* program to convert your Sun CD-ROM drive into a very expensive audio CD player. (It's not so expensive if you already have the CD drive.) We especially like *workman*'s ability to store a database of CD names, artists, and song titles. When we insert our favorite Bob Marley disc, we see "Bob Marley/Exodus" magically appear in the *workman* window. You'll need external speakers or headphones if you wish to actually hear an audio CD.

Xmahjongg presents a solo version of Mah-Jongg, a game involving numbered tiles. The goal in *xmahjongg* is to remove every tile from the display.

There's a number of Mah-Jongg game programs for X, including *xmahjongg* and *xmj*. We find *xmahjongg*, though, to have a much less garish display than *xmj*, and *xmahjongg* uses the default colormap, while *xmj* insists on using its own private colormap. Hence our preference for *xmahjongg* (*xmahjongg* is easier to win, too).

Xsol is a tried and true simple solitaire game, using Vegas-style rules, although you can cheat and go through the deck again and again.

Acquiring X

There's a number of ways you can obtain the sources for the X Window System and a whole plethora of X applications. If you have access to the Internet, you can pick up the latest versions from there. Otherwise, you can watch the *comp.sources.x* Usenet newsgroup or purchase a X source tape or CD-ROM. We find quite a few CD-ROMs available in the $40–$100 range.

Anonymous FTP

If you don't know what anonymous FTP is, chances are you don't have it. Basically, you can use the *ftp* (which stands for file transfer protocol) program to copy files from other sites on a network. If that network happens to be on the Internet, then you can use *ftp* to copy files from generous sites around the world that allow members of the public *ftp* access. Due to a great deal of generosity (and large software packages), you can use *ftp* to acquire zillions of megabytes off the Internet.

 If you're not well versed in it, we cover much more on *ftp* in our books *Teach Yourself Unix* and *Unix in Plain English* (see Appendix A for the details).

N O T E

If you have access to the Internet, there are a number of common locations to obtain the basic X release, which we list in Table 17.2.

Table 17.2   Where to get X source code on the Internet.

Location	Hostname	Internet Address	Directory
Australia	*munnari.oz.au*	128.250.1.21	X.V11/R5
California	*gatekeeper.dec.com*	16.1.0.2	pub/X11/R5
California	*soda.berkeley.edu*	128.32.131.179	pub/X11R5
Denmark	*freja.diku.dk*	129.142.96.1	pub/X11R5
Finland	*nic.funet.fi*	128.214.6.100	pub/X11/R5
France	*nuri.inria.fr*	28.93.1.26	X/X11R5
Germany	*ftp.germany.eu.net*	192.76.144.129	pub/X11/X11R5
Indiana	*mordred.cs.purdue.edu*	128.10.2.2	pub/X11/R5
Israel	*cs.huji.ac.il*	132.65.6.5	pub/X11R5
Italy	*ghost.sm.dsi.unimi.it*	149.132.2.1	pub/X11R5
Kanagawa, Japan	*sh.wide.ad.jp*	133.4.11.11	X11R5
Kwansai, Japan	*ftp.ics.osaka-u.ac.jp*	133.1.12.30	X11R5
Kyushu, Japan	*wnoc-fuk.wide.ad.jp*	133.4.14.3	X11R5
Maryland	*ftp.brl.mil*	128.63.16.158	pub/X11R5
Massachusetts	*crl.dec.com*	192.58.206.2	pub/X11/R5
Massachusetts	*ftp.x.org*	198.112.44.100	pub/R5
Michigan	*merit.edu*	35.1.1.4	pub/X11R5
Missouri	*wuarchive.wustl.edu*	128.252.135.4	packages/X11R5
Montana	*ftp.cs.montana.edu*	192.31.215.202	pub/X.V11R5
New Mexico	*pprg.eece.unm.edu*	129.24.24.10	pub/dist/X11R5
New York	*azure.acsu.buffalo.edu*	128.205.7.6	pub/X11R5
Netherlands	*archive.eu.net*	192.16.202.1	windows/X/R5
North Carolina	*cs.duke.edu*	128.109.140.1	dist/sources/X11R5
Norway	*ugle.unit.no*	129.241.1.97	pub/X11R5
Norway	*nac.no*	129.240.2.40	pub/X11R5
Ohio	*ftp.cis.ohio-state.edu*	128.146.8.52	pub/X.V11R5
Ontario	*ftp.cs.utoronto.ca*	128.100.1.105	pub/X11R5

continued

Location	Hostname	Internet Address	Directory
Switzerland	*nic.switch.ch*	130.59.1.40	software/X11R5
TISN, Japan	*utsun.s.u-tokyo.ac.jp*	133.11.11.11	X11R5
Tokyo	*kerr.iwanami.co.jp*	133.235.128.1	X11R5
Tokyo	*scslwide.sony.co.jp*	133.138.199.1	pub/X11R5
United Kingdom	*src.doc.ic.ac.uk*	146.169.3.7	graphics/X.V11R5
Washington, D.C.	*x11r5-a.uu.net*	192.48.96.12	X/R5
Washington, D.C.	*x11r5-b.uu.net*	137.39.1.12	X/R5

Since the above machines are run by very nice people who are giving away access, try to be friendly when you pick up X sources. There's about 100 megabytes in the basic X distribution, so exercise restraint, especially during business hours. It's also considered bad form to initiate cross-ocean network links when alternate sites are available on your continent.

Contributed X Software

The best possibility to find any program that's not part of the core X release is *ftp.x.org* in the **contrib** directory. Most programmers leave copies of their latest free X programs in this **contrib** directory.

For instance, you can find *xv*, a handy utility for viewing graphics images. The *xv* program displays image files in a number of formats, including GIF and TIFF.

Figure 17.1   Displaying a bitmap with *xv*.

Mail Servers

If you don't have access to the Internet, you can often use a mail server as a proxy to perform the *ftp* access for you by sending a formatted electronic mail message to the mail server's address. Inside this message, you name the files you wish to receive and the machine to get them from. Then the mail server executes the *ftp* program at its site (which is presumably connected to the Internet or the whole thing wouldn't work).

When the mail server acquires the desired files, it mails them back to you, often in many pieces. In addition, mail servers often convert binary files to ASCII text through a standard Unix utility program named *uuencode*.

It seems that whenever we find a working email FTP server, it stops working after a short time. For that reason, we're not listing any FTP mail servers here. The best source of information on this is to check the Usenet newsgroups for names of active FTP mail servers.

The Xstuff Mail Archive

In addition to the handy FTP mail servers, the X Consortium runs a simpler mail server, called xstuff. With the xstuff mail server, you can ask for files that are stored on the X Consortium's machines only. The xstuff mail server won't execute *ftp* for you.

Since the X Consortium is where the X Window System is developed in the first place, this is a central location to pick up just about any X file. We find the xstuff mail server especially helpful in acquiring the period fixes to the X source code (see the section on patches near the end of this chapter).

To use the xstuff mail server, send electronic mail to *xstuff@x.org*. Put the word *help* in the subject line and leave the text of the message blank. The xstuff mail server will respond with detailed directions for accessing the files it can serve.

CD-ROMs

If you're willing to give up on the instant gratification that the Internet provides, there's a number of inexpensive CD-ROMs full of free X sources, usually including the entire X Window System distribution. There's some variance, but usually, on any given X CD-ROM (except for the one accompanying this book) you'll get the entire X11 distribution (the core package that makes up the minimal X Window System as well as the contributed code for the latest release) along with a host of other software, such as the GNU C compilers. We find that CD-ROMs are the best value, because of the huge amount of source code that can be placed on a single compact disc. In fact, buying an X CD-ROM is generally cheaper than backing up the massive X sources to tape.

The Usenet News

You'll also find that new X programs—and updates of old ones—periodically appear on the Usenet newsgroup *comp.sources.x*, which contains only source code for X programs. This, in addition to the aforementioned **contrib** directory on *ftp.x.org*, is one of the best sources for the latest X freeware.

In addition to *comp.sources.x*, a number of other X Window Usenet newsgroups may prove helpful. Most of these are devoted to programming X (no mean feat), as we show in Table 17.3.

Table 17.3   Usenet newsgroups devoted to X.

Newsgroup	Discusses
alt.sources	Program source code, sometimes includes X programs
comp.windows.x	General X Window issues; mostly programming
comp.windows.x.apps	X Window applications
comp.windows.x.i386unix	XFree86
comp.windows.interviews	InterViews C++ programming
comp.windows.x.intrinsics	Programming with the Xt library
comp.windows.x.motif	Motif programming
comp.windows.open-look	Open Look issues; mostly programming
comp.windows.x.pex	PEX 3D programming

Getting Patches for X

X is a moving target. As the X Consortium fixes bugs, they provide for periodic fixes, a form of patch for the X software. The term *patch* comes from a program of the same name that allows developers to ship only the differences in the new release, rather than the entire set of source code. (We cover the *patch* program in more depth in the next chapter.) You can get the X Consortium's patches from the xstuff mail server (see above).

Patches are especially important for Sun Solaris users, because at least with X11 Release 5, you need a patch to compile X on Solaris. These patches are located in the **contrib** directory on the machine named *ftp.x.org*.

Summary

In this chapter, you examined the various methods for acquiring X and various programs in source-code form, via the Internet and via more traditional and mundane means.

In the next chapter, you will learn how to compile and link this source code.

Using *Make* and *Imake*

Topics covered in this chapter include:

* Building X programs
* X programming libraries and what they're used for
* Compiling and linking X programs
* Generating **Makefiles** with *imake*
* Using the *xmkmf* shell script
* Creating an **Imakefile**
* Installing application resource files
* Using the *patch* program to update versions

Working with Free Software

The X Window System, like UNIX, supports a fine tradition in free software. Many individuals, universities, and a few open-minded companies support free software. In fact, the X Window System itself is freely distributable. Unfortunately, the complexities of various X installations, along with variations in UNIX versions, make it difficult to for administrators to compile and install this free software.

The most frustrating problem with free X software is just getting the code to compile. It's hard to complain about what you get for free, yet we find a distressingly small number of programs actually compile and run. To help you avoid hassles with free software, we present some tips that work for us.

Just about all free X programs are written in the C programming language or an object-oriented superset called C++.

One advantage of the X Window System is software portability. C or C++ programs written on one platform can compute just fine on other platforms—at least the user interface (that is, X) portion of the programs. If the program's developers worked with portability in mind, you can expect to get most X programs running on your platforms with a limited amount of effort.

The problem, though, is that every operating system and every site is set up differently. This requires a lot of manual tweaking when you try to compile the supposedly portable X Window applications to your platforms. Part of the answer provided by X is a program called *imake*. (The rest of the answer—as usual—is up to you.)

In this chapter, we provide an overview of the process of converting C program source code into actual executable programs that users can run. We then delve into X-specific conventions for building up X applications and cover *imake*, a program used to generate a **Makefile** for just about every free X program. If you're well-versed on C programming, then jump ahead to the section on X Programming Libraries. If you're not, then the next section can provide a better context for compiling and linking X programs. Even so, we're not out to make you a programmer—if you wanted to be a programmer, then you'd be one.

Building C Programs

C programs begin as a series of C program source-code files. These text files come chock full of C programming language statements, wrapped together in functions. Many of these functions are introduced in standard header files, called include files and usually stored in **/usr/include**.

The C files usually end with a **.c**. The problem is, UNIX systems don't run these files very well. Instead, programmers must compile the C source files into relocatable object modules, which usually end in **.o**. We list some standard file suffixes, or filename extensions, in Table 18.1.

Table 18.1   File suffixes.

Suffix	Use
.c	C source code
.cpp	C++ source code
.C	C++ source code
.cxx	C++ source code
.h	C header file
.o	Compiled object module
.a	Compiled library of object modules

The software tool that does the compiling is called, appropriately enough, the C compiler, one of many UNIX utilities listed in Table 18.2.

Table 18.2   Common UNIX programming utilities.

Program	Use
ar	Builds compiled code into library files
c	C compiler
cc	C++ compiler (note uppercase name)
cpp	C preprocessor, automatically called by the C compiler

continued

Program	Use
ld	UNIX linker, automatically called by the C compiler
make	Program builder, calls **cc**

The C compiler, *cc*, then calls the linker/loader, *ld*, to link together all the object modules with a set of prebuilt programming libraries. The end result is an executable UNIX program.

X Programming Libraries

A library is a set of compiled C functions that programmers can call on. Some programmers build their own libraries. All C programmers use the UNIX system's set of utility libraries.

This stuff is all standard for building any C programs on UNIX. What's different is the set of libraries and include files required by X applications. Most X programs are built using an X toolkit of some sort. (A toolkit is just a fancy name for a C library.) Among the most common toolkits, you'll find Motif, the Open Look Intrinsics Toolkit (OLIT), and the Athena widgets. Unfortunately, many programs don't come right out and tell you what X toolkits are required. You may have to decode the libraries listed in the link command and use these libraries to determine which toolkits you need to look for.

We list the most common libraries in Table 18.3.

Table 18.3   Common X programming libraries.

Library	Meaning
libXaw.a	Athena Widget Set
libXm.a	Motif toolkit
libXt.a	X Toolkit Intrinsics, used by Athena, Motif, and OLIT
libX11.a	Low-level X library

continued

Library	Meaning
libXext.a	X Extensions
libXol.a	Open Look Intrinsics Toolkit, or OLIT
libXpm.a	Free (contributed) X pixmap library
libXmu.a	X Miscellaneous Utilities
libxview.a	XView toolkit
libolgx.a	Low-level routines used by XView

The Motif library is not free, but it comes from most UNIX vendors, including Hewlett-Packard, Sun, IBM, Novell, and SCO. Frequently, though, the Motif libraries are special-cost add-on items. The Xt library, then, is the X toolkit Intrinsics, which supports many X widget sets, such as Motif, OLIT, or the Athena widgets. Most Xt-based programs use just one of the toolkit libraries. The only exception we know of is Lucid *emacs*, which requires both the Motif and Athena widget libraries.

Not all systems have all the libraries listed in Table 18.3. For example, unless you have a SunOS, Solaris, or System V Release 4 system, chances are you won't have the OLIT library. If you do have OLIT, chances are you won't have the Motif library.

The X pixmap library does not ship as a standard part of X. Instead, you must acquire it yourself. It's well worth it, though. (See the previous chapter for more on acquiring X source code.)

The Athena widget library comes with the X releases from the X Consortium, but many vendors, such as Hewlett-Packard, don't ship this. Because the Athena widgets are free, many developers of free software stick to this library, instead of using propriety X toolkits like Motif or OLIT.

The XView library, although no longer emphasized by Sun Microsystems, is becoming more and more popular because it supports an easy-to-learn programming model with a small application programmer's interface. Most new X programs written for Linux or one of the other free UNIX workalikes build on the XView toolkit.

You can find a copy of the XView library in the contributed area of most X FTP sites, such as *ftp.x.org*, and on most X CD-ROMs.

Compiling and Linking X Programs

Once you've figured out which libraries a program needs, you can then try to compile and link the software. In Table 18.4, we list the common ordering for the X programming libraries when used with various toolkits. It's a common error to reverse one of these many libraries on the *cc* command line.

Table 18.4   Common X library orderings.

Program Type	Libraries in Order
Athena	-lXaw -lXmu -lXt -lX11
Athena with X extensions, like SHAPE	-lXaw -lXmu -lXt -lXext -lX11
Motif	-lXm -lXt -lX11
Motif with X extensions, like SHAPE	-lXm -lXmu -lXt -lXext -lX11
OLIT	-lXol -lXt -lX11
Xlib	-lX11
Xlib with X extensions, like SHAPE	-lXext -lX11
XView	-lxview -lolgx -lX11

For example, you can compile a Motif program stored in a C file named *foo.c* with the following command:

```
cc -o foo foo.c -lXm -lXt -lX11
```

Motif programs generally require the Xm, Xt, and low-level X11 libraries.

A common means to compile with the free Athena widget set follows:

```
cc -o foo foo.c -lXaw -lXmu \
    -lXt -lXext -lX11
```

With X11 Release 5, Athena widget programs need the Xaw, Xmu, Xt, Xext, and X11 libraries. The Xext library holds functions for X extensions, including the SHAPE extension, which provides for rounded windows.

You can compile OLIT programs with:

```
cc -o foo foo.c -lXol -lXt -lX11
```

In addition to these basic examples, a number of systems require you to vary the procedure, based on system-specific differences.

Networking Issues for Compiling and Linking

The low-level X library uses a network connection under the hood to communicate between your applications and the X server. Normally, this is some form of TCP/IP or UNIX domain socket. In most cases, your code won't have to deal with this at all. For many versions of UNIX for the Intel architecture, networking is an add-on item. With these systems, you'll need to link in an extra library or two after the low-level X library. For example, on Interactive/SunSoft UNIX System VR3.2 3.0, you can use the following command to compile and link a Motif program:

```
cc -o foo foo.c -lXm -lXt \
     -lX11 -linet
```

The extra *inet* library provides the networking routines. These routines are stored in the default C library (**libc.a**) on most non-Intel systems, such as H-P, Silicon Graphics, or Sun Microsystems.

For SCO systems, you may need to link in the *tlisock*, *socket*, and *nsl_s* libraries, as shown on the following command:

```
cc -o foo foo.c -lXm -lXt -lX11 \
    -ltlisock -lsocket -lnsl_s
```

Locating Include Files and Libraries

Some systems place X include files in nonstandard locations. Sun's OpenWindows, for instance, places include files in **/usr/openwin/include**. If your C compiler can't find these files, you'll generally get a host of compiler errors regarding files not found.

OpenWindows also places the X libraries in **/usr/openwin/lib**. Your command to compile and link an OLIT program becomes:

```
cc -o foo -I/usr/openwin/include foo.c \
     -L/usr/openwin/lib -lXol -lXt -lX11
```

Under HP-UX 9.0.*x*, the X and Motif include files are stored in **/usr/include/X11R5** and **/usr/include/Motif1.2**, respectively. The libraries

----

are stored in **/usr/lib/X11R5** and **/usr/lib/Motif1.2**. You can compile and link a Motif program on an HP-UX 9.0.*x* platform with:

```
cc -o foo -I/usr/include/Motif1.2 \
   -I/usr/include/X11R5 \
   foo.c -L/usr/lib/Motif1.2 \
   -L/usr/lib/X11R5 -lXm -lXt -lX11
```

See Chapter 2 for more on the location of include files and libraries on various platforms.

Even if you have *imake* (which we will cover shortly) and all the libraries and include files, you may still be out of luck when compiling free X programs. Many free X programs are written for a particular machine or operating system. This is to be expected, as you can't demand that authors of free programs buy every conceivable combination of hardware and software to ensure they support your configuration. You may have to tweak the code to get it running. If you do, please send a note to the program's author, so that your fixes can get into the next general release of the program.

Building Programs with *Make*

With large complex programs, many programmers use a building tool called *make* to help manage the process. *Make* is a very simple rule-based engine that aims at compiling and linking C programs. (You can use *make* for other purposes, but it has the most built-in support for building C programs.)

Make provides a few built-in rules (which unfortunately differ by platform), but most of the rules are particular to a given application. Because of this, each application will come with one or more files usually named **Makefile**. This file (there's usually one in each source-code directory) contains the rules to build a particular application.

Armed with these rules, and presuming the rules are properly configured for your system, you can build an X application by simply invoking *make* on the command line. With this, *make* will follow the rules in the **Makefile** and generally compile each source code module in the current directory. Some **Makefiles** are much more complex than this, of course, especially for X programs.

TROUBLE-SHOOTING

A common problem, especially for newcomers to X, is trying to deal with a missing or misconfigured **Makefile**. Due to differences in UNIX versions, many programmers define options in the **Makefile** to ensure that the code compiles properly on a variety of machines. X programs require quite a few options in the **Makefile**, mostly telling the C compiler where the X include files are libraries are located.

With many X programs, though, you'll find no **Makefile** at all, or a **Makefile** that is obviously set up for another UNIX system. Frequently, in place of the **Makefile**, you'll find an odd file named **Imakefile**.

The proper *make* rules, though, vary from system to system, particularly with regard to the libraries of C language routines heavily used by X applications. Thus, the designers of the X Window System include a utility called *imake*.

Imake: Adding Bells and Whistles to *Make*

Imake is a simple-minded program that generates a **Makefile** tuned to your system's setup. *Imake* uses its own rules and builds a **Makefile** from a template file (which describes your system's setup) and a set of rules for building a program, which are stored in a file named **Imakefile**. The end result—if *imake* is configured properly—is a **Makefile** that should work on your system to build an X Window application. Then *make* takes over and builds the X application.

There are three main uses of *imake*. First, should you install the X Window System source code and compile your own X server, you'll use *imake* to configure X for your system.

Second, you use *imake* to install new X program libraries, such as Motif from the Open Software Foundation (OSF). If you license Motif sources from the OSF, then you'll need to compile the Motif sources into the proper programmer libraries on your system. Again, if you purchase the Motif toolkit precompiled from a third-party vendor, or if Motif already comes with your system, then you won't have to bother with this.

Finally, you use *imake* to build X applications, especially the free X applications that you can get from CompuServe, from the *comp.sources.x* Usenet newsgroup, and from various program archive sites on the Internet. This chapter covers this last case, as it is the most common use of *imake*.

Delving into *Imake*

Imake starts by loading in a master template file called **Imake.tmpl** (the **.tmpl** stands for template). This file normally resides in **/usr/lib/X11/config**. The master **Imake.tmpl** executes the following steps to build a **Makefile**.

First, **Imake.tmpl** determines what sort of machine you have, such as a Sun SPARC, and includes (that is, executes the rules in) a file configured for your operating system. The Sun system file is named **sun.cf** (**.cf** stands for configuration). The Silicon Graphics (SGI) file is named **sgi.cf**, and so on. The **sun.cf** file, for example, contains variables to set the version of the operating system and other means to customize *imake* for Sun systems.

These files, like all *imake* configuration files, are normally located in **/usr/lib/X11/config**. You may need to edit the *system*.cf file when you install the X Window sources, but once you've done that, you probably won't need to edit the operating system file again. On systems where X comes preinstalled, you shouldn't need to edit this file.

Second, **Imake.tmpl** includes the file **site.def**, also in **/usr/lib/X11/config**. The **site.def** file should have local customizations. For example, if you want X programs to reside somewhere else than the standard **/usr/bin/X11**, you can configure this in the **site.def** file.

Third, **Imake.tmpl** includes a project-specific file, named **Project.tmpl**. This is used mainly for building the X Window sources from the X Consortium.

Fourth, **Imake.tmpl** includes a set of rules used to build X programs, stored in a file named **Imake.rules**. **Imake.rules** contains a set of generic rules used by *imake*. You shouldn't need to edit this file, but you may want to take a look at the file to see what sort of rules are defined. The syntax won't make a lot of sense, though, as it uses *cpp* macros extensively.

In the last step, **Imake.tmpl** includes the local directory's **Imakefile**. This file describes the high-level rules (using the low-level rules in the **Imake.rules** file) for building a particular X application.

In addition, there's also a **Motif.tmpl** file, a template for Motif programs, and **Motif.rules**, the generic rules for building the Motif libraries and programs that use the Motif libraries.

When all this is done, *imake* uses a program called *makedepend*, along with all the configured rules, for building the **Makefile**.

When you configure *imake,* **you'll spend most of your time working with the site.def and** *system***.cf files.**

NOTE

You should only have to configure *imake* once—if that. Many systems come with *imake* preconfigured. (Some systems don't include *imake,* such as Hewlett-Packard workstations, but look below for the section "Hewlett-Packard Systems" for information on how to get *imake* for H-P systems.)

The main purpose of *imake* is to generate a **Makefile** that is configured to work on your system. To do so, *imake* supports the following command-line parameters, shown in Table 18.5.

Table 18.5   *Imake* command-line parameters.

Option	Meaning
-D*define*	Defines the value following the -D
-I*directory*	Names the directory for the **Imake.tmpl** file
-T*template*	Names the master template file, which defaults to **Imake.tmpl**
-f *filename*	Names the local **Imakefile**, which defaults to **Imakefile**
-s *filename*	Names the output file, defaults to **Makefile**
-e	Imake should build and execute the **Makefile**; using the default avoids executing the **Makefile**
-v	Turns on verbose mode, which prints out *cpp* commands

Although you can call *imake* directly, most users use the *xmkmf* shell script to invoke *imake.*

Xmkmf: A Wrapper Around *imake*

X includes a simple UNIX shell script called *xmkmf*, which serves as an easy front end to *imake*. If you have a directory with an **Imakefile**, you can use *xmkmf* to generate a **Makefile** by changing to the directory with the **Imakefile** and then using the simple command:

```
xmkmf
```

If *imake* is set up properly—a big if—then you'll see the following output and you should now have a **Makefile** in the current directory:

```
imake -DUseInstalled -I/usr/lib/X11/config
```

The commands output to the screen are the commands you could use to invoke *imake* directly.

If you run *xmkmf* and there already is a **Makefile** in your local directory, *xmkmf* will save that **Makefile** to **Makefile.bak** before creating a new **Makefile**. The command will look something like:

```
mv Makefile Makefile.bak
imake -DUseInstalled -I/usr/lib/X11/config
```

Creating Imakefiles

The easiest way to create an **Imakefile** is to use an existing working file as a template and then just fill in the differences. Most simple X programs can use the file below as a template:

```
#
#   As with Makefiles, lines starting
#   with a "#" are comments.
#
LOCAL_LIBRARIES1 = $(XAWLIB) $(XMULIB)\
        $(XTOOLLIB) $(EXTENSIONLIB) $(XLIB)

CDEBUGFLAGS = -g

SRCS1 = file1.c file2.c file3.c file4.c
OBJS1 = file1.o file2.o file3.o file4.o
```

```
INCLUDE_FILES = include1.h include2.h

PROGRAM = xkana

ComplexProgramTarget_1(xkana, $(LOCAL_LIBRARIES1), )
```

This short 400-byte **Imakefile** generates a 10Kbyte **Makefile**. In addition, this **Imakefile** references a number of *imake* variables, listed in Table 18.6.

Table 18.6   Imake variables in the sample Imakefile.

Imake Variable	Used For
LOCAL_LIBRARIES1	Listing of the necessary libraries, using *imake* variables
SRCS1	C program files used to build the program
PROGRAM	Name of the program to build, *xkana* in this example
OBJS1	Object modules to link together to make the program
ComplexProgramTarget_1	*Imake* command to build the whole thing

Unless you have special needs, you can use the *ComplexProgramTarget_1* macro to build your programs.

The library names are also *imake* variables, because these can have different names or locations on different platforms (this is why you spent so much work configuring *imake* in the first place, so that *imake* knows where all these libraries are located). We list the example libraries in Table 18.7.

Table 18.7   Examples of imake library names.

Imake Name	Description	Usual Library
XAWLIB	Athena widget library	libXaw.a
XMULIB	X miscellaneous utilities library	libXmu.a
XTOOLLIB	X Toolkit Intrinsics	libXt.a

continued

Imake Name	Description	Usual Library
EXTENSIONLIB	X extension library	**libXext.a**
XLIB	Low-level X library	**libX11.a**

Using the New Makefile

If all goes well, you shouldn't ever have to read the automatically generated **Makefile**. You should be able to just type *make* on the command line and the program should be built.

N O T E

You should be able to compile most X programs without root access. Only rarely will you need root access to set up setuid root programs. When installing, you may need root permissions to copy the programs into protected directories.

When *make* completes, you're done (if all went well). Unfortunately, it doesn't always work that way. When compiling a new free X application, you may be hit with a problem if *imake* fails to build the **Makefile**. Luckily, programmers often include a simple default **Makefile** for building their application. If this is the case, it's usually a lot easier to customize a **Makefile** for your system than it is to get *imake* working properly.

If *imake* fails completely to build a working **Makefile**, you should look around in the source-code directory for a file named something like **Makefile.ini**, **Makefile.simple**, or **Makefile.orig**.

Even if it can't find one of these files and you do have a configured *imake*, your best bet is often to create your own **Makefile**. If you have an *imake*-generated **Makefile**, the first thing you'll notice is that the file is *huge* and it sets up *make* variables for just about everything you can imagine — and then some. Instead of changing all these options, we usually jump to the end of the **Makefile** and find the commands that actually compile and link the code. At that point, we edit away, typing in options we know work for our system. It's simply easier to edit this trailing section of the **Makefile** than to set up every single *make* variable properly. Be prepared for a number of trials, though, to get the whole thing to work. It's much easier if you have *imake* available and configured for your system.

Hewlett-Packard Systems

H-P systems don't ship with the Athena widget set, Xaw, or the X miscellaneous utility functions, Xmu. Both of these programming libraries are used extensively by free X software because they're both free libraries and they come with the standard X release from the X Consortium.

In addition, H-P systems don't ship with *imake* or the *xmkmf* script. Luckily, though, you can get all of these from a number of anonymous FTP sites, including *hpcvaaz.cv.hp.com* (15.255.72.15). You can also get these from the HP InterWorks user group (care of Carol Relph, InterWorks, 300 Apollo Dr., Chelmsford, MA 01824; 508/436-5115).

Installing X Resource Files

Once you get the code to compile and link, you sometimes have problems getting the programs to run properly. In many cases, what you're missing is the proper X resource file for the application. Sometimes, though, it's hard to tell exactly which file is the resource file and what you should name it.

Luckily, many X programs adopt the convention that a file ending in **.ad**, which stands for application defaults, is the X resource file. For example, the file **XGrab.ad** comes with *xgrabsc*, as the graphical front-end program named *xgrab*.

Usually an application's resource file has the same name as the program, but the first letter is uppercase. If the program name starts with *x*, then the first two letters are normally uppercase, such as a resource file named **XTerm** for the **xterm** program. There are some exceptions, such as the resource file **Xedit** for the **xedit** application. (There's no standard for naming X resource files.) Most applications should come with an X resource file; if the file is named **Foo.ad**, then you have a good chance that the resource file should be named **Foo**.

For testing purposes, you should copy the resource file into your home directory and rename the file to **XGrab** sans the **.ad** suffix. (**XGrab** is just an example name for the example *xgrab* application.)

When you're through testing the application (and presuming it works), you should install the X resource file in your sitewide X application defaults directory, typically **/usr/lib/X11/app-defaults**. Many X programs require the application defaults resource files to be set up properly or they won't work well.

Where to Install X Programs

If the X resource file checks out, the next step is to install the X program. Luckily, many **Imakefiles** set up an *install* target in the **Makefile**, so you can often install the program by typing:

```
make install
```

You probably want to install X applications in some local **bin** directory, such as **/usr/local/bin** and the online manual pages in **/usr/local/man**.

Patching X Sources

Many X programs tend to come in huge distributions, even in source-code form. Because of this, program modifications often come in patch files instead of rereleasing the whole shebang.

A patch file is a file that was produced by the UNIX *diff* utility (which lists differences in files). Armed with the differences between the new version and the old version, the *patch* program can apply the proper changes to update your old program to the latest version.

Patch is a very handy utility, even for non-X programs. If you work much with free X programs, you'll need to learn how to use *patch*, as there's lots of program updates (this is a good thing, as you get bug fixes and new features—all for free). It's easy to run: change to the program's directory and then run *patch*:

```
patch < patchfile
```

The above feeds the patch file named *patchfile* as standard input to the *patch* program. When run, *patch* pumps out a lot of status information and may even ask you a few questions. Generally, the process completes fairly quickly.

All of the periodic fixes to the X Window System source code, and most free X applications, come in the form of *patch* files.

Summary

You'll sometimes need to compile free software for use on your system. The process, while slightly complicated, isn't totally insurmountable if you follow the directions detailed in this chapter.

In the following chapter, you will review some very convenient system-administration utilities.

System-Administration Utilities

Topics covered in this chapter include:

* Using *netload* to monitor system load
* Using *xsystats* to monitor system load
* Reading the meter of *xmeter*
* Dealing with compilation problems
* Determining disk space with *spacetool*
* File and disk-browsing utilities
* Bitmap font tools
* Editing fonts with *xfedor*

Whistle While You Work

There are a number of free X programs that can help make your duties as an administrator more fun—or at least present a better picture of system performance. This chapter briefly introduces a number of free X tools to help you with common system administration duties, including:

❋ Monitoring the system load on a number of machines

❋ Watching the amount of disk space that is used and which users are filling it up

❋ Converting, extracting, and editing fonts (as well as other bitmap images)

These programs are contained on the accompanying CD-ROM disk.

Monitoring the System Load

A number of free X utilities help you monitor system data on both local hosts and hosts across a network. This last feature is very important, as it allows you to detect the beginning of a problem situation before it gets too severe.

Most of these programs operate on the same principle. Each gathers period statistics on some measure of system load, the percent of CPU time used, the number of active processes, or the number of swaps to disk. Each then presents this data in some graphical way, which should make it easier for you to determine whether things are all OK or whether one machine is experiencing problems.

All of this information must be accessible from the UNIX kernel or networking system. Because of this, you may need **root** user access to install some of these programs.

We've found that one of the main problems with X load-monitoring utilities is the lack of standards for accessing this information from the UNIX kernel. Therefore, any load-monitoring program will only support a small number of operating systems, with most supporting SunOS 4.1.*x*, an operating system where accessing the load data is relatively easy. Unfortunately, few of these tools have been ported to many operating systems other than SunOS 4.1.*x*, including Sun's Solaris.

In addition, there's also a number of commercial system-monitoring packages if your needs exceed what these free programs offer.

Using *Xnetload* to Monitor Multiple Machines on a Network

The *xnetload* program uses the remote who daemon, *rwhod*, to monitor a number of machines over the network, displaying all the values in a window on your display. To generate this display, run *xnetload* and pass it the names of the hosts to monitor:

```
xnetload hostname1 hostname2...
```

To monitor two machines, *kevin* and *eric*, you'd use the following *xnetload* command:

```
xnetload kevin eric
```

TROUBLE-SHOOTING

A common error with *xnetload* is:

```
xload: cannot get name list from /hp-ux
```

This means that *xnetload* couldn't read the system data from the UNIX kernel, in this case the Hewlett-Packard HP-UX kernel, /hp-ux. You might also see a similar message regarding access to /dev/kmem.

Compiling Xnetload

We compiled *xnetload* using the *xmkmf* script introduced in the last chapter to generate a **Makefile**, and then we ran *make* to compile all the source code. In fact, we were up and running with the following commands:

```
xmkmf
make
cp XNetload.ad ~/XNetload
xnetload eric
```

In this case, *eric* is a hostname for a machine on our network.

XSysStats

As with most load-monitoring tools, *XSysStats* can display results from multiple machines as well as display different values describing the system load, using color to separate the different graphs. *XSysStats* uses the *rstat* mechanism to gather statistics on machines on your network.

To run *XSysStats*, enter the following command:

```
xsysstats -type type
```

The *type* of data to display is listed in Table 19.1.

Table 19.1 Type of data you can display with XSysStats.

Type Value	Meaning
collisions	Number of Ethernet packet collisions
context	Number of context switches per second
cpu	Percentage of CPU time used
disk	Number of disk transfers per second
errors	Number of Ethernet errors
interrupts	Average number of device interrupts, per second
load1	Average number of jobs for the last 1 minute
load5	Average number of jobs for the last 5 miutes
load15	Average number of jobs for the last 15 minutes
packets	Number of Ethernet packets per second
page	Number of page-ins
swap	Number of swap-ins

To display multiple graphics, you can also use multiple *-type* parameters:

```
xsysstats -type cpu \
  -type disk -type swap &
```

This displays the percentage of CPU time, the number of disk transfers per second, and the number of swap-ins. The data displayed from this command is shown in Figure 19.1.

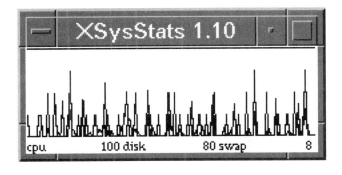

Figure 19.1   Collecting system data with *XSysStats*.

With *xsysstats*, the order of the command-line parameters is important. The *-type* command-line parameters must come before other parameters.

N O T E

After the *-type* command-line parameters, you can choose the hostname to monitor with the *-host* command-line parameter. For example, to monitor the percent of CPU time used on Kevin's machine, you'd use the following command:

```
xsysstats -type cpu -host kevin &
```

Reading the Meter with *Xmeter*

Another load-monitoring utility is *xmeter*. Like *XSysStats*, *xmeter* also uses the *rstat* method to gather statistics on the system load. To launch *xmeter*, use the following:

```
xmeter hostname1 hostname2...
```

You must list each hostname to monitor. To monitor the machines *eric* and *kevin*, use the following:

```
xmeter eric kevin
```

Xmeter presents its data using the same StripChart as used by *xload*, as shown in Figure 19.2.

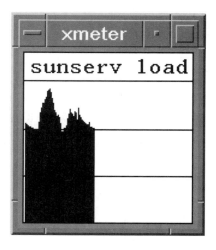

Figure 19.2 *Xmeter* **in action.**

Once you get *xmeter* running, you can switch the type of data gathered for any given host by moving the mouse into the label for the given host and clicking any mouse button.

One neat feature of *xmeter* is the *-fp* command-line parameter. With this parameter, you can specify a program to execute when a monitored host goes down. You can take advantage of this feature to run a program that will alert you to the situation and maybe even take corrective action. The syntax for this option is as follows:

```
xmeter -fp program
```

In the above command, *program* is the name of the program to run when one of the monitored hosts goes down. Of course, there's no guarantee that *xmeter* will actually detect a host going down or that *xmeter* will really launch the program you specify. You certainly don't want to depend on this in safety-critical situations.

Xmeter also offers to launch a program when a given host goes into a warning state.

Other Monitoring Programs

Other system-load-monitoring programs include *xcpustate* and *xtacho*, which presents a neat-looking tachometer display for the system load.

What to Do if None of These Tools Compile or Run

If you're not running SunOS 4.1.*x*, there's a very real possibility that none of these tools will compile or run. We even had troubles on later Sun operating systems, such as Solaris 2.3. In this case, there's not a lot you can do. We've found that most UNIX systems do have a working version of *xload*. With *xload*, you can then login to remote machines and display the data on your local workstation.

This solution isn't nearly as elegant as running one X program to gather statistics from a number of systems, but it will give you some information on networked systems. If you're in this situation, look in Chapter 6 for more on *xload*.

N O T E

On Sun systems, you can also run the *perfmeter* program, which many users prefer to *xload*.

Watching Disk Space Usage

It seems that one of the tasks that always bedevils system administrators is maintaining enough free space on disk. If only those users would stop filling the disks with useless files! We can't help with that, especially since we're recommending a number of very large X programs designed to fill your disk in and of themselves. There are a number of X tools that can help you track disk usage and quickly zoom in on problem areas.

Displaying Data on the Amount of Disk Space Used

Xdu is a graphical front end to the standard UNIX *du* (disk used) utility. To run *xdu*, you pipe the output of *du* into the *xdu* program. For example, the following command generates the disk space used for an entire system and then pipes this output to *xdu*:

```
du / | xdu &
```

After a while (a long while on a systems with large disks), you'll see the *xdu* window appear, as shown in Figure 19.3.

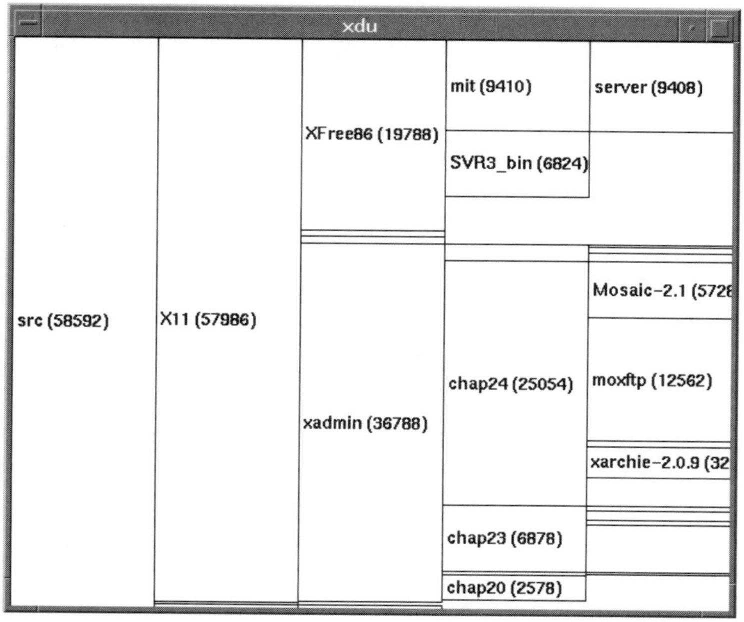

Figure 19.3   Displaying disk space with *xdu*.

Within *xdu*, you can then use the leftmost mouse button to zero in on an area. For example, to zoom in on the **XFree86** directory, click the mouse in the proper box, as shown in Figure 19.4.

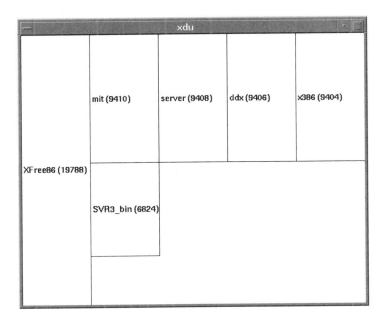

Figure 19.4   Zooming in with *xdu*.

To quit *xdu*, click the rightmost mouse button over the window.

Rocketing into Disk Space with *Spacetool*

Spacetool displays the amount of free space on your disks with a graphical interface, as shown in Figure 19.5.

To compile *spacetool*, you'll need the XView toolkit. *Spacetool* is also very Sun system-specific.

When the disk fills up more than a certain amount (which you can specify), *spacetool* alerts you with changed colors and even by playing an optional audio file. You normally launch *spacetool* without any command-line parameters.

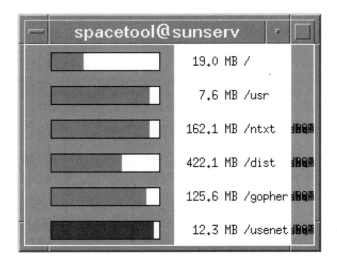

Figure 19.5 *Spacetool*: **where no disk has gone before.**

File and Disk-Browsing Utilities

As UNIX systems become more and more user friendly, most vendors now ship some sort of file and directory-browsing tool. These programs, while not standard across most versions of UNIX, can at least help you get a handle on what is taking up space in the file systems you need to manage.

For example, you can run the COSE common desktop file manager to browse through the directories on disk, as shown in Figure 19.6.

You can also use the Solaris *filemgr* program, as shown in Figure 19.7.

Among the freely available X programs, you can try *xmfm*, a Motif-based file manager, and *xdtm*, a program that tries to put a friendly front end on the UNIX shell and includes disk-browsing capability.

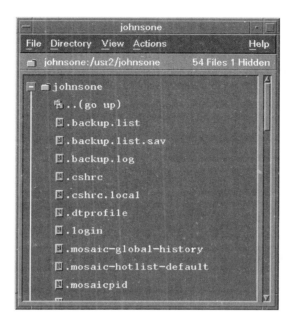

Figure 19.6   The COSE CDE file manager.

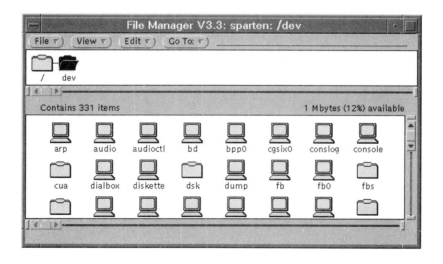

Figure 19.7   The Solaris *filemgr* program.

Bitmap Font Tools

In most cases, you won't need to mess much with system fonts or with creating your own fonts. X comes with literally hundreds of fonts, and this is enough to please even the most picky users. Sometimes, though, you need to mess with fonts, especially to extract a system-specific SNF-formatted font file on one machine and use it on another. One handy set of programs for working with X fonts is the *bdftools* package, which contains three programs for working with X Window fonts: *bdftops* converts a BDF font file into a bitmapped PostScript font; *bintobdf* converts a raw bitmap into a BDF font; and *snftobdf* converts an old-style SNF format font into a BDF font.

Extracting SNF Fonts

Of the programs in the *bdftools* package, *snftobdf* is the most useful if you are running an older version of X, as Release 5 and higher X servers use PCF-formatted fonts rather than the older SNF format. If you have a few of these old SNF fonts around and need to convert them for other X systems, *snftobdf* is the tool for you.

The basic syntax is simple:

```
snftobdf fontfile.snf > fontfile.bdf
```

In the above command, *fontfile.snf* is the name of the SNF-formatted font file, and *fontfile.bdf* is the name of the BDF-formatted file.

Converting Fonts to PostScript

You can use *bdftops* to convert a BDF-formatted font file into a bitmapped PostScript font. Again, the syntax is simple:

```
bdftops fontfile.bdf > fontfile.ps
```

In this case, *fontfile.bdf* is the input BDF-formatted font, and *fontfile.ps* is the output PostScript font.

NOTE *Bdftops* only works with single-byte character fonts. It does not work with double-byte fonts used for Asian languages like Chinese or Japanese.

Extracting Raw Bitmaps into Fonts

The *bintobdf* utility converts a raw bitmap font into a BDF-formatted font. Of course, the documentation doesn't describe what raw bitmap really means, but the program seems designed to extract double-byte Asian fonts, such as GB 2312-1980 (Chinese) or JIS X0208 (Japanese) fonts.

One limitation with *bintobdf*: It assumes that each character in the font is square. This limitation is hard-coded into the program.

Editing Fonts

You learned about a free font editor, *xfed*, in Chapter 7. You can use that program to edit fonts, or you can use one of a number of other bitmap and font-editing programs. *Xfedor* is one such program.

Xfedor is a bitmap editor that allows you to create BDF font files, XBM (X bitmap), XPM (X Pixmap, although it only supports the older XPM-1 files), and mouse cursors. To edit a BDF-formatted font file, use the *-f* command-line parameter, shown as follows:

```
xfedor -f fontfile.bdf
```

The *xfedor* font-editing interface is shown in Figure 19.8.

Some of the more useful command-line parameters supported by *xfedor* are listed in Table 19.2.

Table 19.2   *Xfedor* command-line parameters.

Parameter	Use
-b *bitmapfile*	Edits XBM bitmap file *bitmapfile*
-f *fontfile*	Edits font file *fontfile*

continued

Parameter	Use
-p *pixmapfile*	Edits XPM pixmap file *pixmapfile*
-m *bitmap mask*	Edits two X bitmap files to make a mouse cursor, the cursor *bitmap* and *mask*

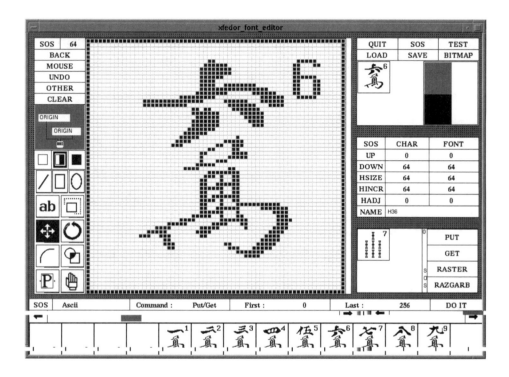

Figure 19.8   Editing a font with *xfedor*.

The original documentation for *xfedor*, contained in the file **xfedor.man**, is in French. For those not literate in French, the English manual file is named **xfedor_a.man**.

Obtaining These Tools

We've included all of the freely available tools on the accompanying CD-ROM; for obvious reasons, we can't supply the commercial software.

However, if your system lacks a CD-ROM drive, you can obtain any of these tools wherever you can get X contributed program sources. Except for *xload*, none of these programs are part of the core X release. Instead, they're all part of the contributed code, which are normally stored under a different directory on systems that provide X applications via anonymous FTP. See Chapter 17 for more on where to look for these programs.

Summary

This chapter covers a slew of convenient system-administration tools, including several graphical tools for monitoring system loads.

In the next chapter, you will examine tools that help you create graphical front ends for text-based applications.

Creating Graphical Front Ends for Text-Based Applications

Topics covered in this chapter include:

* Using Tcl to create interfaces
* Using *wish*
* Tk examples
* Using *xgen*
* Developing *xgen* applications
* Using the COSE windowing Korn shell
* Using Wcl
* Using *Mri*

Front Ends

X is still unfortunately very much a programmer's windowing system. X requires users to learn far too much, especially about esoteric resources and programming toolkits. Even so, there are a number of tools administrators can use to present more of a friendly front end to UNIX applications and hide many of the cryptic details of X. In fact, users are demanding more and more of this.

To help you out, we've found four very useful tools for creating front ends to text-based applications and prototyping new programs. These include:

❋ Tcl (a scripting tool) and the Tk interface toolkit

❋ *xgen*, for making text-based front ends

❋ *dtksh*, the windowing Korn shell with the COSE common desktop

❋ *Wcl*, for those who are X resource-file literate

Tickling Applications

Tcl (Tool Command Language, pronounced "tickle") provides a powerful scripting language used to write programs (scripts) that run independently or embedded in C programs.

Many applications, such as most spreadsheets, offer a built-in customization language, typically called a macro language. Tcl can be viewed as a generic macro language that programmers can embed into a number of applications.

In addition to embedding the Tcl interpreter into your code, you can also use the Tcl shell, called *wish* (for windowed shell—we get to the windowing part shortly). In *wish*, you can enter Tcl commands directly, or you can use *wish* to run your Tcl shell scripts, using a syntax recognized by most UNIX shells. Therefore, you can skip the programming side and use Tcl as a rich, powerful scripting language in its own right. This scripting language also sports a very useful means for scripting X applications.

Both Tcl and UNIX shells use the hash character, #, as a comment marker. If you place the following comment at the beginning of your Tcl script, your UNIX shell will use *wish* to execute the Tcl script:

```
#!/local/bin/wish -f
```

You'll need to place your *wish* path in the comments. We use **/local/bin**, but you may not. In addition, your shells may not support the syntax of placing the actual shell name in the first line's comment, as we discovered to our chagrin on a few systems.

Working with Tcl

Running *wish* is a lot like running a LISP interpreter (only you don't need nearly as many parentheses). You enter commands like the following:

```
expr 555+10
```

and get back the printed results:

```
565
```

The *expr* command calculates the expression you pass to it. You're not allowed to use spaces in the expression.

Much like *ksh* or *csh* shell scripts, you can also set a value into a variable with the *set* command:

```
set var 42
```

Remember that you're working with scripts, so everything is text. Tcl scripts look much like other scripting languages, so you should feel right at home if you've already used *csh*, *sh*, *ksh*, or *perl* scripts. For example, Tcl uses the dollar sign, $, to mean the value of. So, for example, *$var* returns the value of the variable named *var*, while the text string *var* is simply the letters *v-a-r*.

As a scripting language, we find Tcl better than *csh* or *sh*. You will find that Tcl scripts are by and large quite simple, especially when you start adding widgets to the scripts.

Tk: Adding Widgets to Tcl

X Window administrators use Tcl for the Tk extension. Tk is a toolkit for Tcl scripts that adds X Window widgets to the base language.

Tk provides a set of widgets that looks much like those provided by the Motif toolkit. The Tk widgets, though, are accessible from simple Tcl scripting commands. All of this is implemented without the Motif toolkit.

The easiest way to start with Tcl and Tk is to try a few examples.

Tk Examples

Just about the simplest widget you can create is a simple pushbutton widget. The following two-line Tk script creates a pushbutton named **.button** (the leading period is important) and sets the widget's text to display "Hello from Eric & Kevin", as shown in Figure 20.1.

```
button .button -text "Hello from Eric & Kevin"
pack .button
```

Figure 20.1   A sample Tcl script.

The *pack* command sizes the parent window to hold the pushbutton widget and also makes the whole thing visible. This may seem strange, but it's just something you have to remember to do. If you forget, chances are you won't see anything at all on the screen. You can enter the above two commands into the *wish* shell to see the pushbutton. You'll find that working with *wish* is the simplest method for prototyping your Tcl scripts.

In the previous example, we created a widget named **.button**. In a confusing piece of syntax, the top-level widget is named **.** (that's right, a simple period). Widgets that are direct children of the top-level widget are then named with the starting dot, much like UNIX files with an absolute path from the root directory (/).

If you create a pushbutton widget named **button** and this widget is a child of the top-level widget, the full widget name will be **.button**. These full names are important to help separate widgets and provide a hierarchy to the naming, much like disk directories provide a hierarchy for organizing files.

Once you have a widget's name, you can use the Tcl *configure* command to change some attributes of the widget. For example, the following command makes the pushbutton execute the "destroy ." command when activated (that is, when the user pushes the pushbutton):

```
.button configure -command "destroy ."
```

The *-command* parameter specifies that we're configuring the widget's command. The "destroy ." command destroys the widget named **.**; that is, the top-level widget. By destroying the top-level widget, all child widgets (like **.button**) get destroyed as well.

You can also use configure to change a widget's colors, as shown in the following commands:

```
.button configure -foreground black
.button configure -background yellow
.button configure -activebackground maroon
```

If you try this, you'll immediately be repulsed by these colors. When first testing a new tool, we always use garish colors, so that it will be immediately obvious whether or not our commands work.

You can also change aspects of how the Tcl script interacts with the window manager. For example, the following command changes the title of the window:

```
wm title . "Eric and Kevin's Tk Test"
```

Putting this all together, we have the following short Tcl script:

```
#!/local/bin/wish -f
# Tcl/Tk  hello world script.
#
button .button -text "Hello from Eric & Kevin"
.button configure -command "destroy ."
```

```
.button configure -foreground black
.button configure -background yellow
.button configure -activebackground maroon
wm title . "Eric & Kevin's Tk Test"
pack .button
```

When you run this script with *wish*, you'll see the window shown in Figure 20.2.

Figure 20.2   A more extensive Tcl sample.

You can run this script using *wish* on the command line, or, if your current shell supports it, as a separate script. That is, you can run the script with the following command:

```
wish -f filename
```

where *filename* is the name of the script file. If you set the execute permission and your shell supports the initial comment we just described, you can use the filename alone:

```
filename
```

Sending Messages Between Applications

One of the most powerful features Tk provides is the *send* command. *Send* allows any Tk application to send messages (in the form of Tcl commands) to any other application. This provides a handy and transparent means for interprocess communication, which is especially useful for developing client–server applications. For example, you can change the text displayed in our sample "Hello World" application with the following command:

```
send hello {.button configure -text "New Text"}
```

Unfortunately, the Tcl *send* command, as with most X operations, provides a gaping security hole. Any user with access to your X display can cause a Tk program to execute any number of nasty commands—all with your user ID and authorization. Even though this security problem is documented, use the *send* command with care. This obviously is an even bigger security hole if you're running a Tcl script while logged in as the **root** user. In fact, in our version of *wish*, we received an error message when trying to use the *send* command without using the *xauth* security package.

Using Tcl and Tk

Using Tcl is more of a scripting process than programming. Tcl and Tk are most useful for system administrators who want to write small graphical applications, such as providing front-end interfaces to commonly used text-based administrative tools.

In addition to scripting, programmers can also interface to Tcl from C, C++, Ada, and *wish*. Tcl and Tk run on most versions of UNIX. There's also work on porting Tcl to DOS, Macintosh, and VMS.

For More Information on Tcl

Tcl comes with some documentation. In addition, John Ousterhout wrote a book on Tcl and Tk scripting, *An Introduction To Tcl and Tk* (see Appendix A for additional information). For day-to-day problems and answers, you can also look in the Usenet newsgroup *comp.lang.tcl*, where you'll find a boatload of discussion on Tcl.

Using *Xgen* to Generate Program Front Ends

Where Tcl provides a whole scripting language, *xgen* allows you to create a text file that describes an interface. This interface can execute UNIX commands to fill in data and interact with the user. Using this capability, you can create graphical applications that provide a front end to traditional UNIX programs like *tar* or *∂∂*. You can use these *xgen*-generated front ends as prototypes or even make use of them in production environments. *Xgen* is also great for making demo programs that provide an overview of a new subject. For example, one of the demo scripts that comes with *xgen* introduces the program itself.

Basically, *xgen* allows you to write up a script that describes the interface for a program. This script includes all the top-level windows, pulldown menus, and interface widgets. You can set resources — much like X resources — to change the fonts, colors, and other things that X resources traditionally allow. In addition, you can use *xgen* resources to control what happens when the user interacts with the program. When the user clicks the mouse over a pushbutton, for example, you can tell *xgen* to execute a UNIX program in the foreground or background.

It takes a while, though, to get used to the terminology used by *xgen*. *Xgen* uses the term *environment* to describe what most of us would call a *program*. The term environment refers to the fact that *xgen* variables are simply UNIX environment variables.

Within an environment, you can then create shells, which are top-level windows. There are two types of *xgen* shell widgets: menu and commandboard. To get a feel for these, you'll need to try each out.

Inside a shell, you can create interface objects, or widgets, of which *xgen* supports 11 types, listed in Table 20.1.

Table 20.1 *Xgen* widget types.

Xgen Widget	Use
button	User clicks mouse button to perform action
label	Presents static text message
list	Scrolled list of choices for the user
message	Multiline label
multiline	Multiline scrolled text editing
pulldown	Pulldown menu
separator	Three-dimension line to separate widgets
slider	Analog slider, like a scrollbar

continued

Xgen Widget	Use
table	Spreadsheet-like text entry
textentry	Single-line text entry
toggle	On–off switch

One of the most interesting widgets supported by *xgen* is the table widget. (This is really the Xbae Matrix widget for Motif applications from Bellcore.) The table widget acts as a primitive spreadsheet, showing text-entry cells in rows and columns. You can edit each cell inline which is much nicer than some commercial spreadsheet programs that require you to edit only in a special editing area at the top of the spreadsheet. You can set up a scrollbar to scroll the whole table and you can label the rows and columns.

With *xgen*, you must build up widgets in a top–down fashion — create the shell widget before you create a toggle button inside the shell, for example.

Learning *Xgen*

The best way to learn the *xgen* scripting language is to try a few small scripts. The process is really quite simple, and you should be up to speed with most of *xgen* in under a half-hour. Just about the smallest *xgen* script follows:

```
environment xgen_test
{
  menu menu_name
  (
      button Exit
        exit:0
      ;
  )
}
```

To run this script, you pass the filename to the *xgen* program, as in the following:

```
xgen filename
```

When you run this script with *xgen*, you'll see a window like the one shown in Figure 20.3.

Figure 20.3   A sample *xgen* interface.

This script sets up an environment (program) named *xgen_test*. *Xgen* environments use curly braces, { and }, as delimiters, much like C programs. The menu command creates a shell widget. You can use a menu shell or a commandboard shell. Here we use a menu shell named *menu_name*, though we could have replaced the shell type of *menu* with *commandboard*, if we wanted to.

N O T E   Shells in *xgen* are delimited by parenthesis, (and), which is very confusing, especially since it's hard to tell (and) from { and } on a printed page. The use of so many different characters as delimiters is one of the odd quirks associated with *xgen*.

In the previous example, we create one child widget, a **button**, inside the **menu**. The button's name is **Exit**, which is also the text it will display.

The exit:0 resource tells *xgen* that when the button is pressed, the program should exit with a status of 0 (meaning no errors occurred).

You can set a number of resources for each widget. The *xgen* documentation describes the available resources and their possible values. The semicolon, yet another delimiter, ends the button definition.

You can place comments into *xgen* scripts. Just like C programs, delimit comments with /* and */.

To pull this all together, the basic syntax for *xgen* scripts follows this pattern:

```
set global resources

environment environment_name
   set environment resources
{
 menu|commandboard shell_name
   shell resources
```

```
(
  primitive object object_name
    set object resources
  ;
  more primitive objects...
)
}

environment environment_name ...
  /* Can have more environments... */
```

Developing *Xgen* Applications

To flesh out this syntax description, we'll use *xgen* to create a front end to the text-based RCS program. RCS (Revision Control System) maintains different versions of the same file, so you can restore previous versions, if needed. RCS works very well for software developers.

Our very primitive front end for RCS uses the following *xgen* script:

```
/* Global resources. */
font: "*adobe*helv*r*norm*12*"
foreground: black
background: lightgray

environment rcstool
    initialshells:main
{

  commandboard main
    titlestring:"RCS Tool"
    dx:40.0
    y:100
    pane:true
    help:"There is no help."
  (

    label RCS
      titlestring:"RCS Directories"
      ;

    list RCSDirList
      visibleitems:10
      updatefrom: "!ls -1 /usr/local/X11R5"
      ;

    label RCSFiles
      titlestring:"Files in RCS Directory"
```

```
         ;
   list RCSFileList
      listtype:multiple
      visibleitems:10
      updatefrom: "!ls -1 xclock/RCS"
         ;

   pulldown File
      (
      button CheckIn
         titlestring:"Check In"
         setRCSDIR: "[RCSDirList]"
         setRCSFILE:"[RCSFileList]"
         runforeground:"echo $RCSDIR $RCSFILE > /dev/tty"
            ;
      button CheckOut
         titlestring:"Check Out"
            ;
      separator sep
         separatortype:shadowetchedin
            ;
      button Exit
         titlestring:"Exit"
         exit:0
            ;
      )
         ;
   )
}
```

When you run this script, you'll see an interface much like the one shown in Figure 20.4.

In the next few sections, you will examine this script in depth.

At the very beginning of the script, you can set global resources, such as *foreground:black,background:lightgray*, and *font:"*adobe*helv*r*norm*12*"*. These resources apply to all the widgets in the entire script. After the global resources, you can define one or more environments.

Environments form the basic unit of *xgen* scripts. In each *xgen* script, you can define a number of environments. Each environment then holds a number of shell widgets (menu or commandboard). Each shell, in turn, holds a number of primitive objects, such as the list, button, or toggle. You can also add optional environment resources that apply to all the shells within an environment. If you have multiple shells in the environment, then you need to set the *initialshells* resource to specify which shell widget should appear when *xgen* starts up. See the previous script for an example of the *initialshells* resource, where we set the initial shell to be the shell named *main*.

Figure 20.4   A simple *xgen* front end to RCS.

After the environment header comes the shell definitions. You can place multiple shells within each environment. Each shell definition starts with one of two keywords: commandboard or menu. The keyword determines the type of shell.

Both shells offer severely limited layouts. Even so, these limits are acceptable for most front ends to command-line programs. While limited, a large part of the convenience of *xgen* comes from its simplicity.

For each shell, you can set shell resources that apply to an individual shell. For example, look in the previous script under the commandboard main command for a set of shell resources. The *titlestring* resource sets the shell window's title, which appears in the window manager's titlebar. The *∂x:40.0* resource specifies that the shell's X coordinate should be 40 percent of the total screen size. The *y* resource sets the Y coordinate directly. The *pane* resource turns on the commandboard's paned layout. The *help* resource sets the shell's help message, which also creates a help pushbutton on the menubar.

Inside the shell definition, you can set up a number of primitive objects, such as those listed in Table 20.1. With each object, you can set a number of resources. Looking at the previous script again, we see a definition for a scrolled-list object with the list *RCSDirList* command. We set the list to show 10 items at a time with the *visibleitems:10* resource and then use the *updatefrom* resource to fill in the list with the result of a UNIX command. This resource executes a given program (*ls* in our example) and takes the output from the program to fill in the list. Each line of the output goes to a single list item. Our example takes the contents of the **/usr/local/X11R5** directory on our machine and makes a list item from each file in that directory. Like before, the primitive object's definition ends with a semicolon.

One of the most complex objects you can create with *xgen* is a pulldown menu. A pulldown menu requires a number of menu choices, which we place between the opening and closing parentheses that start after the *pulldown File* command.

Each item within a pulldown menu is a primitive object, such as a button or separator. Since the previous script example is a simple prototype to RCS, we provide a button to check in files and one to check them out. The *titlestring:"Check In"* resource sets the text to display in the button named **CheckIn**. We used the *titlestring* resource because it's not a good idea to have spaces in a Motif widget's name.

The **CheckIn** button uses one of the neat features of *xgen*. You can set UNIX environment variables directly from *xgen* scripts. The *setRCSDIR* resource sets the UNIX environment variable RCSDIR (the variable name is everything after *set*). In our example, the RCSDIR environment variable is set to the selected item in the scrolled list named *RCSDirList*. The command to set the RCSDIR environment variable is only executed when the **CheckIn** menu choice gets activated.

While the *RCSDirList* list only allowed a single selection, the *RCSFileList* allows multiple items to be selected at the same time. This capability is set up with the *listtype:multiple* resource. Now, back to the **CheckIn** button. When the user activates the **CheckIn** menu choice, the contents of the *RCSFileList* scrolled list are set into the RCSFILE UNIX environment variable. If there are multiple values selected, then the environment variable gets a comma-delimited set of the selected entries from the scrolled list. Watch out, though, because if you select too many items in the list, you can exceed the available environment variable space, as we discovered right away.

The *runforeground* resource runs a UNIX program or shell script in the foreground as a child process. Our sample *runforeground* command just calls *echo* to print the selected data to the terminal. Your *xgen* scripts, though, can call any programs you want. Running the commands in the foreground means that *xgen* blocks other tasks, awaiting completion of the task. If you don't want *xgen* to block, you can use the *runbackground* command instead of *runforeground*.

Due to a quirk in *xgen*, though, the list itself cannot activate any code. Because of that quirk, we had to set up a pushbutton or other widget to extract the selected items from the list and execute a UNIX program. For this, we set up the **CheckIn** menu choice just described. This quirk reflects one of the biggest limitations in *xgen*: unlike Tcl, there's no logic in *xgen* scripts for conditional branching, loops, or any form of arithmetic. *Xgen* can really only launch UNIX programs or shell scripts. It's then up to the program to take care of anything you need that exceeds *xgen*'s capabilities. Even so, you can do a lot with *xgen*, especially for prototyping.

This *xgen* script should give you a good idea of what sort of prototypes you can build with *xgen*. The *xgen* sources come with a set of test and example scripts that provide good places to begin.

For More Information on *Xgen*

Xgen comes with an online manual file as well as a helpful PostScript paper describing the language. This paper also provides a short tutorial. There are over 20 example files that provide the best resource for learning the *xgen* scripting language.

Using the COSE Windowing Korn Shell

For those who are most familiar with the Korn shell, the COSE common desktop comes with *∂tksh*, a windowing version of *ksh-93*.

In *∂tksh*, Korn shell scripts still work. This is the best part to *∂tksh*, as the syntax should be familiar. In addition, *∂tksh* provides hundreds of windowing commands to allow you to create interfaces for your shell scripts.

But, for better and worse, the *∂tksh* commands are basically the same as the set of X Toolkit functions available for Motif programmers. On the one hand, this means you have a powerful toolkit with a great deal of flexibility. On the other hand, it means you'll need to become a Motif programmer to really make use of *∂tksh*.

We're not trying to turn you into a programmer. To provide a flavor of what *∂tksh* offers, the following script will place two pushbutton widgets inside a Motif row–column widget:

```
button_cb()
{
    echo "button_cb invoked"
}

XtInitialize TOPLEVEL dtkshtest1 \
  DtKshTest1 "$@"

XtCreateManagedWidget ROW row \
  rowColumn $TOPLEVEL \
  foreground:black \
  background:white \
  orientation:HORIZONTAL \
  numColumns:2 \
  packing:PACK_COLUMN

XtCreateManagedWidget PB1 pb \
  pushButton $ROW \
  foreground:black \
  background:white \
  labelString:"Kevin" \
  activateCallback:button_cb

XtCreateManagedWidget PB2 pb2 \
  pushButton $ROW \
  foreground:black \
  background:white \
  labelString:"Eric" \
  activateCallback:button_cb

XtRealizeWidget $TOPLEVEL

XtMainLoop
```

When *∂tksh* executes this script, you'll see the window shown in Figure 20.5.

Figure 20.5   A *dtksh* example.

The Widget Creation Library

Although aimed more at programmers than administrators, the Widget Creation Library, or Wcl, provides a number of useful features, including the ability to prototype a program entirely within X resource files.

Wcl takes advantage of X's powerful concept of resource files. While we find resource files a mixed bag, you can use resources to control much of the look and feel of an application. With resources, you can set fonts, colors, and sizes for most widgets.

However, the main thing you cannot do with resource files is specify the widgets themselves. And that's where Wcl comes in. Wcl extends traditional X resource files not only to specify customizations (resources) on widgets, but the widgets themselves, too, along with widget callbacks. This seems very odd at first, but in a matter of a few short minutes, you'll be creating Motif prototypes (or Athena or OLIT prototypes, since Wcl also supports the free Athena widget set and OLIT).

For your Motif prototypes, Wcl includes a program called *Mri* for Motif resource interpreter. (There's also an *Ari* and an *Ori*.) *Mri* is the prototype engine, which you can use with Wcl resource files.

To show the power of Wcl, we'll prototype a very simple application. From this short example, you should get the basic concepts of Wcl. In the example, though, we make heavy use of X resources. If you don't feel comfortable with this, you may want to review the material in Chapter 8.

Learning Wcl by Example

In the following example, we create an application with a class of "Mri" (the resource class name of the *Mri* application). This application, to keep it simple, will create a pushbutton widget that, when pressed, quits the application. Here's the resource file for our small application.

```
Mri.wcChildren: exit
*exit.wcClass:  xmPushButtonWidgetClass

*exit.activateCallback: WcExitCB
```

This file includes a number of new Wcl-defined resources, such as *wcChildren*. The *wcChildren* resource lists the widgets (by name) that are the children of a particular parent widget. The top-level parent in this case is the name of the *Mri* engine. The *wcClass* resource specifies the class for the given widget, in this case a Motif pushbutton. Here's where some programming experience with Motif helps. Motif programmers should already be aware of the *activateCallback* resource. For the rest of us, this is what gets executed when the user clicks the mouse over the widget. Normally, though, this resource is used with a callback function in a C program. With traditional Motif applications, we cannot specify function pointers in the resource file. This stands the same for Wcl, since resource files are still text. But, with Wcl, we can give function names. In this case, the *WcExitCB* function is built in with the Wcl C programming library, and it, naturally enough, exits the application.

Wcl has a few more built-in callback functions, including *WcSetValueCB*, *WcManageCB*, *WcUnmanageCB*, *WcCreatePopupsCB*, and *WcSystemCB* (which calls the UNIX *system* function).

To make all this magic happen, we need to run *Mri* and ensure that our resource file gets loaded.

Running *Mri*

When you run a Wcl program, you need to tell it about your Wcl resource file. You do this the same as with any X resource file. You can set up an application defaults file in **/usr/lib/X11/app-defaults**, although when you're prototyping this normally isn't a good idea. You can also place a resource file, **Mri** in our case, in your home directory, or you can use the XENVIRONMENT environment variable. XENVIRONMENT names a resource file, so before running the previous program, you can set XENVIRONMENT to the name of the resource file you're using for prototyping. If the file name is **foo**, then you'd use the following commands in the C shell:

```
setenv XENVIRONMENT foo
Mri
```

Where to Get These Programs

The accompanying CD-ROM contains the programs detailed in this chapter. However, if you don't have access to a CD-ROM drive and want to grab code from the Internet, you can do so from *ftp.uu.net* in the **languages/tcl** directory or from *ftp.x.org* in the **/contrib** directory. The latest versions as we write this are Tcl 7.3 and Tk 3.6.

The latest version of *xgen* was developed by Kurt Buehler of the U.S. Army Construction Engineering Research Laboratories (USA-CERL). To find *xgen*, check any archive of contributed X sources, such as the **contrib** directory on *ftp.x.org*.

The best place to get Wcl is on an X contributed software tape, if you can't use the accompanying CD-ROM. The X Consortium, as well as many other groups, sells X11 source tapes.

Summary

In this chapter, you examined several tools that place graphical front ends on top of text-based applications. These tools include Tcl/Tk and *xgen*.

The next chapter covers screen-locking programs for X.

Screen Locking in X

Topics covered in this chapter include:

* How screen-locking programs work
* Obtaining screen-locking programs

Locking the Screen

The basic idea of all X screen-locking programs is the same: when a user steps away from their terminal, a screen locker prevents other users from using the terminal without first authenticating themselves with a password.

Of course, users could just log off the system, but this is a tremendous waste of time—it often takes a few *minutes* for an X environment to start, and who wants to wait that long? Instead, your users can lock their screen for a short while and get everything restored by merely entering their password.

How Screen Lockers Work

Screen-locking programs create a very large window on the screen and tell the window manager to leave this window alone. The screen-locking program then forces that window on top of all other application windows, grabbing all mouse and keyboard events in the process, preventing other applications from accessing the screen. Finally, the screen-locking program puts up some form of login widget, where the user is asked to enter a password.

Other users can type all they want at the terminal, but the keystrokes won't do any good, since the screen-locking program discards all keystrokes, except those entered in the password window.

That's the basic idea, anyway. Some screen savers, such as *xsecure*, tend to get fancy. *Xsecure* uses the *xfishtank* program to present a screen full of fish as the locked-screen backdrop. Others, such as *xlock*, come with all sorts of modes for pretty pictures, including fractals, spinning lines, Sun Microsystems logos, swarms of bees following a wasp, spinning rotors, fireworks, and wiggly worms.

Many X environments come with a screen-locking program built in. For example, both the COSE common desktop and Hewlett-Packard's VUE interfaces come with a screen-lock program you can access from the interface's front panel (indicated by a lock icon). If this is the case in your system, then you don't need to track down any freely available screen-locking programs.

For those lacking such an environment, you'll need to do with one of three free screen-locking programs contained on the accompanying CD-ROM: *xsecure*, *xlock*, and *xnlock*. However, be warned that these programs pose a few challenges, which we unfortunately discovered the hard way. Quite honestly, we've had troubles compiling screen-locking programs on a variety of systems. If you think about it, this makes sense, as all of these programs require you to enter a password, and the system-call routines to verify a password vary between systems.

Obtaining Screen-Locking Programs

We've included *xsecure*, *xlock*, and *xnlock* on the accompanying CD-ROM. However, if your system lacks a CD-ROM drive, you can obtain any of these tools wherever you can get X contributed program sources. To find *xsecure*, *xlock*, *xnlock*, or any number of other screen-locking programs, check any archive of contributed X sources, such as the **contrib** directory on *ftp.x.org*.

Summary

This short chapter covered screen-locking programs.

In the next chapter, you'll learn how to debug applications with *xmon* and *xscope*.

Debugging Applications with *Xmon* and *Xscope*

- - - - - - - - - - - -

Topics covered in this chapter include:

* How to track down odd X errors without source code
* Using *xmon*
* Using *xscope*
* Errors in X
* Decoding error messages
* Filtering error messages
* Obtaining *xmon* and *xscope*

Dealing with Errors

Dealing with X errors can be a frustrating hassle. This is even more so for applications where you don't have the source code and therefore can't try to track down errors in the program logic.

X makes error fixing even harder, in that the nature of X is asynchronous. That is, a program may do something wrong or cause the X server to run out of memory, and only sometime later will the error come to light, since most X applications queue up requests for the X server and then send out large batches. (This cuts down on the network transmission time, which is especially helpful for X terminals.) The X server gets these packets sometime after they were created. At this time, an error may occur, but the application has moved on to other areas in the program's logic. This makes it hard to determine the cause of the problem from the error event.

For example, we once faced an X application that had the ability to knock out an X server. When we tried to report the error, the technical support folks wanted more detailed information—which we found *extremely* hard to acquire, as our X server kept crashing! That was when we discovered two handy tools to help see exactly what in an application is causing an X error: *xscope* and *xmon*. Both act much the same, but *xmon* has a graphical front end, which we find easier to use. Each tool is essentially an X-protocol sniffer. You can watch each X packet as it goes from application to server or server to application.

Xmon and *xscope* are considered pseudoservers. These applications look like X servers, talk like X servers, and quack like X servers, but really all they do is forward on each X packet to the *real* X server after taking note of the packet. As far as an X application is concerned, it's communicating with a real X server, rather than the pseudoserver. The pseudoserver acts as a proxy, forwarding each packet from the application to the real X server and each packet from the real server on to the application.

In and of itself, this doesn't seem very interesting. However, the pseudo X server now has access to each X packet as it gets transmitted. Armed with this knowledge, you can have the pseudoserver try to filter out the information (in the case of *xmon*) to zero in on what is really causing the error.

Both *xscope* and *xmon* print out these X packets as they get forwarded. *Xmon* is essentially the same as *xscope*, but *xmon* provides a graphical front end that filters out unwanted X packets. Because X applications generate thousands of X packets, we advise filtering.

What can you do with this? In most cases, you'll look for X error packets to see what could have caused them. This is a tedious process at best, so avoid it if possible. In some cases, though, a low-level tool like *xmon* or *xscope* is all you really have to track down a problem.

Of course, you really shouldn't ever see these X error messages. X applications should be robust—robust enough to avoid low-level X error messages. Unfortunately, that's not the case. X errors can stop programs dead. Most X programs simply quit when an X error arrives.

That leaves you as system administrator to solve the problem, especially if the problem occurs in a free X application for which you can get no support.

X Errors

X applications send *requests* to the X server. The X server then sends *replies* back. In addition, when an unforeseen event occurs, like the user typing on the keyboard, the X server sends an unannounced packet to the application, called an *event*. When an error occurs, the X server notifies the application through an error event. This is normally what you're looking for with *xmon* and *xscope*.

The X server sends X error events to an application whenever it detects a serious problem. These X errors are reported in terms of X protocol, not in terms of X function calls or application tasks, so it's hard to determine exactly what went wrong, especially if you don't have the source code for the application.

Decoding the Error Message

Programmers can make applications intercept X error events. In this case, usually the programmers came up with a way to handle the events. With many X applications, though, the programmers took the easy way out and let the X toolkit libraries handle the error. Most X toolkits then merely report the error (to standard error) and then exit. In this case, you'll see an error message like the one that follows:

```
X Error of failed request:
 BadDrawable (invalid Pixmap or
    Window parameter)
 Major opcode of failed request:  76 (X_ImageText8)
 Minor opcode of failed request:  0
 Resource id in failed request:  0x0
 Serial number of failed request:  12
 Current serial number in output stream:  13
```

In the previous error message, three pieces of information are important: The X error (*BadDrawable*), the major opcode (*76* or *X_ImageText8*) and the resource ID of the failed request (*0x0*). The serial numbers and minor opcodes don't do you a lot of good.

The *BadDrawable* part tells us that the error involved a bad drawable ID: a bad window or pixmap. Other common errors include *BadName*, meaning usually that the application attempted to load a nonexistent font, *BadMatch*, usually involving attempts to copy data between windows or pixmaps with different depths (such as a monochrome to a 8-bit color window) and *BadAlloc*, the dreaded out-of-memory error. There's not a lot you can do about *BadAlloc* errors, but you can manage most of the rest.

From the opcode, *76* or *X_ImageText8*, we can determine that the error had to do with something called *image text8*. What the heck does this mean? Well, you're just supposed to know this. (Have you figured out yet that X *still* is really a programmer's windowing system?) From our programming experience, we know that *image text* is one way to draw text to a window. The *8* part tells us that it's 8-bit text (probably US ASCII), instead of 16-bit text (Japanese, Chinese, or Korean).

The resource ID of *0x0* (which is really 0, but printed in hexadecimal — C programmers use a leading *0x* to indicate hexadecimal numbers) tells us something very important. In X, any window or pixmap has an ID and the ID must not be 0, as X uses a 0 ID to indicate a bad window or pixmap.

You now know that our error message had to do with an attempt by the application to draw text into a bad window or pixmap. What probably happened was that an error occurred in creating the window or pixmap, but the application didn't check for this error. Instead, it kept the bad window (or pixmap) ID of 0 and tried to draw into it. When drawing into this nonexistent window (or pixmap), the X server generated the error event.

Many error messages aren't this easy to decipher, so you may need to watch the application more closely to see what actually generates the X error. That's where *xscope* and *xmon* come in.

Watching the Errors

Once you've got a good idea of what the error is, you can filter out all the unwanted network packets. As we just described, both *xmon* and *xscope* work alike and make use of a clever trick. You configure *xscope* and *xmon* to sit between the X server and your applications. The X server sits at a known socket ID. *Xscope* and *xmon* connect up to that X server like any normal X application. Then *xscope* monitors the known socket ID for the next X server (or any open slot you care to specify). Applications to be debugged then connect to the *xscope* pseudo X server. *Xscope* prints the X network packets and forwards them to the real X server, so that you actually see your application windows.

NOTE   You don't have to do anything special to your application code—just tell the application to connect up to the *xscope* server. This is very helpful if you don't have the source code for the application.

To start *xscope* on machine *eric*, presenting X server 1 to applications, use:

```
xscope -heric -i1
```

Start your application, say *xterm*, with:

```
xterm -display eric:1
```

That's it. Since *xscope* prints out a huge amount of text, you should be sure to start it from a terminal window, such as that provided by *xterm*, and then don't do anything else in that window, or you'll obscure the *xscope* output. You might also want to redirect the *xscope* output to a file for later viewing. This file will grow large.

Filtering Packets with *Xmon*

Xmon acts mostly the same, except that it allows you to filter X requests, events, errors, and server replies. Since X applications generate storms of network traffic, this greatly enhances *xmon*. The key, of course, is to filter out the unimportant packets, so that the important, error-generating packets aren't swamped in the storm of requests.

Xmon requires a more complex command line than *xscope*. Following our previous example, to have *xmon* connect to the first (and most likely only) X server on machine *eric*, use the following command line:

```
xmonui | xmond -server eric:0 -port 1
```

In the above command, *xmonui* is the user interface program, which you can use to filter out unwanted X events. *Xmond* is the X monitor daemon. The *-port* command-line parameter tells *xmond* to establish itself as the second X server on the machine; that is, *eric:1* in our example.

As with *xscope*, you should start applications you want to debug by telling them to connect to *eric:1*:

```
xterm -display eric:1
```

When you start *xmonui*, you'll see a following window (see Figure 22.1), which allows you to filter out unwanted X packets.

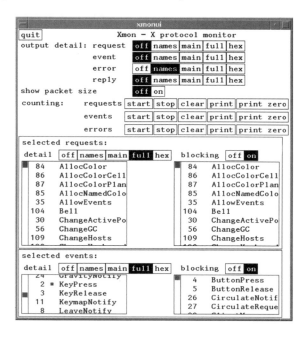

Figure 22.1 The user interface of *xmon*.

You can select the various types of X packets to filter out, which should dramatically cut down on the number of network packets printed out.

Once you print the packets, you should be able to try to track down what the application first does to initiate the X error. Armed with this information, you can either fix the application or call for technical support with enough information to actually track down and fix the problem.

In all the times we've run *xscope* or *xmon*, we've been desperate, since we had no other tools available to help us. There are usually much easier means to track down X errors, if you have the application's source code. If you don't, you may find *xscope* and *xmon*, like we did, to be a tool of last resort.

Obtaining *Xscope* and *Xmon*

We've included *xscope* and *xmon* on the accompanying CD-ROM. However, if your system lacks a CD-ROM drive, you can obtain these tools on an archive site for the *comp.sources.x* newsgroup. (Don't bother looking on *ftp.x.org*; we've never seen either application posted there.)

Summary

In this chapter, you examined the use of *xmon* and *xscope* to debug X applications. These are not exceptionally complicated programs—just *knowing* that they exist puts you ahead of a great many X Window users—and they've worked for us in the past.

In the next chapter, you will learn about various free X programs.

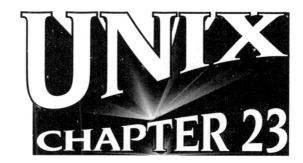

Various Free X Sources

Topics covered in this chapter include:

* Using *xman*
* Using various clock programs
* Using *workman* to play audio CDs

A Lot of Odd and Sods

Now begins our discussion of tools that don't fit into the neat categories as those in Chapters 19, 20, 21, 22, and 24 do. These tools are, by and large, very useful—so useful that we've included them on the accompanying CD-ROM, if they didn't already ship with the standard X release.

Reading Documentation Online

One nice tool that comes with the standard X release is *xman*. This program allows you to read and browse through the traditional UNIX online manual pages—the same data that the *man* program presents.

Xman presents two main windows: a control window and a man-page viewer window. The control window allows you to call up the man-page browser, and the man-page browser does what you'd think—it displays a UNIX man page, as shown in Figure 23.1.

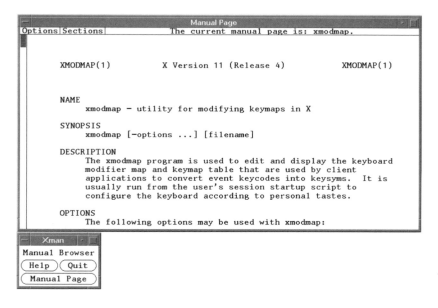

Figure 23.1   Reading man pages with *xman*.

Xman lets you browse through the list of commands with accompanying man pages. If you or your users forget a command, you can search through the list presented by *xman*, as shown in Figure 23.2.

```
┌──────────────────────────── Manual Page ────────────────────────────┐
│Options│Sections│          The current manual page is: xmodmap.      │
│X              XConsortium XStandards  Xau         Xserver    Xsgi     │
│appdefpath     appres      atobm       bdftopcf    bdftosnf   bitmap   │
│bmtoa          bsdinst.sh  dps         dpsexec     editres    endsession│
│f2p            f2ps        fmtosnf     fontview    ico        imake    │
│keyboards      listres     makedepend  maze        mkdirhier  mkfontdir│
│muncher        oclock      puzzle      reaper      resize     rgb      │
│scratchpad     setxkeymap  showpcf     showrgb     snftopcf   startx   │
│twm            userenv     uwm         viewres     wait4wm    xauth    │
│xbiff          xcalc       xcalendar   xclipboard  xclock     xcutsel  │
│xditview       xdm         xdpr        xdpyinfo    xedit      xev      │
│xeyes          xfd         xfig        xfontsel    xgc        xhost    │
│xinit          xkill       xlistscrns  xload       xlogo      xlsatoms │
│xlsclients     xlsfonts    xlswins     xmag        xman       xmh      │
│xmkmf          xmodmap     xpr         xprop       xpsview    xrdb     │
│xrefresh       xscope      xset        xsetroot    xshowcmap  xstdcmap │
│xterm          xwd         xwininfo    xwud                            │
│                                                                      │
│                                                                      │
└──────────────────────────────────────────────────────────────────────┘
```

Figure 23.2   A list of man pages.

Telling Time

Computer users—or computer programmers, anyway—must all be Type A personalities, since there's not only a host of time-telling programs available, and just about every workstation we've seen has one running.

With the standard release of X, you can run *xclock* or the more interesting *oclock* (an oval clock). In addition, there are a number of freeware X clock programs, including a Swiss watch and *moonclock*. The Swiss watch program, *swisswatch*, presents what looks like a railroad clock, as shown in Figure 23.3.

Figure 23.3   A fun way to tell time.

Turning Your Workstation into a Home Entertainment Center

Workman is one of a number of free X tools that help turn a very expensive UNIX workstation into a workplace entertainment center by playing audio compact disks from your UNIX CD-ROM drive.

Through its interface, you can engage a shuffle mode for pseudorandom selection of which songs to play. You can also program in which tracks to play and which to skip, just like a normal CD player on your stereo.

One nice thing about *workman* is the ability to remember the title of a CD, presuming you enter it, of course. Each audio CD has a code that allows *workman* to identify it. You can then type in the disc name, artist name, and all the song names. Once you've done this, *workman* will call up the proper name every time you insert the disc.

Workman plays the audio through the headphones port on the CD drive, not from any speaker system. This means you should plug in any speakers or headphones to the CD drive, not to the computer's audio port.

Installing Workman

For such a seemingly simple program, *workman* requires some low-level access to the CD device. This means you may need **root** privileges to install *workman*.

Workman runs on BSD/386, Hewlett-Packard HP-UX, Linux, Solaris 2, Sony NEWS-OS, SVR4, and Ultrix operating systems. *Workman* comes with a set of directions for installing on each of these operating systems.

NOTE

Workman **requires the XView toolkit. See Chapter 18 for more on how to get this toolkit.**

Obtaining Workman

We got *workman* from its source, the machine *ftp.hyperion.com* in the **/WorkMan** directory, and present it straight to you on the accompanying CD-ROM. We did not include a related "tool"—from this same machine you can grab a database of over 750 audio CDs (also in the **/WorkMan** directory.)

If you can't get *workman* to compile or run, you might want to try a program named *xcdplayer*, which is very similar to *workman*.

Summary

This chapter summarizes some useful X Window programs—providing, of course, that we define *useful* liberally.

The next, and final, chapter covers various X Window tools that ease connection to and usage of the Internet.

Connecting to the Internet with X

Topics covered in this chapter include:

* ✳ Navigating the Internet with free X tools
* ✳ Using *xarchie*
* ✳ Installing and setting up *xarchie*
* ✳ Burrowing through the Net with *xgopher*
* ✳ Finding anything with *Mosaic*
* ✳ X FTP tools
* ✳ Using *xgetftp*

Get Your Kicks on Route 66

With millions of users, the Internet has grown too fast for its own good. Internet users are now faced with an information glut. It's quite hard to track down what you want in the huge number of files, machines, and disks available to search. There are a number of helpful X-based tools to aid in navigation of helpful both the Internet and the network at your local site. These tools include:

❊ *Xarchie*, a front end to the Archie information service

❊ *Xgopher*, a front end to the gopher information server

❊ *Mosaic*, a front end to many different information servers

❊ An assortment of FTP tools

In this chapter, we cover each of these tools and show how to find the information you want, grab the documents, and copy files. And, as a bonus, we've included them on the accompanying CD-ROM.

Finding What You Need with Archie

Xarchie is a graphical front end to the Archie system. Archie is a system that allows queries on where to find programs and other files on the Internet.

The Archie database contains indices for over 2 million files strewn throughout the Internet. *Xarchie* places a friendly front end to an Archie client program.

Installing *xarchie*

Xarchie uses a GNU *Autoconf* configuration script, which must be used before running *xmkmf* to generate a **Makefile**. We ran the following commands to build *xarchie*:

```
sh ./configure
xmkmf
make Makefiles
make depend
```

```
make
cp Xarchie.ad ~/Xarchie
```

The commands may be different for your system. See the *xarchie* documentation for more information.

Before running *make*, we edited the Makefile to comment out this line:

```
#RESOLV_LIB = -lresolv
```

N O T E

See the Makefile for more information.

Xarchie is a large program, so expect it to take a while to compile and link.

Setting Up Archie

Figure 24.1 presents the basic *xarchie* interface, which allows users to set up a query to look for files.

Xarchie comes with a menu full of information on preconfigured Archie sites that can be queried. And, to further make life better, *xarchie* comes with a full reference manual as part of its online help, as shown in Figure 24.2.

Burrowing in the Gopher Hole

While Archie tells you where to get files, *gopher* actually brings the information to you. *Gopher* is an information server that presents information from a server to any number of clients. (The name *gopher* comes from the Golden Gopher mascot of the University of Minnesota, where *gopher* was developed.)

On the server, *gopher* reads a top-level directory, specified when you start up the *gopher* server). Underneath this top-level directory, you can place files of data as well as menu files that *gopher* clients will use to present menus to the user. (However, here's a word of warning: Don't always trust these menus. More than a few times we've run into improperly configured *gopher* servers.)

Users then run a *gopher* client program like *xgopher* or *Mosaic*. The *xgopher* program queries the *gopher* server for a top-level view of the information. Users then see a hierarchical set of menus, as shown in Figure 24.3.

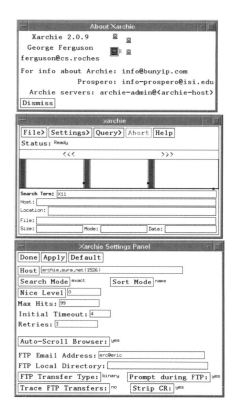

Figure 24.1   Using *xarchie*.

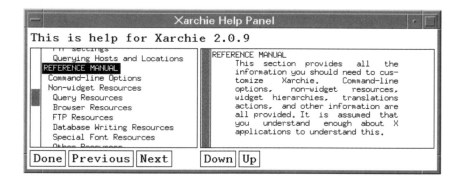

Figure 24.2   *Xarchie*'s online help.

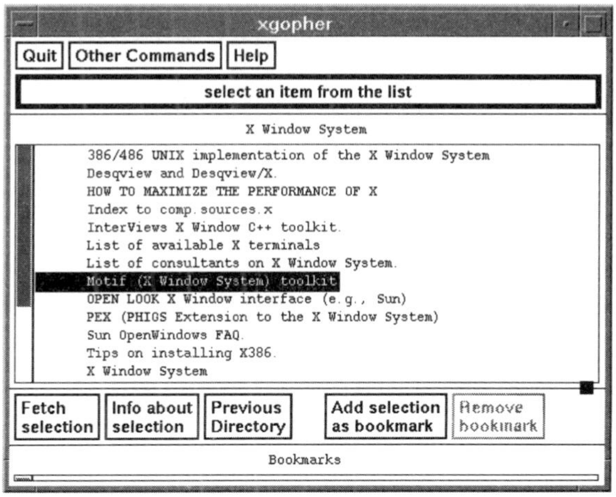

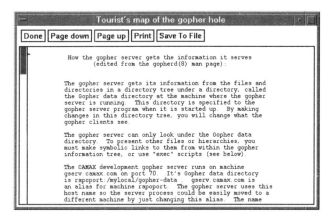

Figure 24.3   Burrowing with _xgopher_.

Each menu choice can either call up a new menu (that is, go down a directory on the _gopher_ server) or display a file of data. (If this file isn't a text file, you can configure _xgopher_ to launch a program that can view the file, such as _xv_ to view an image file.)

For example, when displaying information on _gopher_ itself, you'll see a window like the one shown in Figure 24.4.

Figure 24.4   Viewing information with _xgopher_.

On the Internet, you'll find a number of gopher servers. Even if you don't have access to the Internet, you'll find *gopher* to be very helpful in your position as UNIX system administrator. Why? Because you can use *gopher* on a local network as an easy information-distribution system. For example, you could place documents describing your computer administration policies and then let users query the documents if they need the information.

We find *gopher* worthwhile for distributing answers to frequently asked questions on various subjects like X, Motif, and PEX. On the Usenet news, you'll find periodic messages that contain just these answers. With a *gopher* server, you can then make the latest such documents instantly available to all the users on your network.

None of these users will need to know which machine or filename the documents are stored under. Instead, a gopher client like *xgopher* will present the information in a menu-based format.

Finding It All with Mosaic

In addition to *xgopher*, you can use a tool named *Mosaic* to display *gopher* server data, as shown in Figure 24.5.

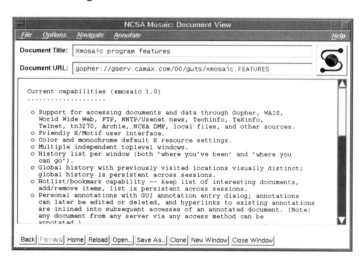

Figure 24.5   Accessing information with Mosaic.

However, *Mosaic* offers a lot more than just viewing *gopher* documents. *Mosaic* ties together a number of diverse information sources into one front-end program. You can view documents from:

❋ *Archie*

❋ FTP

❋ *Gopher*

❋ Local files on your systems' disks

❋ NCSA DMF

❋ Techinfo

❋ Telnet

❋ TeXinfo

❋ Usenet news (even NNTP-acquired news)

❋ WAIS

❋ World Wide Web (WWW)

❋ And much, much, more

It takes a bit of work to set up a *Mosaic*-based information-retrieval system, but it's well worth it, as your users no longer have to worry about all the different and incompatible means for accessing information from all of the previous sources.

Mosaic supports the HTML hypertext format, so that if you have any HTML documents, you can display and interact with them using *Mosaic*. (While you may not have any HTML documents now, HTML is an emerging standard for hypertext documents.)

In addition to the hypertext support, *Mosaic* automatically recognizes a number of popular image formats and then tries to launch viewer programs to display those images. *Mosaic* doesn't actually display the image, but rather forks off another program to do that.

One odd thing about *Mosaic*, though: It expects to find all its help files over the Internet. When you call up help on how to configure *Mosaic*, chances are it will tell you it can't give you any help.

X FTP Tools

With more and more network use, many users ask for friendlier means for accessing the myriad files on your network. So far we've covered a number of tools for information retrieval. X also offers some simple front ends to common networking programs like *ftp*.

One of these, *xgetftp*, uses the Motif toolkit to present a mouse- and menu-driven interface that's far easier to use than cryptic *ftp* commands.

Xgetftp also presents lists of files in a scrolled window, so you have to do a lot less typing when you retrieve files. And you don't need to be on the Internet to take advantage of *xgetftp*—you just need to have a network and the *ftp* program. Again, this program could benefit you and your users even if you're not on the Internet.

Running *Xgetftp*

When you run *xgetftp*, the *-q* command-line parameter makes the program run in quiet mode. Otherwise, *xgetftp* prints out all the responses from FTP to the standard output. (This option can be useful, though, when tracking down a problem with *xgetftp*.) We usually start *xgetftp* with the following command:

```
xgetftp -q
```

When you do so, you'll see an interface to the *ftp* program like the one shown in Figure 24.6.

Other FTP tools

In addition to *xgetftp*, there are a number of other similar tools. Each presents a front end to *ftp* that tries to make life easier on the part of the user. Among the other tools we've seen are *moxftp* and *ftptool*.

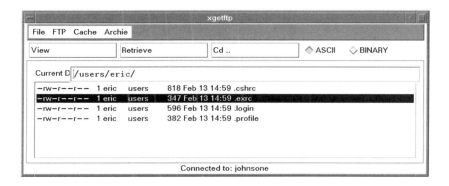

Figure 24.6   A front end to *ftp*.

Summary

We conclude this book with a discussion of popular X-based tools for navigating the wide-open spaces of the information superhighway. And even if your site isn't connected to the Internet, we think you'll still find a lot of use from tools like *xgopher* and *xarchie* for distributing information in-house.

For More Information

During the course of this book we've made reference to a number of vendors and additional sources of information. We've gathered these references in one place—this appendix.

Books

There aren't too many books devoted to UNIX system administration when it comes to X. Therefore, you're going to need to cobble together a set of resources above and beyond this book on your own.

UNIX Commands and Networking

For an introduction to basic UNIX commands, including networking commands like *ftp*, we've put together a few books. We think they're rather nifty, but we're obviously biased.

Teach Yourself UNIX, second edition. Reichard and Johnson, MIS:Press, 1992.

UNIX in Plain English, Reichard and Johnson, MIS:Press, 1994.

For administering TCP/IP networks, we recommend the following:

TCP/IP Network Administration, Craig Hunt, O'Reilly and Associates, 1992.

Books on X Usage

This book covers X Window administration from the point of view of the UNIX system administrator. If you want more of a background on using X programs and especially on writing X resource files, you'll want to check out one of the following.

Using X: Troubleshooting the X Window System, Motif and Open Look, Johnson and Reichard, MIS:Press, 1992.

X Window System Administrator's Guide, Linda Mui and Eric Pearce, O'Reilly and Associates, 1992.

The X Window System in a Nutshell, Ellie Cutler, Daniel Gilly, and Tim O'Reilly, O'Reilly and Associates, 1990.

X Window System User's Guide, Valerie Quercia and Tim O'Reilly, O'Reilly and Associates, 1990.

X and Motif Programming Books

No, we're not trying to turn you into a programmer, but if you need X programming information, there are a huge number of books available. Why so many books? X Window is a difficult programming environment. The following books should prove useful:

Advanced X Window Applications Programming, second edition, Johnson and Reichard, MIS:Press, 1994.

An Introduction to Tcl and Tk, John Ousterhout, Addison-Wesley, 1994.

Power Programming Motif, second edition, Johnson and Reichard, MIS:Press, 1993.

Professional Graphics Programming in the X Window System, Johnson and Reichard, MIS:Press, 1993.

Software Portability with imake, Paul DuBois, O'Reilly and Associates, 1993.

X Window Applications Programming, second edition, Johnson and Reichard, MIS:Press, 1992.

Vendors

Here's where to go for more information on various commercial products discussed in this book.

PC X Servers

Covered in Chapter 15, these X-server packages run under DOS or *Windows*.

DESQview/X, Quarterdeck Office Systems, 150 Pico Blvd., Santa Monica, CA 90405. (310) 392-9851

HCL-eXceed, Hummingbird Communications Ltd., 2900 John St., Unit 4, Markham, ONT L3R 5G3, Canada. (416) 470-1203

PC-Xware, Network Computing Devices, 9590 SW. Gemini Dr., Beaverton, OR 97005. (800) 598-7638

Reflection X, Walker Richer & Quinn, 2185 Eastlake E., Seattle, WA 98102. (800) 92NETWORK

Xvision 5, Visionware, 4500 Bohannon Dr., Suite 280, Menlo Park, CA 94025-1029. (800)949-8474

X Terminals

These are firms that specialize in X-terminal manufacturing. Many leading UNIX vendors, such as Digital Equipment Corp., Hewlett-Packard, and IBM also sell X terminals.

Human Designed Systems (HDS), 421 Feheley Dr., King of Prussia, PA 19406. (800) HDS-1551

Network Computing Devices, 350 N. Bernardo Ave., Mountain View, CA 94043. (415) 694-0650

Tektronix, P.O. Box 1000, Wilsonville, OR 97070. (800) 835-6200

CD-ROMs

We decided to focus on X applications with the CD-ROM that accompanies this book, rather than with the core X Window System itself. If you're interested in purchasing the entire X Window System on CD-ROM, contact one of the following vendors.

Free Software Foundation, 675 Massachusetts Av., Cambridge, MA 02139. (617) 876-3296. *gnu@prep.ai.mit.edu*

O'Reilly and Associates, 103A Morris St., Sebastopol, CA 95472. (800) 998-9938. *order@ora.com*

Prime Time Freeware, 370 Altair Way, Suite 150, Sunnyvale, CA 94086. (408) 738-4832. *ptf@cfcl.com*

Sterling Software, 1404 Fort Crook Road S., Bellevue, NE 68005. (800) 643-NEWS. *cdnews@sterling.com*

Sun User Group, 1330 Beacon St., Suite 315, Brookline, MA 02146. (617) 232-0514. *office@sug.org*

Walnut Creek CD-ROM, 1547 Palos Verde Mall, #260, Walnut Creek, CA 94596. (800) 786-9907. *orders@cdrom.com*

Yggdrasil Computing, P.O. Box 8418, Berkeley, CA 94707. (510) 526-7531. *yggdrasil@netcom.com*

Young Minds, 1910 Orange Tree Ln., Suite 300, Redlands, CA 92374. (909) 335-1350.

In addition, X11R5 source is available on ISO-9660-format CD-ROM for members of the Japan UNIX Society from Hiroaki Obata, *obata@jrd.dec.com*.

Decoding X Errors

This appendix lists a number of common X-related errors messages you may face, along with some techniques to help the situation. Table B.1 lists the most common errors, along with the probable causes.

Table B.1   Common X errors.

Error	Probable Cause
Can't open display	Application not allowed to connect to server or DISPLAY not set
Connection reset by peer	Application not allowed to connect to server
Not authorized to connect to server	X security prevents connection
Cannot connect to server "L"	Different network link expected for X server
XIO: fatal IO error 32	Poorly behaved X application was killed
Command not found	X applications aren't in shell's path
ld.so: warning: older version	Shared-library version mismatch
ls.so not found	LD_LIBRARY_PATH not updated for X libraries
Delete/Backspace key doesn't work	Improper keyboard configuration
vi has wrong number of lines	Improper LINES environment variable
t_bind failed	Restarting X server before all timeouts resolved
General X error	Who knows?

In the rest of this appendix, we expand on Table B.1 and describe what the various messages mean, along with solutions.

X Toolkit Error: Can't open display
Error: Can't Open display

This error can mean one of two things: Either the DISPLAY environment variable is not set up properly, or the application running on a remote system is not allowed to connect to the X server on your local display. Both errors occur when trying to run an X application on a remote machine and trying to display the program on a local X terminal or workstation.

First, check that the DISPLAY environment variable on the remote machine properly names the local workstation or terminal. The DISPLAY environment variable should be in the form of *hostname*:0, where *hostname* is the name of the local display.

If the DISPLAY environment variable is properly set up, the next thing to check is access control. Are programs on the remote system allowed to connect to the local display?

What you do next depends on the security method you have in place: *xhost* or *xauth*. (We covered these schemes in Chapter 12.) The X Display Manager stores a cookie value in the **.Xauthority** in your home directory, or in the file named by the XAUTHORITY environment variable. Once stored in your home directory, X programs must access this file to get the cookie value. If a program doesn't have access to your home directory's **.Xauthority** file, that program cannot get the magic cookie value and therefore cannot connect to your X server. The *xauth* program then helps manage **.Xauthority** files.

If you're using *xhost* case, you must add the hostname of the remote system using the *xhost* command:

```
xhost +hostname
```

where *hostname* is the name of the remote host. Once you execute this command, any program on the given host is allowed to connect to the local X display. (You must type in the *xhost* command in a window that's computing on your local display.) In addition, you can set up a file, **/etc/X0.hosts**, that names preauthorized hosts. You can make one of these files for every X server on a given computer. The file name is **/etc/X*number*.hosts** where number is the display (X server) *number* (starting at 0). *Xhost* can override the entries in this file.

If you're using one of the *xauth* security methods, then you'll need to get the security cookie to the remote host—a process explained in Chapter 12.

XIO: fatal IO error 131 (Connection reset by peer) on X server Segmentation Fault xclock (core dumped)

Like the *can't open display* error described above, this is also an authorization error. The X application (*xclock* in our example above, but it could be any X program) is not allowed to connect to the X server. In fact, on some systems, this will even cause the application to dump core.

Not authorized to connect to server

This message is essentially the same as the *can't open display* error message explained above and encompasses the same solutions.

Cannot Connect to Server "L"

This error, or a similar one, often occurs when you have an Intel-based X system, such as Interactive/SunSoft UNIX System VR3.2 version 3.0. On such a system, the X server is often set up for a certain type of network link, say streams, and you're running an X server set up for a different kind of link, say, TCP/IP sockets. Many Intel-based implementations of UNIX make networking an add-on item, which is where this problem comes from. You won't face this error on most other systems.

We've found that what helps is to set the DISPLAY environment variable from unix:0 to :0, using a command like the following:

```
setenv DISPLAY :0
```

XIO: fatal IO error 32 (Broken pipe) on X server ":0.0" after 15 requests (15 known processed) with 0 events remaining

The connection was probably broken by a server shutdown or KillClient.

This error means that a poorly behaved X application was killed by some other X program, likely, the window manager. For example, if you choose the **Close** choice on the window menu provided by the Motif window manager, it will send a message to the X application to close the window. If the application isn't set up to receive this message, the window manager will simply terminate the application.

The *XIO* part of the previous error message indicates that the problem is a loss of the link between the application and the X server. If the user didn't explicitly kill the program, then something is amiss with the network link between that program and the X server. Network problems are usually serious, so check to make sure that the network links are still up and running.

Command not found

This is a UNIX shell error and not an X error. Most X applications are not stored in the same place as other UNIX applications (not in **/bin** or **/usr/bin**), so you must set up the command path for all users to include the location of the X applications on your system. The normal location is **/usr/bin/X11**, but this does vary by system. We list some common locations in Table B.2.

Table B.2   Common locations for X programs.

Location	System
/usr/bin/X11	Generic X applications
/usr/bin/X11R5	Hewlett-Packard X applications
/usr/vue/bin	Hewlett-Packard VUE applications
/opt/dt/bin	COSE CDE applications
/usr/openwin/bin	Sun OpenWindows and X applications

ld.so: warning: /usr/lib/libX11.so.4.2 has older revision than expected 3

This warning message appears a lot on SunOS systems using shared libraries. The application was compiled with one version of the shared library, and the operating system has a different version available.

On SunOS, for example, **/usr/lib/libX11.so.4.2** is the name of the shared library file (*so* tells us that this is a shared library, because normal—static—UNIX libraries end with *.a*).

If the X programs still run acceptably, don't worry about this warning. If you experience problems, however, you should look into your X installation and check the shared libraries.

N O T E   One of the periodic fixes to X11 Release 5 resulted in an accidental version number mismatch for SunOS shared libraries. Because of this, we treat this warning less seriously than we probably should.

/usr/lib/libX11.so.4.2 not found

This, too, is a shared-library problem, as evidenced by the reference to a file containing the string *.so*. The shared library probably isn't in the library path, held in the LD_LIBRARY_PATH environment variable on many systems, including Sun Solaris systems. On Sun systems, X libraries are not stored in **/usr/lib**, where shared libraries traditionally reside. Instead, Sun systems usually use **/usr/openwin/lib**, so you should check the LD_LIBRARY_PATH environment variable. You may need to set the value to **/usr/openwin/lib**, as shown in the following command:

```
setenv LD_LIBRARY_PATH /usr/openwin/lib
```

Delete/Backspace Key Doesn't Work

If users hit the **Backspace** key and see ^H or ^?, then the wrong key is set up for editing the command line. This problem occurs most often when users log onto remote machines over a network link.

This really isn't an X problem, but instead is a UNIX shell problem. The answer is to use the *stty* program to change what key the shell uses to erase characters. Type in the following command:

```
stty erase erase_key
```

where *erase_key* is the actual key on the keyboard you want for the erase function in the shell. For example, if you want your key labeled **Backspace** to act as the erase key, type in *stty erase* and then press the **Backspace** key. Press the **Return** key to end the command.

vi Text Editor Shows Wrong Number of Lines

This problem hits Hewlett-Packard systems, which have a special patch to correct a bug in the *xterm* application. As a result, the *xterm* window loses track of how tall it is when the user resizes the window. The symptoms become especially apparent when editing files, particularly with the *vi* text editor. In this editor, it's obvious that only some of the lines are in use.

To fix this, update the LINES environment variable to the proper number of lines. To determine the proper number of lines, run the *resize* program, which determines how big the terminal is and tries to set the LINES and

COLUMNS environment variables. Generally, you'll leave the columns at 80, so the COLUMNS environment variable won't be a problem; it's usually the number of lines that is off.

When you run *resize*, it will print out the current settings, as show below:

```
set noglob;
setenv COLUMNS '80';
setenv LINES '52';
unset noglob;
```

On some systems, you'll need to use *eval resize* or type in the new LINES setting manually:

```
eval `resize`
```

If the above command doesn't work, just run *resize* and then set the LINES environment variable based on the number printed by *resize*:

```
setenv LINES 52
```

t_bind failed: Couldn't allocate address
X Tcp port for display 0 is busy, will try again...

On many Intel-based UNIX systems, networking is an extra-cost option. As a result, the networking system isn't always fully integrated with the rest of the operating system. In this case, when the user quits the X server, a number of streams ports are still active until they time out. If the user tries to restart the X server too soon, the streams ports will still be reserved for the last X server session, resulting in the error message.

There's nothing to fix; just wait and the problem will correct itself in a few minutes. If not, you may need to reset the networking system, or, in more serious cases, reboot the server.

When Trying To Quit X, The Window Manager
Starts Up Again

This problem often occurs if you use *xinit* to start X sessions and edit the **.xinitrc** while running X. Since *xinit* executes the **.xinitrc** file, changing the file in midstream can cause problems. The best answer is to quit X and then edit the **.xinitrc** file. Another option is copying **.xinitrc** to another name and edit the copy; when you're done editing, quit X and just move the copy back to **.xinitrc**.

X Error of failed request:
BadDrawable (invalid Pixmap or Window parameter)

Major opcode of failed request: 76 (X_ImageText8)

Minor opcode of failed request: 0

Resource id in failed request: 0x0

Serial number of failed request: 12

Current serial number in output stream: 13

Any errors of this type mean that the X application did something wrong and didn't correct the situation. Often, you can discover what the application did wrong (like trying to load a nonexistent font) from the text of the error message.

About This CD-ROM

The directories on the accompanying CD-ROM are organized around the subject matter, and the location of programs should be obvious. To help you find things, we divided the CD into a number of general categories:

bitmap_tools	Tools to manipulate bitmaps and image files	**fun**	CD players, clocks, and the *xfishtank* (try it)
cpu_load	Programs to monitor system resources	**internet**	Tools to access information on the Internet
debugging	*xscope* and *xmon*	**keyboard**	*xkeycaps*
disk_space	Programs to monitor disk usage	**security**	Screen-locking programs
email_tools	Tools to help with electro\nic mail	**tar**	Tar files of all directories, for systems that don't support long Rock Ridgefile names on CD-ROMs.
font_tools	Font editors and converters		
front_ends	Front ends to UNIX software, such as *xgen* and Tcl	**time_plan**	Tools to help manage what little time you have
		utilities	A calculator, patch, etc.

Most of the UNIX programs on this disk use longer filenames than are allowed by the strict (eight-dot-three) standard for CD-ROMs. (The standard is known as ISO 9660.) Because we wanted to preserve the original software as much as possible, we used the Rock Ridge extensions to ISO 9660, which allows for longer file names. Most UNIX systems, such as SunSoft Solaris and Silicon Graphics IRIX, support Rock Ridge CD-ROMs. But, if your system for some reason does not support Rock Ridge CD-ROMs, you may have trouble reading all the file and directory names (or you may see strangely shortened names). To help you out, we've also included UNIX **tar** files for all the packages, so you can copy the **tar** file (which uses a short filename) onto your hard disk and then extract the X software, which uses longer filenames. These files are compressed. You need to first uncompress a file and then use **tar** to extract its contents. (Also note that the .Z extension on these files was forced to lowercase, e.g., .z, because the ISO 9600 CD-ROM standard does not support mixed-case names.)